Next-Gen Cybersecurity: AI and ML Innovations for Digital Protection

Davide Mancuso

Davide Mancuso is a seasoned cybersecurity expert and technology strategist with over a decade of experience in protecting organizations from the ever-evolving threat landscape. Recognized for his innovative approaches to digital security, Davide has worked with leading global enterprises, governments, and startups to build robust security frameworks that leverage cutting-edge technologies like artificial intelligence (AI) and machine learning (ML).

With a background in computer science and a passion for exploring how emerging technologies can revolutionize traditional practices, Davide has positioned himself at the forefront of the next-generation cybersecurity movement. His work combines technical expertise with a deep understanding of the human and organizational aspects of digital protection, making him a sought-after speaker, consultant, and thought leader in the industry.

Beyond his professional achievements, Davide is an advocate for ethical AI use in cybersecurity and a mentor to aspiring professionals in the field. **Next-Gen Cybersecurity: AI and ML Innovations for Digital Protection** reflects his dedication to empowering individuals and organizations with the knowledge and tools needed to stay ahead in a rapidly changing digital world.

In a world where digital threats grow more sophisticated every day, traditional approaches to cybersecurity can no longer keep up. The integration of artificial intelligence (AI) and machine learning (ML) into cybersecurity offers unprecedented opportunities to detect, respond to, and even predict cyberattacks with remarkable accuracy and speed. **Next-Gen Cybersecurity: AI and ML Innovations for Digital Protection** is your guide to understanding how these transformative technologies are shaping the future of digital defense.

This book is designed for cybersecurity professionals, technology enthusiasts, and decision-makers seeking actionable insights into how AI and ML are revolutionizing the field. Whether you are a seasoned expert or a newcomer to the world of cybersecurity, this book will provide you with the foundational knowledge, advanced strategies, and forward-looking perspectives needed to thrive in this new era of digital protection.

Chapter 1: Introduction to Cybersecurity in the Age of AI

Discover how AI is changing the cybersecurity landscape, addressing the limitations of traditional methods, and providing smarter, faster solutions to defend against modern threats.

Chapter 2: Understanding the Cyber Threat Landscape

Explore the evolving nature of cyber threats, including advanced persistent threats, ransomware, and AI-powered attacks, and learn why automated defense is crucial.

Chapter 3: AI and ML Basics for Cybersecurity Professionals

Gain a solid understanding of the AI and ML concepts, algorithms, and tools that are most relevant to building next-gen cybersecurity systems.

Chapter 4: Next-Gen Intrusion Detection and Prevention Systems

Learn how AI enhances traditional intrusion detection systems, enabling real-time monitoring and adaptive responses to threats.

Chapter 5: Automating Threat Intelligence with AI

Dive into how AI gathers and analyzes threat intelligence, offering predictive insights and faster detection of emerging vulnerabilities.

Chapter 6: Behavioral Analytics and User Anomaly Detection

Understand how AI profiles user behavior to detect insider threats, compromised accounts, and anomalies in real-time.

Chapter 7: The Double-Edged Sword: AI in Cyber Attacks

Examine how cybercriminals use AI to enhance their attacks and explore strategies to counter these AI-driven threats.

Chapter 8: Simulating Attacks with AI

Learn about AI-driven penetration testing and how simulating attacks can help organizations strengthen their defenses.

Chapter 9: Natural Language Processing (NLP) in Phishing Detection

Discover how NLP is revolutionizing phishing detection by analyzing email and text patterns to prevent malicious communication.

Chapter 10: AI in Malware Detection and Reverse Engineering

Explore the role of AI in detecting malware, analyzing its behavior, and uncovering zero-day vulnerabilities.

Chapter 11: Securing IoT with Machine Learning

Delve into the unique challenges of IoT security and how ML solutions protect interconnected devices from vulnerabilities.

Chapter 12: Adversarial Machine Learning: The Next Battlefield

Learn about adversarial ML, where attackers manipulate AI models, and how to defend against these sophisticated techniques.

Chapter 13: Ethics and Privacy in AI-Powered Cybersecurity

Examine the ethical challenges of using AI in cybersecurity, including balancing privacy, transparency, and compliance with global regulations.

Chapter 14: Building a Resilient Cybersecurity Ecosystem with AI

Discover how to integrate AI into a comprehensive cybersecurity strategy, combining human expertise with machine intelligence to future-proof defenses.

This book not only explores the state of AI in cybersecurity today but also provides a vision for the future, empowering you to adapt to and thrive in an era where technology is both the greatest asset and the greatest challenge in digital protection.

1. Introduction to Cybersecurity in the Age of AI

The digital landscape is evolving rapidly, and so are the threats that compromise it. Traditional cybersecurity measures, while foundational, are struggling to keep pace with increasingly sophisticated attacks. This chapter explores how artificial intelligence (AI) is revolutionizing cybersecurity by introducing intelligent, adaptive, and scalable solutions to counter modern threats. From analyzing vast amounts of data in real time to predicting potential vulnerabilities, AI is not just a tool but a game-changer in the fight against cybercrime. This introduction sets the stage for understanding why integrating AI and machine learning into cybersecurity is not just a trend but a necessity for the digital age.

1.1 The Evolution of Cybersecurity: Past to Present

Cybersecurity, in its simplest form, refers to the protection of digital assets from malicious threats, attacks, and unauthorized access. Over the last few decades, the landscape of cybersecurity has evolved dramatically in response to increasingly sophisticated threats and the rapid advancement of technology. From its humble beginnings with rudimentary firewalls and antivirus software to the adoption of artificial intelligence (AI) and machine learning (ML) in modern-day defense strategies, the evolution of cybersecurity reflects the growing complexity of digital environments and the constant arms race between security professionals and cybercriminals. This chapter explores the historical progression of cybersecurity, from its early days to the present, and highlights how innovations in technology have shaped the field.

The Early Days of Cybersecurity: The 1970s to Early 1990s

Cybersecurity as a discipline began to take shape in the 1970s when computer systems began to become interconnected. Early on, security measures were minimal, and most computers were isolated systems with limited communication between them. In the early 1970s, organizations began to recognize the need for secure systems, particularly as more businesses began adopting computing for operations. One of the first notable events in cybersecurity history was the development of the ARPANET (Advanced Research Projects Agency Network), which laid the groundwork for the modern Internet. As ARPANET grew in size and connectivity, security became a growing concern.

One of the earliest cybersecurity technologies was the password, which was introduced to protect data from unauthorized access. However, the first real breakthrough in network security came in 1983 with the development of the first firewall. Created by researchers at the Digital Equipment Corporation (DEC), the firewall was designed to filter incoming and outgoing traffic, offering a basic level of security for computer networks. It was simple but effective for the time, blocking access from external networks while allowing internal communications to flow freely.

During the late 1980s and early 1990s, the rise of the Internet and email opened new avenues for cyberattacks, such as viruses, worms, and other forms of malware. In response, companies began developing more sophisticated protection measures. The first antivirus software emerged during this period, providing protection against common viruses such as the Brain virus, which was one of the first examples of malware targeting PCs. Antivirus software worked by detecting known malware signatures and blocking them from infecting systems.

The Expansion of the Internet and Early Cybercrime: 1990s to Early 2000s

The 1990s saw the explosion of the World Wide Web, making the Internet a central part of everyday life for millions of people. As more businesses, government agencies, and individuals connected to the Internet, the threat landscape expanded exponentially. Cybercriminals realized that with the growth of the Internet came the opportunity to exploit vulnerabilities for financial gain or political motives. During this period, hackers and viruses became more prominent, with attacks ranging from simple denial-of-service (DoS) attacks to defacing websites and launching email-based scams.

The early days of the Internet also witnessed the rise of phishing attacks, which became one of the most common forms of social engineering. Hackers would impersonate legitimate entities like banks or government agencies to steal sensitive information, such as passwords or credit card details. Cybercrime started to take on a more organized and profitable nature, as criminal groups began to operate in a similar way to legitimate businesses, creating a new class of digital criminal organizations. In response, businesses and governments started to understand the need for more robust cybersecurity measures.

Firewalls evolved in the late 1990s with the introduction of stateful inspection firewalls, which analyzed the state of network connections and could better detect unusual behavior. By this time, many organizations were also adopting intrusion detection systems (IDS), which were designed to detect unauthorized access or suspicious activities on a network. Antivirus software also became more sophisticated, offering real-time protection and heuristic scanning to identify new threats based on behavior rather than known signatures alone.

The Rise of Advanced Persistent Threats (APTs): 2000s to Early 2010s

The 2000s saw the rise of more advanced cyber threats, especially Advanced Persistent Threats (APTs). These were highly sophisticated, targeted attacks often attributed to nation-states or well-funded criminal groups. Unlike earlier attacks, which were typically opportunistic, APTs involved long-term, strategic efforts to infiltrate an organization's network, steal sensitive information, or cause significant damage. This new form of attack pushed the cybersecurity industry to evolve once again, focusing not just on protecting data but on maintaining the overall integrity of networks against sophisticated, multi-stage attacks.

During this period, cybersecurity began to shift toward defense-in-depth strategies, in which multiple layers of security were implemented to protect against various types of threats. Encryption became widely used to secure sensitive data, and the concept of multi-factor authentication (MFA) was introduced to reduce the risk of unauthorized access. Additionally, the increasing use of virtual private networks (VPNs) allowed organizations to create secure connections between remote users and internal systems.

One of the most significant developments in the 2000s was the rise of cloud computing. As businesses began to move their infrastructure to the cloud, it became crucial to ensure that data stored remotely was secure from cyberattacks. Cloud security models began to evolve to accommodate this shift, requiring a new set of best practices and security frameworks. The security-as-a-service model emerged, where cloud providers began offering specialized security tools like cloud firewalls, intrusion prevention systems, and data encryption services.

The growth of mobile devices and the advent of the smartphone also introduced new cybersecurity challenges, as mobile apps and devices became prime targets for malware. The early 2010s saw the first major mobile malware outbreaks, leading to the development of mobile-specific security solutions and app store screening protocols to help prevent malicious apps from being distributed.

AI and ML-Driven Cybersecurity: 2010s to Present

The past decade has witnessed the integration of artificial intelligence (AI) and machine learning (ML) in cybersecurity, dramatically shifting the landscape once again. The ability to analyze vast amounts of data in real-time and detect complex patterns has enabled AI-driven security tools to identify threats faster and more accurately than traditional methods. AI and ML are now used in threat intelligence gathering, intrusion detection, malware analysis, and incident response, transforming how organizations protect their networks.

One of the most significant advancements in recent years has been the use of behavioral analytics to detect anomalies and identify potential security breaches. Machine learning models are now capable of learning what "normal" activity looks like and can quickly identify deviations from this baseline, which often signal an attack or intrusion. AI is also used to automate routine security tasks, such as patching vulnerabilities or scanning for threats, allowing security teams to focus on higher-level strategic concerns.

Another major trend in modern cybersecurity is the use of blockchain technology for secure data storage and transactions, as well as the rise of zero-trust security models. With zero-trust, no one, whether inside or outside the network, is trusted by default, and continuous verification is required for every user and device accessing systems.

As cybercriminals continue to use AI and other technologies to launch sophisticated attacks, the cybersecurity industry is constantly adapting. With the ongoing development of quantum computing, new challenges and opportunities will emerge, and the arms race between attackers and defenders will continue to evolve.

The evolution of cybersecurity from its early days of basic password protection and firewalls to the AI-powered defense systems of today reflects the dynamic nature of the digital world. As technology continues to advance, so too will the tactics and strategies used by both defenders and attackers. The next frontier in cybersecurity will likely be shaped by quantum computing, AI-driven threat detection, and automated defenses, ensuring that the fight for digital security is always at the cutting edge. The history of cybersecurity serves as a reminder that in the digital age, security must always evolve to stay one step ahead of those who seek to exploit it.

1.2 Traditional Approaches and Their Limitations

As the digital world has grown more interconnected, the approaches to cybersecurity have evolved significantly. In the early days of computing and networking, cybersecurity was largely reactive and focused on basic methods to prevent and detect unauthorized access. Traditional cybersecurity approaches, which emerged in response to relatively simple threats, have played an essential role in securing systems for decades. However, as cyberattacks have become more sophisticated and pervasive, these traditional methods are proving to be increasingly ineffective against modern threats. This section explores the traditional cybersecurity strategies and highlights their limitations, shedding light on the need for advanced solutions such as artificial intelligence (AI) and machine learning (ML) to address the evolving digital security landscape.

1. Signature-Based Detection

One of the earliest and most widely used methods of detecting and preventing cyber threats is signature-based detection. This approach relies on a database of known patterns or "signatures" of malware, viruses, or malicious activities. Signature-based detection works by comparing incoming data or files to a pre-established list of known threats. If a match is found, the system can flag the potential danger and take preventive action, such as blocking the file or alerting security personnel.

While this method was effective in the early days of cybersecurity, it has significant limitations, particularly in today's dynamic threat landscape. The most obvious drawback is its inability to detect zero-day attacks—new and previously unknown threats that have not yet been added to the signature database. Additionally, signature-based systems are less effective against polymorphic malware, which changes its code or appearance in order to avoid detection. Attackers can create variations of malicious software that evade traditional signature-based defenses by altering their code or structure, rendering this approach insufficient for modern threats.

2. Rule-Based Intrusion Detection Systems (IDS)

Intrusion Detection Systems (IDS) are designed to monitor network traffic and identify suspicious activities that could indicate an attempted security breach. Traditional IDS solutions often operate on rule-based systems, where predefined rules are used to flag suspicious events. These rules are typically based on known attack patterns or behavior, such as unauthorized access attempts or unusual network traffic.

While rule-based IDS systems were effective in identifying common attacks, they come with several limitations:

False Positives: Rule-based IDS can generate a high volume of false alarms, flagging normal behavior as suspicious. This can overwhelm security teams and lead to the misallocation of resources.

Static Nature: Rule-based systems rely on manually configured rules, which means they are not adaptive. As cybercriminals evolve their tactics, static rule sets can become outdated, leaving organizations vulnerable to new, more sophisticated attacks.

Limited Contextual Understanding: Rule-based IDS lacks the ability to understand the context behind specific actions, making it less effective in identifying complex, multi-step attacks that unfold over time.

Due to these limitations, traditional IDS systems often fail to detect advanced threats, such as Advanced Persistent Threats (APTs), which are stealthy and persistent, often involving multiple stages and exploiting zero-day vulnerabilities.

3. Antivirus Software and Firewalls

Antivirus software and firewalls have long been considered the cornerstone of network defense. Antivirus software typically scans files, applications, and systems for known threats and malware, blocking or quarantining suspicious files. Firewalls, on the other hand, act as a barrier between internal networks and external ones, filtering traffic and preventing unauthorized access.

While both tools have provided essential protection for decades, they face several challenges in the modern cybersecurity environment:

Malware Evasion: Modern malware is increasingly capable of bypassing traditional antivirus defenses. For example, fileless malware, which operates directly in memory rather than leaving traditional files behind, is difficult for antivirus software to detect. Similarly, attackers may use techniques like polymorphism or obfuscation to hide the true nature of the malware, making it harder for antivirus software to recognize it.

Limited Threat Intelligence: Traditional antivirus solutions often rely on databases of known signatures and patterns, which means they are reactive rather than proactive. This approach struggles to address the rapidly evolving nature of threats, such as new forms of ransomware, advanced malware, and emerging attack vectors.

Firewall Limitations: While firewalls are essential for controlling access to a network, they are often ineffective in protecting against attacks that originate from within the network or from trusted insiders. Moreover, modern attacks, such as application-layer attacks or social engineering, may bypass firewalls entirely, targeting vulnerabilities in specific software or exploiting human behavior.

Traditional firewall configurations also struggle to handle the complexities introduced by cloud computing, mobile devices, and remote work environments. With an increasingly distributed workforce, securing endpoints beyond the traditional network perimeter becomes a challenging task.

4. Human-Dependent Security Monitoring

In many traditional cybersecurity models, human intervention plays a central role in monitoring and responding to threats. Security teams are tasked with manually analyzing logs, interpreting alerts, and deciding on the appropriate actions to mitigate potential threats. While human expertise is indispensable, this approach has its drawbacks:

Human Error: Security professionals, like any other workers, are prone to mistakes. A minor oversight in monitoring or misinterpretation of an alert can lead to a significant security breach. Given the increasing volume and complexity of data, it is difficult for human teams to keep up with the scale of potential threats.

Resource Constraints: Many organizations face resource limitations, which can lead to security teams being overworked and understaffed. As a result, security analysts may overlook important alerts or delay responses to critical issues. This can leave systems vulnerable to attacks, especially when threats are rapidly evolving.

Slow Response Times: Cyber threats often require swift responses to mitigate damage. Manual intervention is typically slower than automated systems, which means that attackers may gain enough time to cause significant harm before a human security professional can act.

5. Static Security Models

Traditional security models were often based on a perimeter-defense approach, where the focus was on creating a strong defense at the network boundary. This was based on the assumption that threats typically originated from external sources, and once an attacker breached the network perimeter, the internal systems were considered trusted. This model led to the development of approaches such as demilitarized zones (DMZs) and network segmentation, which attempted to isolate critical systems from potential threats.

However, this model has been rendered increasingly ineffective due to several factors:

Cloud Computing: The rise of cloud services has created new attack surfaces that lie outside the traditional perimeter. Data and applications are no longer confined to on-premise systems, making it harder to protect everything within a secure perimeter.

Mobile and IoT Devices: The proliferation of mobile devices and Internet of Things (IoT) devices further complicates perimeter-based security models. These devices often connect to corporate networks without the same level of security controls as traditional endpoints.

Insider Threats: The perimeter model assumes that insiders are trusted, but this is no longer the case. Insider threats, whether intentional or accidental, have become a significant security risk. These threats cannot be easily mitigated by traditional perimeter defenses alone.

6. The Need for Advanced Security Approaches

As cyber threats continue to evolve in complexity and sophistication, it is clear that traditional cybersecurity approaches are no longer sufficient to protect against modern threats. Signature-based detection, rule-based intrusion detection, and human-dependent monitoring cannot keep up with the volume of data, the speed of attacks, or the evolving tactics of cybercriminals. Today's organizations need to adopt more adaptive, intelligent, and automated solutions to address these challenges.

In the next section, we will explore how advanced technologies like artificial intelligence (AI) and machine learning (ML) are stepping in to fill the gaps left by traditional cybersecurity methods, enabling organizations to stay ahead of emerging threats and build more robust, resilient security infrastructures. These advanced tools offer the ability to analyze vast amounts of data in real-time, predict potential vulnerabilities, and automate responses to attacks, providing the agility and speed required to defend against the next generation of cyber threats.

1.3 AI's Role in Transforming Digital Defense

As cyber threats have grown increasingly complex and pervasive, traditional cybersecurity approaches—such as signature-based detection, firewalls, and antivirus software—have shown significant limitations. These methods are often reactive, relying on known attack patterns and manual interventions, which leaves organizations vulnerable to emerging and sophisticated threats. In contrast, artificial intelligence (AI) has emerged as a game-changing technology in cybersecurity, providing dynamic, adaptive, and proactive defense mechanisms capable of transforming the way digital security is approached. This section delves into the role of AI in revolutionizing digital defense, exploring its capabilities, benefits, and applications in modern cybersecurity.

1. Proactive Threat Detection and Prevention

One of the most significant advantages of AI in cybersecurity is its ability to move beyond reactive security measures and enable proactive threat detection and prevention. Traditional security tools typically operate on a signature-based approach, where only known threats are identified and blocked. This method is limited by its inability to detect new, unknown threats—often referred to as zero-day attacks—or to respond to polymorphic malware that changes its appearance to evade detection.

AI, particularly machine learning (ML), overcomes these limitations by analyzing vast amounts of data from multiple sources and identifying patterns of behavior that are indicative of malicious activity. Instead of relying on pre-existing signatures or human input, AI systems are capable of learning from ongoing data inputs, allowing them to detect anomalies in real-time. By establishing a baseline of "normal" network behavior, AI can identify deviations from this baseline that may indicate an attack in progress. Whether it's an advanced persistent threat (APT), insider threats, or network intrusions, AI can spot unusual behavior, even if it's a completely new attack vector.

Moreover, AI can anticipate potential threats before they manifest by continuously learning from historical data and analyzing patterns that human experts might miss. This capability enables security systems to act preemptively, blocking threats before they have the chance to cause significant damage.

2. Automating Incident Response

AI's ability to automate response actions is another critical transformation it brings to digital defense. In traditional security setups, once an intrusion or attack is detected, security teams must analyze the event, determine its severity, and take appropriate action. This process can be time-consuming and prone to human error, and delays in response may give attackers more time to infiltrate systems or steal sensitive information.

With AI, incident response can be automated in a way that's faster and more accurate. For example, AI-driven Security Information and Event Management (SIEM) systems can automatically correlate logs from various security devices and sources, identify patterns that suggest a cyberattack, and trigger predefined responses. This might include blocking access from malicious IP addresses, isolating affected systems, or alerting security teams to the threat.

AI can also use orchestration to streamline response processes. In situations where an attack is detected, AI can take immediate corrective actions, such as quarantining infected files, removing malicious code, or even conducting a system rollback to a previous safe state. This automation not only speeds up response times but also reduces the strain on security teams, enabling them to focus on more complex tasks.

Furthermore, AI systems can learn from each attack, improving their decision-making over time. This self-improvement helps them stay ahead of new threats and adjust their responses based on the success or failure of past actions.

3. Threat Intelligence and Predictive Analytics

Threat intelligence involves the collection and analysis of data regarding potential or existing cyber threats. The goal is to stay ahead of attackers by understanding their tactics, techniques, and procedures (TTPs). While traditional methods of gathering threat intelligence relied heavily on human analysts and static data sources, AI has revolutionized this field by enabling predictive analytics and the ability to process and analyze vast amounts of information in real-time.

AI-driven predictive analytics leverages historical attack data, current threat trends, and patterns to forecast future attacks and vulnerabilities. For example, AI can use machine learning algorithms to identify emerging malware strains, phishing campaigns, or exploit attempts, allowing organizations to prepare for and defend against new threats before they materialize. This type of proactive threat intelligence helps businesses take preemptive actions, such as updating security protocols or blocking known attack vectors, even before an actual attack occurs.

In addition, AI can enhance threat intelligence by analyzing dark web data, social media platforms, and other unstructured data sources for signs of upcoming attacks or data breaches. This can help organizations monitor threats from external sources, such as criminal groups or state-sponsored attackers, and gain early warning signs of potential cybercriminal activities.

4. Behavioral Analytics and User Anomaly Detection

Another critical area where AI is transforming digital defense is in behavioral analytics. Unlike traditional security models, which focus on identifying specific attack signatures, behavioral analytics uses AI and machine learning to understand how users and systems typically behave within a network. By analyzing large volumes of data, AI can learn patterns and create a baseline of "normal" activity for individual users, devices, and systems.

Once this baseline is established, the AI system can monitor ongoing activity for any deviations or anomalies. For example, if a user who typically logs into a system during business hours suddenly accesses the network at night from a different geographic location, AI can flag this behavior as suspicious. Similarly, if a device exhibits unusual data transfer patterns or attempts to access restricted areas of the network, AI can trigger an alert or take automated actions, such as requiring multi-factor authentication (MFA) or restricting access.

Behavioral analytics powered by AI is particularly effective in detecting insider threats—individuals who exploit their legitimate access to systems for malicious purposes. By recognizing subtle changes in user behavior, AI can identify potential risks from employees or contractors without the need for manual monitoring of each user's actions.

This capability also extends to bot detection, as AI can distinguish between human and automated behaviors, preventing malicious bots from infiltrating systems or performing fraudulent activities such as credential stuffing or spamming.

5. AI for Vulnerability Management

Identifying and addressing vulnerabilities is a critical component of cybersecurity, but the sheer volume of potential vulnerabilities in modern IT systems makes this task increasingly difficult. AI is transforming vulnerability management by enabling more efficient scanning, prioritization, and remediation of security flaws.

Traditional vulnerability management systems may rely on periodic scans or manual input from security teams to identify vulnerabilities. These systems can be slow to detect new threats or fail to prioritize vulnerabilities effectively, leading to missed opportunities to patch or mitigate critical risks.

AI-powered vulnerability management tools, on the other hand, can continuously scan systems for vulnerabilities and prioritize them based on risk assessment models. AI algorithms can consider factors such as exploitability, the criticality of the affected system, and the presence of active attacks targeting specific vulnerabilities. This allows organizations to address the most pressing security gaps first, reducing their overall risk exposure.

Additionally, AI can automate the patching process for known vulnerabilities, ensuring that updates are applied promptly and consistently, without the need for manual intervention. This can significantly reduce the time window during which systems are exposed to attacks.

6. AI in Securing IoT and Cloud Environments

The increasing adoption of Internet of Things (IoT) devices and cloud computing has created new security challenges, as these technologies often operate outside of traditional perimeter defenses. AI has become indispensable in securing these environments by continuously monitoring and defending against threats in real-time.

In the case of IoT, where devices often lack built-in security measures, AI can monitor device behavior for signs of compromise and protect against attacks such as botnet-driven distributed denial-of-service (DDoS) attacks or malware targeting vulnerable IoT devices. Similarly, in cloud environments, AI can ensure secure access management, detect unauthorized access to cloud resources, and even identify and mitigate attacks targeting cloud-based applications.

AI is fundamentally transforming the landscape of digital defense, moving organizations from reactive and manual security models to proactive, intelligent, and automated systems. By harnessing the power of AI and machine learning, cybersecurity teams can detect threats earlier, respond faster, and better defend against the complex and rapidly evolving cyber threat landscape. As AI technologies continue to improve, they will play an increasingly central role in ensuring the resilience of organizations against emerging cyber risks, enabling more adaptive and dynamic defenses that are necessary to protect critical data and digital infrastructures in an interconnected world.

1.4 Key Benefits of AI-Driven Cybersecurity Solutions

The growing complexity and volume of cyber threats, coupled with the rapid pace at which technology evolves, have highlighted the need for more sophisticated cybersecurity solutions. Traditional methods, such as signature-based detection and human intervention, often fall short in addressing the dynamic and multi-faceted nature of modern cyberattacks. In contrast, artificial intelligence (AI) has emerged as a transformative force in cybersecurity, providing numerous benefits that enhance an organization's ability to protect its digital infrastructure. This section explores the key advantages of AI-driven cybersecurity solutions and why they are essential for organizations striving to stay ahead of cybercriminals and safeguard their sensitive data.

1. Enhanced Threat Detection and Prevention

One of the primary benefits of AI-driven cybersecurity solutions is their ability to significantly enhance threat detection and prevention. Traditional security systems typically rely on known signatures or predefined rules to detect threats, which leaves gaps when it comes to identifying new, evolving, or sophisticated attacks. AI, particularly machine learning (ML), addresses these gaps by enabling systems to learn and adapt over time.

AI-driven systems can continuously analyze vast amounts of data from various sources and identify patterns of behavior that indicate potential security threats. Whether it's identifying new malware variants, spotting anomalies in network traffic, or detecting unusual user behavior, AI can detect previously unseen threats that traditional systems might miss. By establishing a baseline of normal behavior, AI can flag deviations from this pattern in real-time, allowing organizations to detect cyberattacks, such as Advanced Persistent Threats (APTs), much earlier.

In addition, AI's ability to recognize new threats means it can detect zero-day attacks—those that exploit previously unknown vulnerabilities—in real time. AI is also capable of analyzing previously undetected attack vectors, helping to prevent security breaches that might otherwise go unnoticed.

2. Automation of Incident Response

The speed and complexity of modern cyberattacks demand rapid responses to mitigate damage. In traditional security setups, manual intervention is required to analyze and respond to threats, which can introduce delays and human error. AI can automate much of the incident response process, providing faster, more accurate, and more consistent defense mechanisms.

AI-driven Security Information and Event Management (SIEM) systems can continuously monitor logs, identify suspicious patterns, and trigger predefined responses. These responses can include blocking malicious traffic, isolating infected systems, or even shutting down compromised user accounts. By automating these processes, AI reduces the time it takes to respond to attacks, ensuring that security teams can act before an attack escalates.

Moreover, AI systems can orchestrate responses across different tools and platforms, allowing for a coordinated defense. This eliminates the need for manual intervention across multiple security systems and ensures a quicker and more effective resolution of incidents.

AI's ability to learn from past incidents also helps refine and improve response actions. By analyzing previous threats and their outcomes, AI can continuously improve its decision-making processes, ensuring that responses become increasingly more effective over time.

3. Reduction of False Positives

One of the ongoing challenges with traditional security systems, particularly Intrusion Detection Systems (IDS) and Intrusion Prevention Systems (IPS), is their tendency to generate a high volume of false positives. These are alerts for suspicious activities that, upon further investigation, turn out to be benign. High rates of false positives can overwhelm security teams, leading to alert fatigue, where real threats are overlooked due to an excess of irrelevant alerts.

AI-driven solutions help address this issue by significantly reducing false positives. Machine learning algorithms can analyze data more deeply, distinguishing between normal user behavior and true anomalies. Over time, AI systems become better at identifying genuine threats, ensuring that alerts are more accurate and meaningful.

By focusing on detecting only the most relevant threats, AI allows security teams to prioritize their resources more effectively, reducing the burden of unnecessary investigations. This means that security professionals can devote their attention to the most critical issues, improving the overall efficiency of the security team.

4. Improved Response Times and Speed of Mitigation

AI's speed in identifying and responding to security incidents is one of its most valuable attributes. Unlike traditional systems, which can take significant time to process incoming data, identify threats, and recommend actions, AI systems can quickly analyze large volumes of data in real time, detect anomalies, and take action.

For instance, when AI detects a ransomware attack in progress, it can immediately isolate the affected system, preventing the ransomware from spreading to other parts of the network. Similarly, AI can swiftly detect a phishing attempt and block malicious emails before they reach an employee's inbox. This rapid response time is critical in preventing attackers from causing significant damage.

AI-driven systems can also prioritize threats based on severity, ensuring that high-priority incidents are dealt with immediately. This time-sensitive defense minimizes the window of opportunity for cybercriminals to exploit vulnerabilities and increases an organization's ability to prevent data breaches and minimize damage.

5. Scalability and Adaptability

The digital landscape is expanding rapidly, with organizations increasingly adopting technologies such as cloud computing, mobile devices, and Internet of Things (IoT) devices. These technological advancements create more entry points for potential attacks and make traditional, perimeter-based security approaches insufficient. AI-powered solutions excel in scaling and adapting to these changes.

AI systems are not constrained by physical infrastructures or specific device types, which allows them to extend their reach across diverse environments. Whether it's securing cloud infrastructure, IoT networks, or mobile devices, AI can dynamically adapt to new technologies and network configurations without requiring significant manual intervention.

As the scale of digital networks continues to grow, AI's ability to process and analyze large amounts of data in real time becomes an essential capability. It can monitor millions of endpoints, devices, and applications, enabling organizations to secure vast and complex environments that would be unmanageable with traditional security tools.

Moreover, AI-powered systems learn and evolve based on new data and emerging threat landscapes. As cybercriminals adapt and develop new techniques, AI continuously updates its detection and response mechanisms to stay ahead of attackers.

6. Enhanced Threat Intelligence

Threat intelligence is a critical component of any cybersecurity strategy, as it involves gathering, analyzing, and utilizing information about potential threats and attackers. AI plays a significant role in enhancing threat intelligence by analyzing vast amounts of structured and unstructured data from diverse sources, including network logs, social media, and the dark web.

By using natural language processing (NLP) and machine learning techniques, AI can automatically extract actionable insights from these data sources, identifying new tactics, techniques, and procedures (TTPs) used by attackers. This real-time analysis can provide organizations with early warnings about emerging threats, enabling them to take proactive measures to defend against them.

AI also helps enhance the accuracy and relevance of threat intelligence. It can analyze trends over time, highlight the most pertinent threats to a specific organization, and deliver predictive threat intelligence that anticipates future attack vectors. This predictive capability allows organizations to bolster their defenses ahead of time, reducing the likelihood of successful attacks.

7. Enhanced User and Entity Behavior Analytics (UEBA)

AI plays a critical role in User and Entity Behavior Analytics (UEBA), which involves the detection of unusual or potentially malicious activity within an organization by analyzing user and system behavior. By leveraging machine learning and AI, UEBA systems can build profiles of normal activity for each user or device and detect deviations from those patterns.

For example, AI can identify when a user is accessing sensitive files they don't typically use, or when a device is communicating with external servers in a way that is inconsistent with its normal usage. These behavioral anomalies could indicate insider threats, compromised accounts, or advanced persistent threats.

By continuously monitoring user behavior and system activity, AI-powered UEBA systems provide ongoing vigilance, alerting organizations to risks as soon as they arise. This makes AI essential in detecting threats that are difficult to identify with traditional signature-based methods, such as insider attacks or credential theft.

AI-driven cybersecurity solutions are transforming how organizations defend against cyber threats by offering proactive, adaptive, and intelligent defense mechanisms. From enhancing threat detection and prevention to automating incident response and reducing false positives, AI delivers several key benefits that make it an indispensable tool in the modern cybersecurity landscape. As cyber threats continue to evolve and grow more sophisticated, AI will play a critical role in enabling organizations to stay one step ahead, protecting critical systems and sensitive data from an ever-expanding range of attacks. AI's ability to scale, adapt, and continuously learn ensures that it remains at the forefront of cybersecurity innovation, providing a strong foundation for future digital defense strategies.

1.5 Challenges in Adopting AI for Cyber Defense

While the potential benefits of AI-driven cybersecurity are immense, organizations face a range of challenges when it comes to adopting and implementing these advanced technologies. The evolving nature of both AI and cyber threats, the complexity of integration, and concerns over effectiveness, cost, and ethical considerations are just a few of the obstacles organizations must navigate to fully leverage AI for digital protection. In this section, we explore the key challenges associated with adopting AI for cybersecurity, highlighting both technical and organizational hurdles that need to be addressed.

1. Complexity of AI Models and Implementation

AI and machine learning (ML) models, especially those used in cybersecurity, are often complex and resource-intensive. Developing and implementing effective AI-driven security systems requires a deep understanding of machine learning algorithms, data science, and the specific nuances of cybersecurity threats. The technical expertise needed to build, train, and fine-tune these systems is often a significant barrier for many organizations, especially smaller businesses that may lack the resources for such specialized talent.

In addition to the technical complexity, integrating AI models into existing security infrastructures can be challenging. Many organizations still rely on legacy systems that are not designed to work seamlessly with modern AI-based tools. As a result, integrating AI-based cybersecurity tools with existing security solutions such as firewalls, intrusion detection systems (IDS), and Security Information and Event Management (SIEM) platforms can lead to compatibility issues, requiring significant effort and additional investment to ensure smooth interoperability.

Moreover, AI systems often require large volumes of labeled data to train the models effectively. Gathering and curating this data can be time-consuming and expensive. Without high-quality data, AI models may not function optimally, leading to inaccurate predictions or missed threats. This dependency on vast datasets is one of the critical hurdles in developing AI cybersecurity solutions that can effectively counter a broad range of evolving cyber threats.

2. Data Privacy and Security Concerns

AI systems in cybersecurity rely heavily on large datasets to identify patterns and detect anomalies. However, gathering and processing this data often involves analyzing sensitive information, including personal identifiable information (PII), financial data, and other confidential business data. This creates a significant data privacy and security concern, particularly in industries with strict regulatory requirements like healthcare, finance, and government.

For instance, the use of AI in monitoring network traffic or user behavior may require analyzing individuals' actions, which can raise privacy issues. If not implemented properly, AI systems could inadvertently expose sensitive data, either through vulnerabilities in the system or by being improperly configured. Moreover, there is the risk of data breaches—if an AI system's data storage or processing environment is compromised, attackers could gain access to critical security data or even use the AI system against the organization.

Organizations must ensure compliance with regulations such as the General Data Protection Regulation (GDPR) in Europe or the California Consumer Privacy Act (CCPA) in the U.S., which place strict limitations on how data can be collected, processed, and stored. As AI becomes more pervasive in cybersecurity, it's crucial for organizations to implement strong data protection protocols and ensure transparency in how their AI models process sensitive data.

3. High Costs of AI Implementation and Maintenance

Implementing AI for cybersecurity can be a costly endeavor. The initial investment in AI technologies—such as advanced machine learning models, cloud services, and AI-enabled cybersecurity tools—can be substantial. Small and medium-sized enterprises (SMEs), in particular, may find these costs prohibitive, as the technology requires not only purchasing advanced software but also significant investments in hardware (e.g., powerful computing resources), data storage, and training datasets.

Beyond the upfront costs, there is an ongoing maintenance cost associated with AI-driven cybersecurity systems. These systems require continual monitoring, regular updates, and adjustments as cyber threats evolve. The maintenance of AI models often requires highly specialized personnel, including data scientists, machine learning experts, and cybersecurity professionals, which can add to the overall expense.

Additionally, as AI systems evolve, organizations may need to upgrade their systems or expand their infrastructure to accommodate new tools and technologies. This ongoing need for upgrades and improvements can result in sunk costs over time, leading to concerns about the long-term financial sustainability of AI adoption for cybersecurity.

4. Bias and Accuracy of AI Models

AI and machine learning models are only as good as the data they are trained on. One of the significant challenges of adopting AI in cybersecurity is ensuring that these systems are accurate and unbiased. If AI models are trained on incomplete, biased, or unrepresentative data, they can produce inaccurate results, which could lead to false positives or false negatives.

For example, an AI system that detects anomalies in network traffic might mistakenly flag a legitimate user's activity as suspicious or fail to recognize a new type of attack due to lack of training data. Such errors can undermine the effectiveness of the system, lead to unnecessary alerts, or—worse—miss critical threats altogether.

Bias in AI models is also a significant concern, especially when it comes to identifying threats based on certain user behaviors. If the training data includes historical biases (such as overemphasizing certain attack vectors), the AI model may incorrectly classify certain types of activities as more likely to be malicious than others. Addressing these biases requires careful data selection, preprocessing, and regular model testing and updates.

Moreover, as AI systems are often opaque ("black-box" models), it can be difficult for cybersecurity professionals to understand why a model made a particular decision. This lack of transparency can be problematic, especially in critical decision-making scenarios where human oversight is necessary to verify AI-driven conclusions.

5. Over-reliance on AI and the Human Element

Another challenge in adopting AI-driven cybersecurity solutions is the potential for organizations to become overly reliant on the technology and neglect the human element of cybersecurity. While AI systems are powerful and can provide invaluable support, they are not infallible. Cybersecurity professionals must continue to play an essential role in overseeing AI-driven defenses, interpreting results, and making complex decisions that may require human judgment and intuition.

AI is not a replacement for skilled cybersecurity professionals. For example, AI may struggle with understanding the context of certain threats or handling complex, multifaceted incidents that require human intervention. A successful cybersecurity strategy should combine AI's strengths in automation, anomaly detection, and real-time threat analysis with the experience and expertise of human analysts who can assess and address potential risks.

Organizations must ensure that AI tools complement, rather than replace, the role of human professionals. Training and collaboration between AI systems and human experts will be key in ensuring that both AI and human knowledge are utilized to create a robust defense against cyberattacks.

6. Adversarial Attacks on AI Systems

While AI is a powerful tool for defending against cyberattacks, it is also vulnerable to adversarial attacks. These attacks involve manipulating the input data that AI systems use to make decisions, causing them to misclassify information or make incorrect decisions. For example, an attacker could subtly alter network traffic or modify input data in such a way that the AI fails to detect a malicious activity.

Adversarial attacks are an emerging challenge for AI-driven cybersecurity, as attackers learn to exploit vulnerabilities in machine learning algorithms. These attacks can potentially compromise the very security systems designed to prevent them, leading to false conclusions and allowing attackers to bypass defenses.

Developing AI models that are resilient to adversarial manipulation requires ongoing research and innovation. Security teams must implement safeguards and continuously test AI models to identify vulnerabilities and improve their ability to withstand such attacks.

7. Ethical and Legal Concerns

Finally, the adoption of AI in cybersecurity raises various ethical and legal concerns. The use of AI for behavioral monitoring, intrusion detection, and even automated decision-making introduces questions about privacy, consent, and the potential for misuse. For example, AI systems used for monitoring employee activity or analyzing personal data could raise concerns about surveillance and data privacy violations.

Organizations must carefully navigate these ethical challenges, ensuring that their use of AI complies with privacy laws and regulations, while also maintaining transparency and accountability. This includes implementing clear policies on how AI systems are used, ensuring that they do not infringe upon individuals' rights, and providing users with the ability to understand and control how their data is being processed.

Adopting AI-driven cybersecurity solutions presents several challenges, from technical complexity and data privacy concerns to biases in AI models and ethical considerations. These challenges must be carefully addressed to ensure the successful implementation and operation of AI in cybersecurity. Despite these obstacles, the potential benefits of AI—such as enhanced threat detection, faster response times, and the ability to scale and adapt to new threats—make it a crucial component of modern cybersecurity strategies. By overcoming these challenges and ensuring the responsible use of AI, organizations can unlock its full potential in protecting against the evolving and increasingly sophisticated landscape of cyber threats.

2. Understanding the Cyber Threat Landscape

The cyber threat landscape has grown more complex and unpredictable, fueled by advancements in technology and the increasing interconnectivity of our digital world. This chapter delves into the variety of threats organizations face today, from traditional malware and ransomware to sophisticated advanced persistent threats (APTs) and AI-driven attacks. It also examines the rise of cybercrime ecosystems, where attackers collaborate and innovate like legitimate businesses. By understanding the scope, scale, and nature of these threats, readers will gain a clearer picture of why modern cybersecurity requires advanced tools and strategies powered by AI and machine learning.

2.1 Overview of Cyber Threats: Malware, Ransomware, and APTs

In the digital age, organizations and individuals face an ever-growing range of cyber threats, each becoming more sophisticated, stealthy, and damaging. The complexity of cyberattacks has evolved as cybercriminals continuously develop new techniques to bypass traditional security measures. Among the most common and damaging forms of cyber threats are malware, ransomware, and Advanced Persistent Threats (APTs). This chapter provides an overview of these three major cyber threats, describing how they work, their impact, and the challenges they pose for cybersecurity professionals.

1. Malware: The Foundation of Cyber Attacks

Malware (short for malicious software) is one of the most common and persistent threats in the cyber landscape. Malware refers to any software designed to disrupt, damage, or gain unauthorized access to computer systems, networks, or devices. It comes in various forms, each with a unique purpose, but all share the common goal of compromising the confidentiality, integrity, or availability of a system.

Types of Malware:

- **Viruses**: These are self-replicating programs that attach themselves to legitimate files or software. Once executed, they can spread to other systems, corrupting files, and disrupting system operations.

- **Trojans**: These are deceptive programs that appear legitimate but actually carry out harmful actions once installed. Unlike viruses, they do not self-replicate but rely on the user's actions to be executed.
- **Worms**: These are self-replicating programs that spread independently across networks, often exploiting vulnerabilities to infect multiple devices without user interaction.
- **Spyware**: This type of malware is designed to secretly gather information from a system, such as keystrokes, login credentials, and browsing habits, and send that information to cybercriminals.
- **Impact of Malware**: Malware can cause significant damage to organizations by corrupting files, stealing sensitive data, or disrupting business operations. It can also create backdoors for future attacks, allowing cybercriminals to maintain long-term access to the system without detection. Additionally, certain types of malware can be used to launch distributed denial-of-service (DDoS) attacks, which overwhelm systems and networks, rendering them inoperable.

The sheer variety of malware means that cybersecurity teams must be prepared to recognize and defend against different attack vectors. Traditional signature-based antivirus tools often struggle to detect new or modified malware strains, making behavioral analysis and AI-driven detection critical in identifying unknown threats.

2. Ransomware: A Growing Threat to Businesses and Individuals

Ransomware is a particularly insidious form of malware that has seen a sharp rise in recent years. Ransomware attacks involve encrypting the victim's data, making it inaccessible, and then demanding a ransom in exchange for the decryption key. In some cases, cybercriminals also threaten to release sensitive data publicly unless the ransom is paid.

How Ransomware Works:

- **Infection**: Ransomware typically spreads through phishing emails, malicious advertisements, or exploiting software vulnerabilities. Once executed, it encrypts the victim's files and locks them out of their own systems.
- **Ransom Demand**: After encryption, a ransom note is displayed, instructing the victim on how to pay the ransom (usually in cryptocurrency, such as Bitcoin) to receive the decryption key.
- **Payment and Decryption**: Once the ransom is paid, the victim may or may not receive the decryption key. Even if the decryption key is provided, there's no guarantee that the files will be restored to their original state.

Types of Ransomware:

- **Crypto-ransomware**: This type encrypts the victim's files, making them unreadable without the decryption key.
- **Locker ransomware**: Instead of encrypting files, this type locks users out of their devices, preventing them from accessing their systems.
- **Double extortion ransomware**: A newer variant, this type involves both encrypting the victim's data and stealing it. The attackers then threaten to release the stolen data unless the ransom is paid.
- **Impact of Ransomware**: Ransomware attacks can be devastating for organizations, often leading to data loss, financial costs, reputational damage, and operational downtime. In addition to the immediate ransom payment, businesses may face the costs associated with system recovery, legal actions, and regulatory fines, especially if customer data is involved. In some cases, even if the ransom is paid, the decryption key may be faulty or the attackers may demand additional payments.

The rise of ransomware-as-a-service (RaaS) platforms has made it easier for cybercriminals with limited technical skills to launch these attacks, further amplifying the threat. These platforms provide attackers with ready-made ransomware tools and infrastructure for a fee, contributing to the widespread nature of ransomware attacks.

3. Advanced Persistent Threats (APTs): A Stealthy and Long-Term Danger

An Advanced Persistent Threat (APT) is a highly sophisticated and targeted cyberattack often carried out by well-funded, organized groups (such as nation-state actors or criminal organizations). APTs are characterized by their long-term nature, as the attackers infiltrate networks and systems to maintain a persistent, often undetected, presence for months or even years. The goal of APTs is not to cause immediate disruption but rather to steal sensitive data, monitor systems, or gain long-term access for espionage or other strategic purposes.

How APTs Work:

- **Initial Intrusion**: APTs typically start with a spear-phishing attack, which targets specific individuals within an organization. Attackers may use social engineering tactics to trick the victim into downloading malicious attachments or clicking on malicious links.

- **Establishing a Foothold**: Once inside the network, attackers install backdoors or remote access tools (RATs) that allow them to maintain control over the system and move laterally within the organization's network.
- **Data Exfiltration and Espionage**: Over time, the attackers gather intelligence, stealing sensitive data, intellectual property, and confidential business or government information. APTs can also engage in surveillance of internal communications, tracking key personnel or monitoring operational activities.
- **Persistence**: APTs are designed to be difficult to detect and even harder to remove. Attackers frequently change tactics, encrypt their communications, and hide their presence by using legitimate system processes to carry out their activities.
- **Impact of APTs**: The damage from APTs is often insidious because the attackers aim to remain undetected for long periods. As a result, data theft or espionage may go unnoticed for months or years, leading to severe financial, reputational, and security consequences. High-profile targets for APTs include government agencies, military organizations, financial institutions, and large corporations that hold valuable or sensitive data.

Because APTs can persist within a system for extended periods, detection often requires sophisticated threat-hunting techniques, advanced intrusion detection systems (IDS), and the use of AI-powered systems to detect abnormal behavior across networks. Once an APT has established a foothold, responding to the attack requires extensive resources and expertise, as the attackers may have left behind multiple entry points and backdoors.

4. The Evolution of Cyber Threats

The cyber threat landscape is constantly evolving, and malware, ransomware, and APTs are becoming increasingly sophisticated. Cybercriminals are leveraging AI, machine learning, and other advanced technologies to refine their attack techniques, automate processes, and target organizations with greater precision. For example, AI can be used to develop more convincing phishing emails, or to automate the discovery of vulnerabilities in systems.

Moreover, the growth of the Internet of Things (IoT) and cloud computing has expanded the attack surface, providing cybercriminals with new opportunities to exploit weak points in connected devices, networks, and infrastructure. This makes defending against cyber threats even more challenging, as attackers can exploit a variety of attack vectors and attack surfaces that may be overlooked by traditional security tools.

Cyber threats such as malware, ransomware, and APTs represent some of the most significant dangers facing organizations today. While each of these threats operates differently, they all share the ability to cause severe financial damage, disrupt operations, and compromise sensitive information. As cybercriminals become more sophisticated and develop new tactics, cybersecurity professionals must adapt and evolve their defenses accordingly. The use of AI and machine learning in cybersecurity is essential to detect, analyze, and respond to these threats effectively, offering organizations a fighting chance against the constantly evolving world of cybercrime.

2.2 The Role of Automation in Modern Attacks

As cyber threats become more complex and prevalent, attackers are increasingly leveraging automation to enhance the scale, speed, and sophistication of their attacks. Automation enables attackers to exploit vulnerabilities more efficiently, adapt to defenses in real-time, and target multiple systems simultaneously, often with minimal human intervention. This shift toward automated attacks represents a significant challenge for cybersecurity professionals, who must counter these threats with equally advanced and adaptive defenses.

This section explores how automation is transforming the cyberattack landscape, examining the tools, techniques, and implications of automated threats.

1. Automating Reconnaissance and Target Selection

The first stage of any cyberattack is reconnaissance, during which attackers gather information about potential targets. Automation has revolutionized this process by enabling cybercriminals to scan vast numbers of networks, systems, and devices in a fraction of the time it would take manually.

Key Techniques in Automated Reconnaissance:

- **Vulnerability Scanning**: Automated tools like Nmap or Shodan allow attackers to scan networks for open ports, outdated software, or misconfigured systems. These tools can quickly identify weak points that can be exploited.
- **Web Scraping and Data Mining**: Attackers use bots to scrape public data from websites, forums, and social media platforms to collect information about individuals or organizations, such as employee names, email addresses, or system configurations.

- **Domain and Subdomain Enumeration**: Automated tools can identify domain and subdomain structures to map out an organization's digital footprint, searching for unprotected or forgotten assets.

By automating reconnaissance, attackers can rapidly build detailed profiles of their targets, identifying the most vulnerable entry points. This makes attacks more targeted and efficient, reducing the time and resources needed to achieve their goals.

2. Automated Exploitation of Vulnerabilities

Once vulnerabilities are identified, attackers use automation to exploit them at scale. Automated tools can execute predefined scripts or commands to exploit specific weaknesses in software, networks, or devices.

Examples of Automated Exploitation:

- **Exploit Kits**: These are prepackaged tools that contain a variety of exploits for known vulnerabilities. Once deployed, exploit kits automatically detect and attack the specific vulnerabilities present in a target system.
- **Brute Force and Credential Stuffing**: Automated scripts can attempt thousands (or even millions) of username-password combinations in a short amount of time. These tools can leverage stolen credentials from data breaches, testing them against other systems where users might have reused the same login details.
- **Botnets**: Large networks of compromised devices, or bots, can be controlled remotely to perform automated attacks. Botnets are often used to deliver malware, conduct distributed denial-of-service (DDoS) attacks, or mine cryptocurrency.

By automating exploitation, cybercriminals can efficiently launch attacks against multiple targets, including individuals, enterprises, and governments. The use of automation also allows attackers to adapt quickly, modifying their tools to bypass newly implemented security measures.

3. Weaponizing Artificial Intelligence and Machine Learning

Attackers are increasingly incorporating AI and machine learning (ML) into their automated attack strategies, allowing them to refine their tactics and improve success rates. By analyzing large datasets and learning from past attacks, AI-driven systems can identify patterns, predict vulnerabilities, and optimize attack methods.

Applications of AI in Automated Attacks:

- **Phishing Campaigns**: AI can generate highly convincing phishing emails by analyzing target behaviors, preferences, and communication styles. Automated systems can also personalize these attacks in real time, increasing the likelihood of success.
- **Evasion Techniques**: Attackers use AI to develop malware that can adapt its behavior to avoid detection by traditional security tools. For example, malware may change its code or execution patterns to evade signature-based antivirus software.
- **Deepfake Technology**: Automation combined with AI can create realistic fake audio, video, or text content to deceive individuals or compromise organizations through social engineering.

These advancements highlight the growing sophistication of automated attacks, blurring the line between human and machine-driven cyber threats. AI-powered automation enables attackers to innovate and escalate their methods, presenting a significant challenge for defenders.

4. Scaling Attacks with Automation

Automation allows cybercriminals to scale their operations, targeting a vast number of systems or organizations simultaneously. This capability is particularly evident in large-scale attacks such as ransomware campaigns, DDoS attacks, and supply chain compromises.

Scaling Techniques:

- **Ransomware-as-a-Service (RaaS):** Platforms offer ready-made ransomware tools to attackers, complete with automated deployment systems. These tools can encrypt files across hundreds or thousands of systems in minutes.
- **Automated Phishing Campaigns**: Bots can send millions of phishing emails or messages in a single campaign, each tailored to the recipient to improve the likelihood of success.
- **DDoS Attacks**: Botnets are used to flood systems with automated traffic, overwhelming servers and causing outages. Advanced botnets can dynamically adjust their attack patterns to counter mitigation efforts.

Automation not only increases the efficiency of these attacks but also lowers the barrier to entry for less-skilled attackers, democratizing access to sophisticated tools and techniques.

5. Challenges in Countering Automated Attacks

The use of automation in cyberattacks poses several challenges for defenders. Traditional security tools and manual processes are often ill-equipped to handle the speed and scale of automated threats, necessitating the adoption of equally advanced defensive strategies.

Challenges Include:

- **Speed of Attacks**: Automated threats can execute thousands of actions in seconds, leaving little time for human responders to detect and counter them.
- **Adaptability of Attackers**: Automation allows attackers to modify their tactics dynamically, making static or rigid defense mechanisms ineffective.
- **Resource Strain**: Automated attacks, such as DDoS campaigns, can overwhelm an organization's resources, causing systems to fail even if the attack is ultimately detected and blocked.

To combat these challenges, organizations must embrace automation and AI in their defenses, leveraging tools that can detect and respond to threats in real time. Proactive threat hunting, behavioral analytics, and machine learning models are essential components of modern cybersecurity strategies.

Automation has fundamentally transformed the cyber threat landscape, enabling attackers to launch faster, larger, and more sophisticated attacks than ever before. From automating reconnaissance and exploitation to weaponizing AI and scaling operations, automation has become a cornerstone of modern cybercrime. Defenders must recognize the scale of this challenge and adopt equally advanced strategies to counter automated threats, ensuring that security measures evolve as quickly as the tactics they are designed to prevent.

2.3 The Rise of AI-Driven Threats

Artificial Intelligence (AI) is a double-edged sword in the realm of cybersecurity. While it empowers defenders with advanced tools to detect and mitigate threats, it simultaneously offers cybercriminals unprecedented opportunities to enhance their attack methods. AI-driven threats are revolutionizing the cyber threat landscape, making attacks more sophisticated, adaptive, and difficult to counter. This section delves into the rise of AI-driven threats, exploring their characteristics, examples, and the challenges they pose to modern digital defense.

1. Characteristics of AI-Driven Threats

AI-driven cyber threats distinguish themselves from traditional attacks in several ways:

- **Adaptability**: AI systems can analyze defenses in real time and adjust attack strategies accordingly. For instance, they can alter malware behavior to avoid detection or switch targets based on a system's vulnerabilities.
- **Scalability**: Using AI, attackers can automate the launch of large-scale, personalized attacks, such as phishing campaigns, at a scale previously unattainable.
- **Sophistication**: AI-driven attacks can mimic human behavior, making them harder to distinguish from legitimate activities. This is especially evident in social engineering and impersonation schemes.
- **Speed**: AI systems can execute complex attack chains far more quickly than a human could, increasing the chances of success before detection.

These traits make AI-driven threats particularly challenging for cybersecurity professionals, as traditional tools often struggle to keep pace with their speed and complexity.

2. Examples of AI-Driven Threats

AI-driven threats span a wide range of attack types, leveraging the capabilities of machine learning and automation to enhance their effectiveness.

1. AI-Powered Phishing Attacks

Traditional phishing campaigns often rely on generic messages sent to large numbers of recipients. AI, however, enables attackers to craft highly personalized phishing emails by analyzing social media profiles, email communication patterns, and other data sources. These emails mimic language and tone, increasing the likelihood of recipients falling for the scam.

2. Deepfake Impersonation

Deepfake technology uses AI to create hyper-realistic fake videos, audio, or images. Attackers use deepfakes to impersonate executives in business email compromise (BEC) scams, convincing employees to transfer funds or share sensitive information. Deepfakes can also be used for misinformation campaigns, undermining trust in individuals or organizations.

3. Malware with AI-Based Evasion

AI-powered malware can dynamically adapt its behavior to evade detection. For example, such malware may monitor the environment in which it is operating and delay execution until it detects an unprotected or low-surveillance setting. It can also alter its code to avoid signature-based detection.

4. AI-Enhanced Ransomware

Ransomware is becoming more dangerous with AI integration. AI can optimize encryption processes, ensuring that files are locked faster and more comprehensively. It can also identify high-value data to target first, increasing the likelihood of ransom payment.

5. AI in Cyber Espionage

Attackers use AI to analyze massive amounts of data stolen during breaches, identifying patterns, valuable insights, or potential leverage points for espionage. This allows them to sift through datasets quickly and effectively, turning raw data into actionable intelligence.

3. The Role of Generative AI in Threat Creation

Generative AI, such as advanced natural language models and image synthesis tools, is being weaponized by cybercriminals to enhance their operations. These tools allow attackers to create convincing and realistic artifacts for use in cyberattacks.

- **Social Engineering**: Generative AI can write personalized messages or create realistic fake profiles to gain the trust of victims in phishing or spear-phishing campaigns.
- **Code Generation**: AI tools can generate malicious code or scripts, significantly lowering the technical barrier for less-experienced attackers. For example, attackers can ask generative AI tools to create scripts that exploit vulnerabilities or automate system reconnaissance.
- **Fake Evidence**: Attackers can generate fake documents, contracts, or other materials to manipulate victims in scams or legal disputes.

Generative AI tools, accessible to the general public, empower a wider range of actors to execute sophisticated cyberattacks, blurring the line between skilled hackers and opportunistic criminals.

4. Challenges in Addressing AI-Driven Threats

AI-driven threats present unique challenges for cybersecurity professionals and organizations, including:

- **Detecting AI-Generated Content**: The realism of AI-generated phishing emails, deepfakes, and other artifacts makes it challenging to distinguish them from legitimate communications. Traditional detection methods, such as keyword analysis or content filtering, often fail against such advanced tactics.
- **Speed and Scale**: The rapid execution of AI-driven attacks overwhelms conventional defenses. For instance, AI can launch thousands of unique phishing emails within minutes, outpacing manual or semi-automated detection systems.
- **Lack of Preparedness**: Many organizations lack the tools or expertise to detect and respond to AI-driven threats effectively. Legacy systems and outdated cybersecurity practices are particularly vulnerable.
- **Resource Gap**: Cybercriminals often use AI to exploit weaknesses in underfunded or understaffed cybersecurity teams, targeting organizations that lack the resources to defend against such sophisticated attacks.

5. Defensive Strategies Against AI-Driven Threats

To counter AI-driven threats, organizations must adopt advanced, proactive defenses that incorporate AI themselves. Key strategies include:

- **Behavioral Analytics**: AI-based systems can analyze user behavior to detect anomalies indicative of malicious activity, such as unauthorized access or unusual data transfers.
- **AI-Powered Threat Detection**: Leveraging AI in cybersecurity tools enables organizations to identify and respond to threats more quickly. For instance, machine learning models can detect subtle indicators of phishing or malware.
- **Continuous Monitoring**: Real-time monitoring of networks and endpoints allows for the early detection of AI-driven threats, reducing the window of opportunity for attackers.
- **Training and Awareness**: Organizations must educate employees about the risks of AI-driven attacks, such as deepfakes and phishing emails, empowering them to recognize and report suspicious activity.

- **Partnerships and Intelligence Sharing**: Collaborating with industry groups and threat intelligence platforms helps organizations stay informed about emerging AI-driven attack trends and tactics.

The arms race between attackers and defenders in the realm of AI is ongoing, with each side striving to outpace the other. Investing in cutting-edge technologies and fostering a culture of cybersecurity awareness are essential to staying ahead.

AI-driven threats represent a paradigm shift in the cybersecurity landscape, introducing new levels of sophistication, adaptability, and scale to cyberattacks. From phishing campaigns enhanced by machine learning to deepfake-driven impersonation scams, these threats challenge traditional defenses and demand innovative responses. As attackers continue to weaponize AI, it is imperative for organizations to embrace advanced technologies, proactive strategies, and collaborative efforts to combat this new generation of cyber threats effectively. In the battle between defenders and attackers, AI is both the ultimate tool and the ultimate challenge.

2.4 Cybercrime Ecosystems: Actors, Markets, and Tools

The modern cybercrime ecosystem has evolved into a sophisticated and highly organized network of actors, markets, and tools. It operates like a parallel economy, enabling malicious activities at scale, while offering specialized services for those with varying technical capabilities. This ecosystem thrives on anonymity and decentralization, allowing cybercriminals to collaborate, innovate, and evade law enforcement. This section explores the key elements of the cybercrime ecosystem, focusing on the individuals and groups involved, the underground marketplaces that facilitate transactions, and the tools that make cyberattacks increasingly accessible and effective.

1. Key Actors in the Cybercrime Ecosystem

The cybercrime ecosystem is diverse, with actors ranging from lone hackers to large, organized groups. Each plays a distinct role in the success of the ecosystem.

1. Script Kiddies

Often inexperienced and unskilled, these individuals rely on prebuilt tools and scripts to conduct low-level attacks. While their technical capabilities are limited, the accessibility of powerful tools allows them to cause significant disruption.

2. Hacktivists

Hacktivists use cyberattacks to promote political, ideological, or social causes. Their actions often target governments, corporations, or institutions they perceive as unethical, focusing on website defacements, data breaches, or denial-of-service attacks.

3. Cybercriminal Gangs

These organized groups operate like traditional criminal organizations, with specialized roles such as developers, testers, operators, and money launderers. They target high-value entities, focusing on ransomware, financial fraud, or data theft.

4. Nation-State Actors

Governments and state-sponsored groups leverage cybercrime for espionage, sabotage, or political gain. Their attacks are often advanced, persistent, and highly targeted, as seen in Advanced Persistent Threats (APTs).

5. Insiders

Employees, contractors, or associates with authorized access to systems often play a role in cybercrime, either deliberately (e.g., selling credentials) or accidentally (e.g., falling victim to phishing schemes).

2. Cybercrime Markets and Underground Economy

The underground economy is a thriving marketplace where cybercriminals exchange goods, services, and tools. These markets often operate on the dark web, accessible only through anonymity-preserving networks like Tor.

1. Dark Web Marketplaces

These marketplaces are hubs for buying and selling illegal goods and services, including stolen data, malware, exploit kits, and forged documents. Popular platforms often mimic legitimate e-commerce sites with ratings, reviews, and dispute resolution systems.

2. Ransomware-as-a-Service (RaaS)

RaaS platforms provide ransomware tools to other criminals for a share of the profits. This "as-a-service" model democratizes cybercrime, enabling even unskilled actors to launch sophisticated attacks.

3. Bulletproof Hosting Services

These providers offer hosting services with minimal regulation and high tolerance for illegal activities, allowing cybercriminals to store malicious files, operate phishing campaigns, or host command-and-control servers.

4. Cryptocurrency Exchanges and Mixers

Cryptocurrencies like Bitcoin and Monero are the primary mediums of exchange in the cybercrime ecosystem. Mixers or tumblers obscure the origin of funds, making it difficult to trace transactions.

5. Information Brokers

These actors sell stolen personal or corporate data, including credit card details, login credentials, and proprietary information. Data breaches fuel this market, which in turn enables further crimes like identity theft and fraud.

3. Tools of the Trade: Enabling Cybercrime

The tools used by cybercriminals have become increasingly sophisticated and user-friendly, lowering the technical barriers to entry. These tools are often sold or shared within the ecosystem, further expanding its reach.

1. Exploit Kits

These prepackaged toolkits allow attackers to exploit known vulnerabilities in software or systems. Often paired with automated delivery mechanisms, they require minimal expertise to use.

2. Malware Variants

Customizable malware, including trojans, ransomware, and spyware, is readily available on underground markets. Some variants are equipped with advanced evasion techniques, such as polymorphism and sandbox detection.

3. Phishing Kits

Phishing kits simplify the process of creating convincing fake websites or emails. Many come with templates for specific industries or platforms, increasing their effectiveness.

4. Botnets

Botnets, networks of compromised devices, are rented out to execute distributed denial-of-service (DDoS) attacks, spam campaigns, or cryptocurrency mining.

5. AI-Powered Tools

AI has entered the cybercrime toolkit, enabling enhanced phishing campaigns, automated vulnerability detection, and adaptive malware. These tools make attacks more scalable and harder to detect.

4. The Lifecycle of a Cybercrime Operation

Cybercrime operations often follow a structured lifecycle, involving multiple actors and tools. Understanding this process is crucial for developing effective countermeasures.

Reconnaissance

Attackers gather intelligence about their target, often using automated tools or purchased data from information brokers.

Initial Access

This step involves exploiting vulnerabilities, phishing, or buying access credentials from dark web marketplaces.

Payload Delivery

The chosen malware or exploit is deployed, often using methods like email attachments, malicious links, or compromised websites.

Command and Control (C2)

Once the payload is active, it connects to a C2 server for instructions, allowing attackers to manage the operation remotely.

Monetization

The end goal is profit, achieved through extortion (e.g., ransomware), theft (e.g., financial fraud), or resale (e.g., stolen data).

5. The Role of Collaboration in Cybercrime

Collaboration is a defining feature of the cybercrime ecosystem, enabling actors to combine their skills and resources for maximum impact.

- **Forums and Communities**: Cybercriminals share knowledge, tools, and advice on underground forums, fostering innovation and reducing barriers to entry.
- **Partnerships and Affiliates**: Many cybercrime operations rely on affiliate models, where multiple parties share profits based on their contributions, such as delivering ransomware or laundering funds.
- **Global Networks**: Cybercrime knows no borders, with actors from different countries collaborating on complex, multinational operations.

The cybercrime ecosystem is a well-oiled machine, driven by a diverse cast of actors, underground markets, and powerful tools. Its structure mirrors legitimate economies, complete with specialization, collaboration, and innovation. This complexity makes it a formidable adversary for cybersecurity professionals and law enforcement. Understanding the inner workings of this ecosystem is critical for anticipating threats, disrupting operations, and developing proactive defenses. As the cybercrime economy continues to grow, collaboration among defenders, enhanced threat intelligence, and advanced tools will be essential to staying ahead of this ever-evolving menace.

2.5 The Growing Complexity of Attack Surfaces

The modern digital landscape has expanded far beyond traditional IT systems, creating a vastly more complex and interconnected attack surface. This evolution has been driven by advancements in cloud computing, mobile technology, the Internet of Things (IoT), remote work, and digital transformation initiatives. While these innovations offer unprecedented convenience and productivity, they also introduce numerous vulnerabilities, exposing organizations to an increasing array of cyber threats. In this section, we explore how attack surfaces have grown, the challenges they pose to cybersecurity, and strategies to mitigate the risks associated with them.

1. Defining the Attack Surface

The attack surface encompasses all potential points where a malicious actor can attempt to gain unauthorized access to a system, exploit vulnerabilities, or disrupt operations. It includes:

- **Digital Assets**: Servers, databases, endpoints, cloud services, and web applications.
- **Network Interfaces**: Open ports, protocols, APIs, and wireless networks.
- **User Interactions**: Employee endpoints, personal devices, and external contractors.
- **Supply Chains**: Third-party vendors, software integrations, and outsourced services.

The attack surface is no longer confined to on-premises systems, expanding to include mobile devices, IoT endpoints, and virtual environments, which complicates efforts to monitor and secure it effectively.

2. Factors Driving the Expansion of Attack Surfaces

Several key trends have contributed to the rapid growth and complexity of attack surfaces:

1. Digital Transformation

Organizations are adopting cloud computing, SaaS platforms, and AI-driven tools to streamline operations. These technologies require external connections and integrations, increasing the number of entry points for attackers.

2. Remote Work and BYOD

The shift to remote work has blurred the boundaries between personal and professional devices. Employees accessing corporate networks from untrusted devices or insecure networks create additional vulnerabilities.

3. Internet of Things (IoT)

IoT devices, from smart thermostats to industrial sensors, often lack robust security measures. These devices are frequently connected to critical systems, providing potential entry points for attackers.

4. Supply Chain Dependencies

Cyberattacks targeting third-party vendors or partners can indirectly compromise an organization. Supply chain attacks, such as those involving malicious updates to trusted software, have become a significant concern.

5. Shadow IT

Unauthorized software and hardware used by employees, often without the knowledge of IT departments, contribute to an unmonitored attack surface. These shadow assets often lack proper security configurations.

6. Sophisticated Threat Actors

As cybercriminals and nation-states grow more adept at exploiting these expanded surfaces, their ability to identify and leverage weaknesses increases, making even minor oversights potentially catastrophic.

3. Examples of Emerging Attack Surfaces

The following examples highlight the diverse and growing nature of attack surfaces:

1. Cloud Services

Cloud infrastructure introduces risks such as misconfigured storage buckets, insecure APIs, and excessive permissions. Attackers exploit these vulnerabilities to gain unauthorized access or exfiltrate data.

2. API Endpoints

APIs are integral to modern applications, enabling communication between services. However, poorly secured APIs can be exploited to bypass authentication or inject malicious code.

3. IoT Networks

IoT devices, such as smart cameras or industrial control systems, often use default passwords and unpatched firmware. Once compromised, these devices can serve as entry points to critical networks or participate in botnet attacks.

4. Social Engineering Entry Points

As organizations adopt collaboration tools and social platforms, phishing campaigns targeting employees have become increasingly sophisticated, exploiting human vulnerabilities rather than technical flaws.

5. Industrial Control Systems (ICS)

Critical infrastructure sectors, such as energy and manufacturing, rely on ICS that were not originally designed with cybersecurity in mind. These systems are now frequently targeted by ransomware and APT groups.

4. Challenges in Managing Complex Attack Surfaces

Securing an ever-growing attack surface poses several challenges for organizations:

1. Visibility

Organizations often lack full visibility into all assets, connections, and potential vulnerabilities. Shadow IT, in particular, complicates the task of identifying and securing all entry points.

2. Dynamic Environments

Cloud environments and virtualized infrastructures are highly dynamic, with new instances, containers, and microservices being deployed regularly. This constant change makes traditional security measures inadequate.

3. Resource Constraints

Managing a complex attack surface requires skilled personnel and advanced tools. Many organizations struggle to allocate sufficient resources to address these demands.

4. Human Error

Misconfigurations, such as leaving databases publicly accessible or failing to revoke outdated permissions, are common contributors to attack surface vulnerabilities.

5. Insider Threats

Employees, whether malicious or negligent, represent a significant risk. Poor security awareness or intentional misuse of access can compromise systems from within.

5. Strategies to Mitigate the Risks of Expanding Attack Surfaces

Organizations can take several steps to reduce the risks associated with complex attack surfaces:

1. Conduct Continuous Asset Discovery and Monitoring

Automated tools can help organizations identify all assets, including those in shadow IT, and continuously monitor them for vulnerabilities.

2. Implement Zero Trust Architecture

Zero Trust principles require all users and devices to authenticate and verify their identity before accessing resources, regardless of their location within the network.

3. Use Advanced Threat Detection Tools

AI-driven cybersecurity tools can analyze network traffic, detect anomalies, and respond to threats in real time, improving defense against advanced attacks.

4. Enforce Strong Identity and Access Management (IAM)

Organizations should adopt multi-factor authentication (MFA), enforce least privilege access, and regularly review user permissions to reduce insider risks.

5. Secure the Supply Chain

Regularly assess the security posture of third-party vendors and partners. Contracts should include provisions for compliance with cybersecurity standards and protocols.

6. Conduct Regular Penetration Testing

Simulating attacks helps identify weaknesses in the attack surface, enabling organizations to address vulnerabilities before they can be exploited.

7. Educate Employees

Security awareness training can reduce the likelihood of social engineering attacks and improve adherence to cybersecurity policies.

The growing complexity of attack surfaces reflects the rapid pace of technological innovation and digital integration. While these advancements provide immense value, they also expose organizations to a wider array of threats. Effective management of this complexity requires a combination of visibility, proactive strategies, and advanced tools. By adopting a comprehensive approach to attack surface management, organizations can reduce vulnerabilities, enhance their defensive posture, and stay ahead of evolving cyber threats. As the digital landscape continues to expand, the importance of securing every possible entry point cannot be overstated.

3. AI and ML Basics for Cybersecurity Professionals

Artificial intelligence (AI) and machine learning (ML) are reshaping cybersecurity, but understanding their core principles is essential for harnessing their potential effectively. This chapter introduces the foundational concepts of AI and ML, including key algorithms like classification, clustering, and neural networks, with an emphasis on their relevance to cybersecurity applications. Readers will explore how these technologies process data, identify patterns, and make predictions that enhance defense mechanisms. By the end of this chapter, cybersecurity professionals will have a solid grounding in AI and ML, empowering them to apply these tools strategically in their work.

3.1 Essential Concepts in Artificial Intelligence

Artificial Intelligence (AI) is at the heart of many modern technologies, powering innovations across industries, including cybersecurity. To effectively understand AI's transformative potential in digital defense, it's crucial to grasp its foundational concepts. AI encompasses a wide range of techniques and methods, from simple rule-based systems to advanced machine learning and neural networks. This section introduces the essential concepts of AI, providing a foundation for understanding its application in cybersecurity.

1. What Is Artificial Intelligence?

AI refers to the simulation of human intelligence by machines, enabling them to perform tasks that typically require human cognition, such as problem-solving, learning, reasoning, and decision-making. The goal of AI is not just to execute tasks but to do so in a way that improves over time through experience or additional data. AI systems can be broadly classified into two categories:

- **Narrow AI**: Designed for specific tasks (e.g., spam filtering, facial recognition). This is the most common form of AI in use today.
- **General AI**: A theoretical form of AI capable of performing any intellectual task that a human can do. It remains largely in the realm of research and science fiction.

2. Key Components of AI

To build effective AI systems, several core components and techniques are used:

1. Data

AI systems rely on vast amounts of data to learn and make decisions. This data can include structured datasets, like databases, or unstructured data, like emails, images, and audio recordings.

2. Algorithms

An algorithm is a set of rules or instructions that the AI follows to solve problems or make decisions. These can range from simple decision trees to complex neural networks.

3. Training and Learning

AI models are "trained" on datasets, allowing them to learn patterns and correlations. Training involves feeding data into the system and adjusting its parameters to improve accuracy. The learning process can be categorized as:

- **Supervised Learning**: Using labeled data (e.g., images tagged as "cat" or "dog") to teach the AI.
- **Unsupervised Learning**: Identifying patterns in unlabeled data.
- **Reinforcement Learning**: Learning through trial and error, receiving rewards or penalties based on actions.

4. Model Evaluation

After training, AI models are tested on new data to evaluate their performance. Metrics such as accuracy, precision, recall, and F1-score are used to measure their effectiveness.

3. Machine Learning: The Foundation of AI

Machine Learning (ML) is a subset of AI focused on enabling systems to learn and improve without being explicitly programmed. ML techniques include:

1. Regression

Used for predicting continuous outcomes (e.g., predicting stock prices based on historical data).

2. Classification

Categorizes data into predefined groups (e.g., identifying spam vs. legitimate emails).

3. Clustering

Groups data based on similarities, without pre-labeled categories (e.g., segmenting customers based on purchasing behavior).

4. Decision Trees and Random Forests

Tree-like models that split data into branches based on decision rules. Random forests combine multiple trees for better accuracy.

4. Neural Networks and Deep Learning

Deep Learning is a subset of ML that uses neural networks with multiple layers to analyze and interpret complex data. Neural networks are modeled after the human brain, consisting of interconnected "neurons" that process information.

- **Structure of Neural Networks**: Neural networks are composed of input layers (data), hidden layers (processing), and output layers (results).
- **Deep Neural Networks**: Neural networks with multiple hidden layers are called deep networks, enabling them to handle tasks like image recognition, language processing, and anomaly detection.
- **Convolutional Neural Networks (CNNs):** Specialized for image processing.
- **Recurrent Neural Networks (RNNs):** Ideal for sequential data like time series or language.

5. Natural Language Processing (NLP)

NLP enables AI systems to understand, interpret, and respond to human language. It powers applications like chatbots, sentiment analysis, and language translation. Key techniques include:

- **Tokenization**: Breaking text into smaller units, such as words or phrases.
- **Named Entity Recognition (NER):** Identifying entities like names, dates, and locations in text.
- **Sentiment Analysis**: Determining the emotional tone of a text.

In cybersecurity, NLP is crucial for detecting phishing emails, analyzing threat reports, and automating incident responses.

6. Reinforcement Learning

Reinforcement Learning (RL) involves teaching AI to make decisions in dynamic environments by rewarding desired outcomes and penalizing undesired ones. It's particularly useful in cybersecurity for adaptive defenses, such as optimizing firewall rules or managing resource allocation during an attack.

7. Key Ethical Considerations in AI

As powerful as AI is, its use raises important ethical concerns:

- **Bias in Algorithms**: AI can perpetuate or amplify biases present in training data, leading to unfair outcomes.
- **Privacy Concerns**: AI systems often require large amounts of personal data, raising questions about data security and consent.
- **Transparency**: Many AI systems, especially deep learning models, operate as "black boxes," making it difficult to understand their decision-making process.

Addressing these concerns is essential for building trust in AI applications, especially in sensitive areas like cybersecurity.

8. AI in Cybersecurity: A Preview

Understanding these essential concepts provides a strong foundation for exploring how AI can transform cybersecurity. AI and ML are not just tools but also strategic assets, enabling organizations to detect threats, respond to incidents, and predict future vulnerabilities with unprecedented speed and accuracy. By leveraging AI, cybersecurity professionals can shift from reactive to proactive defense strategies, staying ahead of an ever-evolving threat landscape.

AI's foundational concepts—spanning machine learning, neural networks, NLP, and reinforcement learning—form the building blocks for its application in cybersecurity. By grasping these ideas, professionals can better appreciate AI's potential to enhance digital defense while remaining mindful of the ethical challenges it introduces. As we delve deeper into AI's role in cybersecurity, these essential concepts will serve as a guiding framework for understanding its transformative impact.

3.2 Machine Learning Models and Their Applications

Machine learning (ML) models are the engines that drive modern AI systems, enabling machines to learn patterns, make predictions, and solve complex problems. These models come in various forms, each suited to specific types of tasks. In cybersecurity, ML models have proven invaluable for detecting anomalies, predicting threats, and automating defenses. This section explores the key types of machine learning models and their practical applications in enhancing digital security.

1. Types of Machine Learning Models

Machine learning models can be broadly categorized into three types based on their learning approach:

1. Supervised Learning Models

Supervised learning involves training a model on a labeled dataset, where the input data and its corresponding output (label) are known. The model learns to map inputs to the correct outputs and can then predict the output for new, unseen data.

Examples: Linear regression, logistic regression, support vector machines (SVMs), and decision trees.

Applications in Cybersecurity:

- Detecting spam emails by classifying them as spam or legitimate.
- Identifying malware based on labeled datasets of malicious and benign files.

2. Unsupervised Learning Models

Unsupervised learning models work with unlabeled data, finding hidden patterns or structures within it. These models are particularly useful when labeled datasets are unavailable.

Examples: Clustering (e.g., K-means) and dimensionality reduction techniques (e.g., Principal Component Analysis, PCA).

Applications in Cybersecurity:

- Anomaly detection, such as spotting unusual user behaviors that may indicate a compromised account.
- Grouping similar attack patterns for better threat intelligence.

3. Reinforcement Learning Models

Reinforcement learning (RL) involves training a model to make decisions in an environment by maximizing rewards over time. The model learns from its interactions with the environment and refines its strategies based on feedback.

Examples: Q-learning, Deep Q-Networks (DQN).

Applications in Cybersecurity:

- Optimizing intrusion detection systems (IDS) by dynamically updating rules based on evolving threats.
- Automated threat response strategies, such as isolating compromised systems.

2. Key Machine Learning Models and Techniques

Below are some of the most widely used machine learning models and their relevance to cybersecurity:

1. Linear Regression and Logistic Regression

- **Purpose**: Linear regression predicts continuous values, while logistic regression predicts probabilities for classification problems.
- **Applications**: Identifying the likelihood of a system compromise based on historical indicators, such as login frequency and unusual access times.

2. Decision Trees and Random Forests

- **Purpose**: Decision trees split data based on features to make predictions, while random forests combine multiple trees for greater accuracy.
- **Applications**: Classifying whether an event (e.g., a login attempt) is legitimate or malicious based on multiple factors like location, time, and device type.

3. Support Vector Machines (SVM)

- **Purpose**: SVMs find the optimal boundary between different classes in the data.

- **Applications**: Malware classification by distinguishing malicious code from benign code based on features like byte sequences and API calls.

4. Clustering Models (e.g., K-means)

- **Purpose**: Group similar data points into clusters based on their features.
- **Applications**: Grouping users based on behavior to detect outliers that may indicate insider threats or compromised accounts.

5. Neural Networks and Deep Learning

- **Purpose**: Neural networks simulate the human brain to learn complex patterns in data. Deep learning, with its multiple layers, excels in tasks like image and speech recognition.
- **Applications**: Identifying phishing emails by analyzing textual patterns and visual elements in messages.

6. Ensemble Learning Models

- **Purpose**: Combine multiple models to improve predictive performance. Examples include Boosting (e.g., Gradient Boosting) and Bagging (e.g., Random Forests).
- **Applications**: Enhancing the accuracy of intrusion detection systems by aggregating predictions from different models.

3. Applications of ML Models in Cybersecurity

ML models are transforming the cybersecurity landscape by enabling more intelligent, adaptive, and proactive defenses. Key applications include:

1. Threat Detection and Prevention

- **Anomaly Detection**: Unsupervised learning models analyze baseline behaviors in network traffic or user activity to detect deviations that could signal attacks.
- **Malware Detection**: Supervised models classify files as malicious or safe based on features extracted from known malware datasets.

2. Intrusion Detection Systems (IDS)

- **Signature-Based Detection**: Supervised learning models identify known attack patterns.

- **Behavioral Analysis**: Anomaly detection models identify unexpected behaviors that may indicate new or unknown threats.

3. Phishing Email Detection

NLP techniques in supervised learning classify emails based on language patterns, sender details, and embedded links to detect phishing attempts.

4. Network Traffic Analysis

Clustering models group similar traffic patterns, identifying unusual spikes or flows that could indicate a DDoS attack or data exfiltration attempt.

5. Fraud Detection

Supervised models monitor financial transactions for anomalies, such as unusually large purchases or access from suspicious locations.

6. Automated Threat Intelligence

Clustering and natural language processing models group and analyze threat reports, extracting actionable insights for defense teams.

7. Securing IoT Devices

ML models monitor device behavior to identify potential compromises, such as unexpected network activity from IoT endpoints.

4. Challenges in Using ML Models for Cybersecurity

Despite their advantages, ML models face several challenges in cybersecurity applications:

1. Data Quality and Availability

- High-quality, labeled data is often hard to obtain, especially for supervised learning.
- Threat landscapes evolve rapidly, making existing datasets obsolete.

2. Model Interpretability

Deep learning models often act as "black boxes," making it difficult to understand their decision-making process, which can hinder trust and adoption.

3. Adversarial Attacks

Attackers can exploit weaknesses in ML models, such as introducing adversarial examples (e.g., subtly altered inputs designed to mislead the model).

4. Scalability

Training and deploying ML models at scale, especially in dynamic environments like cloud infrastructures, can be resource-intensive.

5. False Positives

Overly sensitive models may flag legitimate activities as threats, creating alert fatigue for cybersecurity teams.

5. Future Trends in ML Models for Cybersecurity

Advancements in ML are driving innovative applications in cybersecurity, including:

- **Federated Learning**: Enables training ML models across distributed datasets without centralizing data, preserving privacy while enhancing collaboration.
- **Graph Neural Networks (GNNs):** Analyze relationships between entities (e.g., users, devices, or IP addresses) for threat detection in complex networks.
- **Explainable AI (XAI):** Focuses on making ML models more transparent and interpretable, critical for building trust in AI-driven decisions.

Machine learning models form the backbone of modern AI systems, enabling rapid detection, prediction, and prevention of cyber threats. From supervised learning for malware classification to unsupervised learning for anomaly detection, these models empower cybersecurity professionals to stay ahead of adversaries. While challenges like adversarial attacks and data quality persist, ongoing advancements in ML technologies promise even greater resilience and adaptability in securing digital ecosystems. Understanding and leveraging the right ML models is essential for building an effective, AI-powered cybersecurity framework.

3.3 Key Algorithms in Cybersecurity: Clustering, Classification, and Anomaly Detection

In the field of cybersecurity, machine learning algorithms have emerged as essential tools for identifying, analyzing, and mitigating threats. Three categories of algorithms—clustering, classification, and anomaly detection—stand out for their ability to address different aspects of security challenges. Each offers unique capabilities for understanding patterns, distinguishing between safe and malicious activities, and uncovering hidden anomalies. This section explores these algorithms, their mechanics, and how they are applied to fortify digital defenses.

1. Clustering Algorithms

Overview

Clustering algorithms belong to the realm of unsupervised learning, where the goal is to group similar data points without prior labels. These algorithms identify inherent patterns or structures within data, making them ideal for tasks like segmenting network traffic or profiling user behavior.

Key Clustering Algorithms

K-Means Clustering

- Divides data into a predefined number of clusters by minimizing the variance within each cluster.
- **Application**: Detecting unusual network behaviors by grouping similar traffic patterns and flagging outliers.

Hierarchical Clustering

- Creates a tree-like structure of clusters, merging or splitting them based on similarities.
- **Application**: Grouping related malware families for better analysis and threat intelligence.

DBSCAN (Density-Based Spatial Clustering of Applications with Noise)

- Identifies clusters based on density and can detect noise points (outliers).

- **Application**: Identifying suspicious login attempts that deviate significantly from normal patterns.

Applications in Cybersecurity

- **Traffic Analysis**: Clustering helps identify DDoS attacks by detecting unusually dense traffic patterns.
- **Threat Intelligence**: Grouping malware samples based on shared features to uncover new variants.
- **Insider Threat Detection**: Profiling employee behaviors to flag deviations that may indicate malicious activity.

2. Classification Algorithms

Overview

Classification algorithms are part of supervised learning, where the model learns to assign data points to predefined categories based on labeled training data. These algorithms are extensively used in tasks that require distinguishing between safe and malicious entities.

Key Classification Algorithms

Logistic Regression

- Predicts binary outcomes (e.g., malicious or benign) by modeling the probability of an event occurring.
- **Application**: Phishing email detection by analyzing email features like sender address and content.

Decision Trees and Random Forests

- Decision trees use a hierarchical structure of rules to classify data, while random forests improve accuracy by combining multiple decision trees.
- **Application**: Malware classification by analyzing file properties and execution behavior.

Support Vector Machines (SVMs)

- Finds the optimal boundary between different classes in high-dimensional spaces.

- **Application**: Detecting spam emails or classifying network traffic as normal or malicious.

Naive Bayes

- Uses probability and Bayes' theorem to classify data based on feature independence assumptions.
- **Application**: Detecting spam or malware in datasets with clear feature distributions.

Neural Networks

- Deep learning models like Convolutional Neural Networks (CNNs) and Recurrent Neural Networks (RNNs) are highly effective for complex classification tasks.
- **Application**: Identifying phishing websites by analyzing URL structures and page content.

Applications in Cybersecurity

- **Email Security**: Filtering phishing and spam emails by classifying them as malicious or legitimate.
- **Malware Detection**: Identifying malicious software based on behavioral or static analysis.
- **Access Control**: Authenticating users based on biometric data like fingerprints or voice patterns.

3. Anomaly Detection Algorithms

Overview

Anomaly detection focuses on identifying data points or patterns that deviate significantly from the norm. It is particularly effective for uncovering unknown threats or zero-day attacks, where predefined signatures or labels are unavailable.

Key Anomaly Detection Algorithms

Isolation Forest

- Detects anomalies by randomly partitioning the data and identifying points that require fewer partitions to isolate.

- **Application**: Spotting compromised devices in a network based on abnormal behavior.

One-Class SVM

- Trains a model on normal data to identify instances that deviate from the learned norm.
- **Application**: Detecting fraudulent transactions or unauthorized access attempts.

Autoencoders

- Neural networks that compress and reconstruct data; anomalies are identified when reconstruction errors exceed a threshold.
- **Application**: Detecting unusual patterns in system logs or network traffic.

Principal Component Analysis (PCA)

- Reduces dimensionality to identify variations that may indicate anomalies.
- **Application**: Identifying unusual patterns in high-dimensional datasets like security event logs.

Applications in Cybersecurity

- **Intrusion Detection Systems (IDS):** Anomaly detection is key to identifying unusual patterns in network traffic or system activity.
- **Fraud Detection**: Flagging abnormal transactions or behaviors that deviate from typical customer profiles.
- **IoT Security**: Monitoring device activity for unexpected behaviors that may indicate compromise.

4. Combined Use of Algorithms

In practice, clustering, classification, and anomaly detection are often used in combination to build robust cybersecurity systems. For example:

- **Intrusion Detection Systems (IDS):** Anomaly detection identifies unknown threats, while classification confirms the nature of the threat.
- **Endpoint Security**: Clustering profiles device behaviors, classification detects malware, and anomaly detection spots deviations in activity.

- **Threat Hunting**: Clustering identifies attack patterns, while classification and anomaly detection validate and highlight suspicious behaviors.

5. Challenges and Considerations

While these algorithms are powerful, their effectiveness depends on overcoming certain challenges:

- **Data Quality**: Algorithms require accurate, relevant, and representative data to perform well.
- **False Positives and Negatives**: Overly sensitive models may flag harmless activities, while less sensitive ones may miss threats.
- **Evolving Threats**: Attackers constantly adapt, requiring algorithms to be regularly updated or retrained.
- **Scalability**: Algorithms must handle large-scale, real-time data in dynamic environments without performance degradation.

Clustering, classification, and anomaly detection algorithms are integral to modern cybersecurity strategies. Each serves a distinct purpose, from uncovering hidden patterns to categorizing threats and identifying unknown anomalies. By leveraging these algorithms, cybersecurity professionals can enhance their ability to detect, respond to, and prevent a wide range of threats. However, maximizing their potential requires addressing challenges like data quality, adaptability, and scalability. As cyber threats evolve, these algorithms will remain a cornerstone of AI-powered defenses, ensuring a proactive approach to safeguarding digital ecosystems.

3.4 Neural Networks and Deep Learning in Threat Analysis

The rise of complex and sophisticated cyber threats has necessitated equally advanced solutions for detection, analysis, and mitigation. Neural networks, especially deep learning models, have emerged as transformative tools in cybersecurity. With their ability to learn intricate patterns and relationships in data, these models empower cybersecurity professionals to tackle challenges like malware detection, intrusion prevention, and phishing identification with unprecedented precision. This section delves into how neural networks and deep learning are shaping threat analysis in the digital age.

1. Understanding Neural Networks and Deep Learning

Neural Networks

Neural networks are computational models inspired by the structure and function of the human brain. They consist of interconnected nodes (neurons) organized in layers:

- **Input Layer**: Accepts data inputs, such as network logs or file features.
- **Hidden Layers**: Perform computations to extract patterns and insights.
- **Output Layer**: Produces predictions or classifications, such as whether traffic is malicious.

Deep Learning

Deep learning refers to neural networks with multiple hidden layers (deep neural networks, or DNNs). These models excel at learning hierarchical representations of data, making them ideal for complex cybersecurity tasks.

2. Key Architectures in Threat Analysis

Different deep learning architectures are optimized for various cybersecurity use cases:

1. Feedforward Neural Networks (FNNs)

- **Overview**: Data flows in one direction, from input to output.
- **Applications**: Basic tasks like binary classification (e.g., is an email phishing or legitimate?).

2. Convolutional Neural Networks (CNNs)

Overview: Specialize in processing grid-like data, such as images or sequences.

Applications:

- Analyzing static malware files by examining byte sequences or binary code.
- Detecting phishing websites through image-based pattern recognition.

3. Recurrent Neural Networks (RNNs)

Overview: Process sequential data by maintaining a memory of previous inputs. Variants like Long Short-Term Memory (LSTM) networks are particularly effective.

Applications:

- Detecting threats in real-time by analyzing network traffic or log sequences.
- Identifying patterns in attack campaigns over time.

4. Autoencoders

Overview: Unsupervised models that compress and reconstruct data. Deviations in reconstruction highlight anomalies.

Applications:

- Spotting unusual system behaviors or detecting zero-day attacks.

5. Generative Adversarial Networks (GANs)

Overview: Consist of two networks (generator and discriminator) that compete to improve performance.

Applications:

- Simulating realistic attack scenarios for training threat detection systems.
- Generating synthetic data for testing models without compromising sensitive information.

3. Applications of Neural Networks in Threat Analysis

Neural networks enable robust threat analysis across various domains of cybersecurity:

1. Malware Detection

- **Deep Learning Techniques**: Neural networks analyze file metadata, behavior, and code to detect malware. CNNs can process file headers, while RNNs analyze execution patterns.
- **Impact**: Faster detection of polymorphic malware, which changes its appearance to evade traditional signatures.

2. Phishing Detection

- **Deep Learning Techniques**: Models analyze text, URLs, and images to identify phishing emails or websites.

- **Impact**: Enhanced protection against socially engineered attacks targeting individuals or organizations.

3. Intrusion Detection Systems (IDS)

- **Deep Learning Techniques**: RNNs and LSTMs monitor real-time network traffic, identifying anomalies indicative of intrusions.
- **Impact**: More accurate detection of insider threats and external attacks in dynamic environments.

4. Threat Intelligence

- **Deep Learning Techniques**: Natural Language Processing (NLP) models like Transformer-based architectures (e.g., BERT) process threat reports and extract actionable insights.
- **Impact**: Accelerated threat analysis from large volumes of unstructured data.

5. Behavioral Analytics

- **Deep Learning Techniques**: Autoencoders and GANs model normal user or device behavior, flagging deviations that may signal compromise.
- **Impact**: Early detection of account takeovers or rogue devices.

4. Advantages of Neural Networks in Threat Analysis

1. Handling Complex Data

Neural networks excel at processing diverse data types, such as text, images, and sequences, enabling them to analyze complex cyber threat scenarios.

2. Adaptability

Deep learning models can learn and adapt to evolving threat patterns, making them effective against zero-day attacks and novel malware variants.

3. Automation

By automating threat detection and response, neural networks reduce the workload on cybersecurity teams, allowing them to focus on high-priority tasks.

4. Scalability

Neural networks can process large-scale data, such as enterprise-wide network logs, to identify threats in real time.

5. Challenges in Using Neural Networks for Threat Analysis

Despite their potential, neural networks face several challenges:

1. Data Requirements

Deep learning models require large, high-quality datasets for training. In cybersecurity, labeled data is often scarce or outdated.

2. Computational Costs

Training and deploying neural networks demand significant computational resources, which can strain budgets and infrastructure.

3. Interpretability

Deep learning models often operate as "black boxes," making it difficult to explain their decisions—a critical issue in industries requiring accountability.

4. Adversarial Attacks

Attackers can manipulate neural networks by introducing subtle adversarial examples designed to mislead the model.

5. Overfitting Risks

Models trained on narrow datasets may fail to generalize to new threats, reducing their effectiveness in dynamic environments.

6. Future Directions

The application of neural networks in cybersecurity continues to evolve, with promising trends such as:

1. Explainable AI (XAI)

Developing interpretable models to enhance trust and usability in critical systems.

2. Federated Learning

Enabling collaborative threat analysis without centralizing sensitive data, preserving privacy.

3. Real-Time Deep Learning

Deploying lightweight, optimized models for real-time threat detection on edge devices.

4. Advanced Architectures

Adopting state-of-the-art models like Vision Transformers (ViTs) for malware analysis and GPT-based models for phishing detection.

Neural networks and deep learning are revolutionizing threat analysis by providing sophisticated tools to detect and prevent cyberattacks. Their ability to process complex, high-dimensional data enables them to address the growing sophistication of cyber threats effectively. However, overcoming challenges like data availability, interpretability, and adversarial resilience will be crucial to fully realize their potential. As the field advances, these technologies will continue to play a pivotal role in creating smarter, faster, and more adaptive cybersecurity solutions.

3.5 Tools and Platforms for AI-Powered Cybersecurity

As cyber threats grow in scale and sophistication, the cybersecurity landscape has seen a surge in tools and platforms leveraging artificial intelligence (AI) to enhance digital defense. These solutions offer automated, intelligent, and scalable mechanisms to detect, analyze, and mitigate cyberattacks. From malware analysis platforms to user behavior analytics tools, the integration of AI into cybersecurity operations has fundamentally transformed the way organizations protect their digital ecosystems. This section explores key tools, platforms, and technologies driving AI-powered cybersecurity.

1. AI-Driven Cybersecurity Tools

AI-driven tools provide specialized capabilities for various aspects of cybersecurity, such as threat detection, network monitoring, and endpoint protection. Here are some widely used tools:

1. Darktrace

Overview: A leading AI-powered platform that uses machine learning to detect and respond to threats autonomously.

Key Features:

- Behavioral analytics for anomaly detection.
- Autonomous response capabilities with its "Antigena" module.

Use Case: Identifying insider threats and advanced persistent threats (APTs).

2. Cylance

Overview: A predictive endpoint protection solution powered by AI and machine learning.

Key Features:

- Pre-execution malware prevention without relying on traditional signatures.
- Lightweight agent for real-time protection.

Use Case: Blocking unknown malware and ransomware before execution.

3. CrowdStrike Falcon

Overview: A cloud-based endpoint protection platform using AI to deliver real-time threat intelligence.

Key Features:

- Threat hunting with the "Falcon OverWatch" module.
- Behavioral-based detection of attacks like credential theft.

Use Case: Detecting and responding to ransomware attacks.

4. Vectra AI

Overview: Specializes in network detection and response (NDR) using AI.

Key Features:

- Identifies lateral movement within networks.
- Threat prioritization for faster response.

Use Case: Detecting compromised accounts and lateral threat propagation.

5. Splunk with AI Modules

Overview: A data analytics platform incorporating AI for security information and event management (SIEM).

Key Features:

- Real-time monitoring of security events.
- Predictive analytics for proactive threat mitigation.

Use Case: Log analysis and correlation for advanced threat detection.

2. Platforms Supporting AI-Driven Cybersecurity

In addition to standalone tools, comprehensive platforms integrate multiple AI-powered cybersecurity features into unified ecosystems:

1. IBM Security QRadar

Overview: A SIEM platform enhanced with AI and machine learning.

Key Features:

- Automated threat detection and prioritization.
- AI-driven incident response workflows.

Use Case: Streamlining security operations and improving threat visibility.

2. Microsoft Defender for Endpoint

Overview: A cloud-based endpoint protection platform leveraging AI for threat analysis.

Key Features:

- Advanced threat analytics and automated remediation.
- Integration with Azure Sentinel for expanded capabilities.

Use Case: Providing seamless endpoint-to-cloud protection.

3. Palo Alto Networks Cortex XDR

Overview: A detection and response platform that integrates AI with endpoint, network, and cloud security.

Key Features:

- Automated root cause analysis.
- Proactive threat hunting with AI-driven insights.

Use Case: Reducing dwell time for sophisticated attacks.

4. Elastic Security

Overview: An open-source platform offering unified security analytics with AI.

Key Features:

- Behavioral anomaly detection.
- Integration with the Elastic Stack (Elasticsearch, Logstash, Kibana).

Use Case: Customizable solutions for real-time data analysis and threat hunting.

3. Categories of AI-Powered Cybersecurity Platforms

AI-powered cybersecurity solutions span several categories, each addressing specific challenges:

1. Endpoint Detection and Response (EDR)

- **Focus**: Protecting individual devices like laptops, servers, and IoT devices.

- **Examples**: CrowdStrike Falcon, CylancePROTECT.

2. Network Detection and Response (NDR)

- **Focus**: Monitoring network traffic to identify anomalies and threats.
- **Examples**: Vectra AI, Darktrace.

3. Security Orchestration, Automation, and Response (SOAR)

- **Focus**: Automating repetitive security tasks and orchestrating incident responses.
- **Examples**: Splunk Phantom, IBM Resilient.

4. Threat Intelligence Platforms (TIPs)

- **Focus**: Aggregating and analyzing threat intelligence from various sources.
- **Examples**: Recorded Future, Anomali ThreatStream.

5. Cloud Security Platforms

- **Focus**: Ensuring the security of cloud environments through AI-powered insights.
- **Examples**: Microsoft Defender for Cloud, Prisma Cloud by Palo Alto Networks.

4. Benefits of AI-Powered Cybersecurity Tools

The integration of AI into cybersecurity offers several advantages:

1. Proactive Threat Detection

AI models identify threats before they cause harm, such as detecting malware pre-execution.

2. Faster Incident Response

Automated analysis and response workflows reduce the time taken to address threats.

3. Scalability

AI-driven platforms handle vast datasets, ensuring comprehensive protection in large-scale environments.

4. Real-Time Insights

Continuous monitoring and analysis provide up-to-the-minute threat intelligence.

5. Reduced Human Workload

By automating repetitive tasks, AI tools allow human experts to focus on complex threats.

5. Challenges in Adopting AI-Powered Cybersecurity Tools

While AI-powered cybersecurity tools are powerful, their adoption comes with challenges:

1. False Positives

Overly sensitive models may flag benign activities as threats, leading to alert fatigue.

2. High Costs

Many advanced tools require significant investment in infrastructure and training.

3. Data Privacy Concerns

Cloud-based platforms must ensure that sensitive data remains protected during processing.

4. Skill Requirements

Effective use of AI tools requires expertise in data science and machine learning, which may be scarce.

5. Adversarial AI

Attackers may use adversarial techniques to exploit vulnerabilities in AI models.

6. Future of AI Tools in Cybersecurity

As cyber threats evolve, AI-powered cybersecurity tools are expected to advance in several ways:

1. Enhanced Automation

Future platforms will automate not just detection but also complex response actions, reducing human intervention further.

2. Explainable AI (XAI)

Tools will offer greater transparency, allowing security teams to understand and trust AI-driven decisions.

3. Collaborative AI Models

Federated learning and other collaborative models will enable organizations to share insights without compromising data privacy.

4. Integration with Emerging Technologies

AI tools will integrate with blockchain and quantum computing to offer stronger, tamper-proof security measures.

AI-powered tools and platforms are transforming the cybersecurity landscape, enabling organizations to detect, analyze, and respond to threats with unmatched speed and accuracy. From endpoint protection to network monitoring and incident response, these tools provide critical layers of defense in an increasingly digital world. Despite challenges like high costs and skill requirements, the ongoing evolution of AI in cybersecurity ensures that these tools will remain indispensable for safeguarding digital ecosystems against ever-evolving threats.

4. Next-Gen Intrusion Detection and Prevention Systems

Traditional intrusion detection and prevention systems (IDS/IPS) are often limited by static rules and signature-based methods, making them insufficient against advanced and evolving threats. This chapter explores how AI and machine learning are transforming IDS/IPS into dynamic, adaptive systems capable of detecting anomalies, predicting potential breaches, and responding in real time. Readers will learn about the differences between anomaly-based and signature-based detection, explore real-world applications of AI-powered IDS/IPS, and understand how these systems reduce false positives while improving detection accuracy. This chapter demonstrates why next-gen intrusion systems are a cornerstone of modern cybersecurity strategies.

4.1 Enhancing Traditional IDS/IPS with AI

Traditional Intrusion Detection Systems (IDS) and Intrusion Prevention Systems (IPS) have long served as cornerstones of cybersecurity, offering critical capabilities to detect and block malicious activities within networks. However, the rise in sophisticated and evolving threats, such as zero-day exploits, advanced persistent threats (APTs), and polymorphic malware, has exposed the limitations of conventional IDS/IPS technologies. By incorporating artificial intelligence (AI), these systems are being significantly enhanced to meet the demands of modern cybersecurity challenges.

1. Limitations of Traditional IDS/IPS

Traditional IDS/IPS tools rely heavily on predefined rules and signature-based detection mechanisms. These approaches, while effective for known threats, face challenges in handling emerging threats:

- **Static Rules**: Dependence on manually crafted rules limits adaptability to dynamic attack vectors.
- **Signature-Based Limitations**: Cannot detect zero-day exploits or novel malware variants without prior knowledge.
- **False Positives and Negatives**: High false positive rates can overwhelm security teams, while false negatives miss critical threats.
- **Scalability** Issues: Struggle to manage the massive volume of data generated by modern networks.

2. The Role of AI in Enhancing IDS/IPS

AI introduces dynamic capabilities to IDS/IPS, allowing them to evolve from reactive tools to proactive defense mechanisms. Key enhancements include:

1. Machine Learning (ML) for Anomaly Detection

- AI-driven IDS/IPS leverage ML algorithms to analyze network traffic patterns and baseline normal behaviors.
- Anomalous activities, such as unusual login locations or atypical data transfers, are flagged as potential threats.

2. Behavior-Based Detection

Unlike signature-based methods, AI models detect threats by understanding how malicious activities deviate from typical patterns, even without prior signatures.

3. Adaptive Threat Responses

AI enables real-time adaptation to new attack vectors by continuously learning from network behavior and attack data.

4. Threat Intelligence Integration

AI can ingest threat intelligence feeds and incorporate them into detection models, enhancing the system's ability to recognize emerging threats.

5. Reduction of False Positives

Advanced algorithms filter noise and reduce false positives by cross-referencing alerts with contextual data, improving accuracy.

3. AI Techniques for IDS/IPS

AI employs a variety of techniques to improve IDS/IPS functionality:

1. Supervised Learning

- **Usage**: Training on labeled datasets to classify traffic as benign or malicious.

- **Examples**: Detecting specific malware types based on historical data.

2. Unsupervised Learning

- **Usage**: Identifying unknown threats by clustering unusual behaviors without labeled data.
- **Examples**: Spotting anomalies in encrypted traffic or unexpected user actions.

3. Neural Networks

- **Usage**: Deep learning models analyze high-dimensional data, such as packet metadata, for complex threat patterns.
- **Examples**: Detecting sophisticated attacks like data exfiltration over covert channels.

4. Natural Language Processing (NLP)

- **Usage**: Analyzing textual data, such as network logs or threat reports, to extract insights.
- **Examples**: Understanding indicators of compromise (IoCs) in unstructured logs.

5. Reinforcement Learning

- **Usage**: Allowing IDS/IPS systems to learn from interactions with attackers and adapt to evolving tactics.
- **Examples**: Automatically modifying firewall rules to block ongoing attacks.

4. Key Benefits of AI-Enhanced IDS/IPS

Integrating AI into IDS/IPS systems offers several benefits:

1. Proactive Threat Detection

Detect zero-day attacks and sophisticated threats that bypass traditional mechanisms.

2. Speed and Scalability

Analyze vast amounts of data in real-time, making it suitable for enterprise-level environments.

3. Continuous Learning

AI models improve over time, adapting to new threats without requiring manual updates.

4. Resource Optimization

By automating detection and response, AI reduces the workload on cybersecurity teams.

5. Threat Contextualization

Provide enriched alerts by correlating anomalies with broader threat intelligence.

5. Real-World Applications of AI in IDS/IPS

AI-enhanced IDS/IPS systems are being deployed across industries to improve cyber defense:

1. Darktrace

Uses AI to detect threats in real time, offering autonomous responses to anomalies.

2. Cisco Secure IPS

Combines ML with traditional detection mechanisms to provide proactive protection.

3. Snort with AI Enhancements

Open-source IDS/IPS now integrating AI models to improve detection accuracy.

4. Palo Alto Networks Next-Gen Firewall (NGFW)

Includes AI-powered threat detection and prevention, integrating with their Cortex platform.

6. Challenges in AI-Enhanced IDS/IPS

While AI significantly improves IDS/IPS capabilities, challenges remain:

1. Data Requirements

AI models require large, high-quality datasets for effective training, which may not always be available.

2. Computational Overhead

AI-powered systems may require more processing power, potentially increasing costs.

3. Adversarial Attacks

Attackers may use adversarial AI techniques to mislead or bypass detection systems.

4. False Positives

Despite improvements, AI systems can still generate false positives, requiring manual review.

5. Integration Complexity

Incorporating AI into existing IDS/IPS solutions may involve significant time and resource investments.

7. The Future of AI-Enhanced IDS/IPS

AI-powered IDS/IPS systems will continue to evolve with advancements in machine learning, automation, and threat intelligence:

1. Autonomous Defense

Future systems will combine detection and prevention with autonomous response capabilities.

2. Explainable AI (XAI)

Models will become more interpretable, allowing security teams to understand decision-making processes.

3. Edge Computing Integration

AI models deployed on edge devices will enable real-time detection in decentralized networks.

4. Collaborative AI Models

Federated learning will allow organizations to share detection insights while preserving privacy.

5. Advanced Behavioral Analytics

Incorporation of multi-layered behavioral data (user, device, and application) will enhance threat detection precision.

AI-enhanced IDS/IPS systems represent a significant leap forward in cybersecurity, addressing the limitations of traditional approaches and enabling organizations to stay ahead of increasingly sophisticated threats. By integrating advanced AI techniques, these systems offer faster, more accurate, and scalable solutions for detecting and preventing cyberattacks. While challenges remain, ongoing advancements in AI and machine learning ensure that IDS/IPS systems will remain critical components in the defense against modern cyber threats.

4.2 AI-Driven Anomaly vs. Signature-Based Detection

Cybersecurity has evolved significantly with the advent of advanced technologies like Artificial Intelligence (AI) and Machine Learning (ML). Traditionally, Intrusion Detection Systems (IDS) and Intrusion Prevention Systems (IPS) relied on signature-based detection methods, which focused on identifying known attack patterns or signatures. While effective at recognizing familiar threats, this approach has limitations when facing novel or sophisticated attacks. On the other hand, AI-driven anomaly detection offers a more dynamic and adaptive approach. This section explores the differences between AI-driven anomaly detection and traditional signature-based detection, examining their strengths, weaknesses, and applications.

1. Signature-Based Detection

Signature-based detection is the oldest and most established method used in network security, where security tools rely on pre-defined patterns or "signatures" of known threats to identify malicious activities. A signature typically consists of a unique pattern or sequence of bytes, behaviors, or network traffic indicative of a specific attack or malware.

How It Works:

- **Signature Database**: Security tools maintain a repository of known attack signatures, each corresponding to a particular threat (e.g., a piece of malware or a known attack technique).
- **Traffic Scanning**: The IDS/IPS scans network traffic and compares it against the signatures in the database.
- **Alert Generation**: If a match is found, the system triggers an alert and may block the malicious activity.

Advantages of Signature-Based Detection:

- **High Accuracy for Known Threats**: It is highly effective at detecting known threats that have been documented and added to the signature database.
- **Low False Positives**: Since it only flags patterns that match known signatures, the chances of generating false positives (i.e., alerts for non-threatening activities) are lower.
- **Simplicity**: Signature-based methods are relatively easy to implement and do not require complex training or modeling.

Limitations of Signature-Based Detection:

- **Inability to Detect Unknown Threats**: Signature-based detection can only identify previously known threats. It is ineffective against novel or polymorphic malware that doesn't match any known signature.
- **Frequent Updates Required**: To stay effective, the signature database must be constantly updated with new signatures as attackers develop new methods.
- **Evasion Techniques**: Attackers can modify their techniques to avoid detection, such as by encrypting payloads or altering malware code, making it difficult for signature-based systems to detect new variants.
- **Scalability Issues**: As the volume of traffic increases, the need for an extensive and continually updated signature database grows, which can overwhelm traditional systems.

2. AI-Driven Anomaly Detection

AI-driven anomaly detection, on the other hand, leverages machine learning and statistical models to detect deviations from established "normal" network behaviors, rather than relying on signatures of known threats. By establishing baselines of what is considered "normal," AI systems can identify activities that fall outside this range, potentially indicating malicious behavior.

How It Works:

- **Baseline Behavior Modeling**: AI systems use historical data to learn and model what is normal for the network, including typical user behavior, traffic patterns, and system interactions.
- **Anomaly Identification**: Once the model is established, the system continuously monitors network activities, identifying any deviations from the baseline.
- **Alert Generation**: Any behavior deemed unusual or suspicious is flagged for investigation, even if it doesn't correspond to a known signature.

Advantages of AI-Driven Anomaly Detection:

- **Detection of Unknown Threats**: One of the biggest advantages of anomaly detection is its ability to identify previously unseen threats, such as zero-day attacks, novel malware, or insider threats, which may not have a predefined signature.
- **Adaptive and Dynamic**: AI systems can continuously learn and adapt to changes in network behavior, which is crucial in environments where the network is constantly evolving, such as in the case of new applications, systems, or users.
- **No Need for Signature Updates**: Since anomaly detection is based on behavior rather than signatures, there is no need to frequently update a signature database to stay effective.
- **Contextual Awareness**: AI-based systems can incorporate contextual information such as time, user roles, or geographical location to more accurately detect suspicious activities and reduce false alarms.

Limitations of AI-Driven Anomaly Detection:

- **False Positives**: While AI systems are designed to reduce false positives, anomalies don't always equate to malicious activities. Legitimate changes in user behavior, network traffic, or system usage may be flagged as suspicious, leading to potential alert fatigue.
- **Data and Training Requirements**: For AI-driven systems to be effective, they need vast amounts of data for training and baseline modeling. Without proper data, the system may struggle to accurately distinguish between normal and anomalous behaviors.
- **Complexity and Resource Intensive**: The implementation of AI models requires significant computational resources, and setting up a well-trained model can be

time-consuming. The models also need ongoing monitoring and tuning to avoid drift in their detection capabilities.

- **Adaptation Period**: AI-driven systems require an initial "learning" period to understand baseline behaviors, which may leave systems vulnerable during the early stages of deployment.

4. Use Cases and Applications

Both signature-based and AI-driven anomaly detection are valuable, but they serve different needs within a cybersecurity strategy.

Signature-Based Detection Use Cases:

- **Legacy Systems**: Organizations with older infrastructure may rely on signature-based detection for known malware and vulnerabilities.
- **Specific, Well-Defined Threats**: Environments where specific threats are prevalent (e.g., certain types of worms or ransomware) may benefit from signature-based methods.
- **Network Perimeter Defense**: Signature-based systems are often effective in detecting attacks at the perimeter, where threats are well-understood.

AI-Driven Anomaly Detection Use Cases:

- **Zero-Day and Polymorphic Attacks**: AI-driven systems excel in detecting novel, evolving threats that cannot be captured by signature databases.
- **Insider Threat Detection**: Anomaly detection is effective at spotting suspicious internal activities, such as unauthorized data access or privilege escalation, which may not match any signature.
- **Cloud and Hybrid Environments**: AI's ability to adapt to dynamic network conditions and detect unusual patterns makes it ideal for modern cloud and hybrid infrastructures.

AI-driven anomaly detection and signature-based detection both have distinct advantages and play important roles in modern cybersecurity defense. While signature-based detection remains effective for defending against known threats and is easier to implement and manage, it struggles to cope with the ever-evolving nature of cyber threats. AI-driven anomaly detection offers a powerful solution for detecting unknown, sophisticated attacks, but it comes with challenges such as a higher rate of false positives and greater resource requirements. The most effective cybersecurity strategies will likely combine both approaches—using signature-based detection for known threats and AI-driven anomaly detection to protect against new and evolving dangers. By leveraging both, organizations can achieve comprehensive, adaptive, and robust protection against a wide range of cyber threats.

4.3 Real-Time Monitoring with ML Algorithms

In the rapidly evolving landscape of cybersecurity, real-time monitoring is essential to quickly identify and respond to emerging threats. Traditional methods, such as manual reviews and rule-based systems, struggle to keep pace with the speed, volume, and sophistication of modern cyberattacks. This is where Machine Learning (ML) algorithms play a critical role. ML has transformed real-time monitoring by enabling systems to detect, analyze, and respond to threats faster and more efficiently than ever before.

This section delves into the significance of real-time monitoring using ML algorithms, the types of algorithms involved, their benefits, and the challenges they address in modern cybersecurity environments.

1. The Need for Real-Time Monitoring

As cyberattacks become more sophisticated and persistent, organizations face an increasing number of threats each day. This includes everything from phishing campaigns to advanced persistent threats (APTs), which require quick identification and response. Real-time monitoring helps cybersecurity teams:

- **Identify Intrusions Quickly**: Timely detection of threats is essential to prevent data loss, unauthorized access, or system compromise.
- **Minimize Response Time**: The faster a threat is detected, the quicker it can be mitigated, reducing the potential damage.
- **Enhance Operational Efficiency**: By automating threat detection and response, real-time monitoring frees up resources and allows security teams to focus on higher-level tasks.

2. The Role of Machine Learning in Real-Time Monitoring

Machine Learning enhances real-time monitoring by automating the detection of suspicious patterns in network traffic, system logs, and user behaviors. Traditional methods rely on predefined rules and signatures to flag known threats. However, these approaches struggle to identify new, unknown, or emerging threats. ML algorithms, on the other hand, learn from historical data, adapt to new patterns, and can identify even the subtlest deviations from normal behavior.

Key ML Algorithms Used in Real-Time Monitoring:

1. Supervised Learning

- **How it Works**: Supervised learning algorithms are trained on labeled data sets, where each input is associated with a correct output (e.g., benign or malicious). The model learns to classify future data based on patterns observed in the training data.
- **Common Applications**: Identifying specific types of attacks, such as malware or brute force login attempts, based on previously labeled threat data.
- **Algorithms**: Logistic Regression, Support Vector Machines (SVM), Decision Trees, and Random Forests.

2. Unsupervised Learning

- **How it Works**: In contrast to supervised learning, unsupervised learning algorithms do not rely on labeled data. Instead, they try to identify hidden patterns or anomalies by analyzing data's natural structure.
- **Common Applications**: Anomaly detection, where the model is tasked with identifying abnormal behavior in network traffic or user actions.
- **Algorithms**: K-Means Clustering, DBSCAN (Density-Based Spatial Clustering of Applications with Noise), and Autoencoders.

3. Semi-Supervised Learning

- **How it Works**: A hybrid approach that uses a combination of labeled and unlabeled data to improve the performance of the algorithm. Semi-supervised learning can be particularly useful when labeled data is scarce but large amounts of unlabeled data are available.
- **Common Applications**: Identifying zero-day attacks, where only limited labeled data is available for training, and many attacks have not yet been classified.
- **Algorithms**: Gaussian Mixture Models (GMM) and Semi-Supervised Support Vector Machines (S3VM).

4. Reinforcement Learning

- **How it Works**: Reinforcement learning models continuously learn and adapt based on feedback from their actions. This makes them ideal for environments where threat landscapes change frequently.
- **Common Applications**: Automated incident response, where the model learns from real-world attacks to improve the speed and accuracy of its responses.
- **Algorithms**: Q-Learning, Deep Q Networks (DQN), and Policy Gradient Methods.

3. Key Features and Benefits of Real-Time ML Monitoring

ML-powered real-time monitoring systems offer several benefits that traditional methods simply cannot match:

1. Continuous Learning and Adaptation

- ML algorithms continuously improve by learning from new data. Unlike static rule-based systems, they can adapt to evolving attack methods, ensuring the system remains effective even as new threats emerge.
- For example, as an AI model encounters new attack vectors or novel malware strains, it updates its understanding of malicious behavior and refines its detection capabilities.

2. High Accuracy and Reduced False Positives

- Traditional signature-based systems can suffer from high false positive rates, generating alerts for activities that are normal in the context of the network. ML algorithms, especially unsupervised models, learn the "normal" patterns of network traffic, reducing false alarms by identifying true anomalies.
- This means that security teams can focus on investigating real threats rather than wasting time on benign activities.

3. Real-Time Threat Detection

- ML algorithms excel at processing large volumes of data in real-time, which allows for rapid identification of malicious activity. Traditional systems may only detect threats after they have caused damage or been discovered by an analyst, whereas ML systems can detect and respond to threats as they happen.

4. Scalability

- ML models are highly scalable and can handle vast amounts of data across large networks. This is particularly important for organizations with complex, distributed networks or those with large-scale operations.
- The ability to process massive volumes of data in real-time allows ML algorithms to monitor every corner of a network without slowing down, ensuring that all traffic and behavior are analyzed.

5. Proactive Threat Hunting

- ML systems can be used not only to respond to active attacks but also for proactive threat hunting. By continuously analyzing historical data and identifying patterns, ML algorithms can pinpoint weaknesses in the system or predict potential attack vectors before they are exploited.
- This proactive approach helps organizations stay ahead of attackers, reducing the risk of successful breaches.

4. Challenges in Implementing Real-Time ML Monitoring

While the benefits of real-time ML monitoring are clear, the implementation of such systems is not without challenges:

1. Data Quality and Quantity

ML algorithms require large amounts of high-quality data to be effective. Without sufficient data, particularly labeled data, models may struggle to learn the correct patterns and behaviors. Inadequate or noisy data may result in inaccurate predictions, leading to false positives or missed threats.

2. Model Training and Overfitting

- Training an ML model requires careful attention to avoid overfitting, where the model becomes too tailored to the training data and loses its ability to generalize to new or unseen situations. This is particularly challenging in cybersecurity, where new attack methods are continuously developed.
- Proper model validation and testing are essential to ensure that the ML algorithms can perform effectively in the real world.

3. Latency and Performance

- While ML algorithms are typically faster than traditional manual methods, the computational load required for real-time monitoring can introduce latency. In time-sensitive environments, even slight delays in detecting a threat can be detrimental.
- To minimize latency, organizations may need to invest in high-performance computing infrastructure or optimize their ML models for faster inference.

4. Resource Intensive

- ML-based monitoring requires significant computational resources, including processing power, memory, and storage. Organizations must invest in robust infrastructure, such as GPUs or cloud-based solutions, to handle the demands of real-time data analysis.
- Smaller organizations or those with limited budgets may face difficulties in implementing such systems.

5. Complexity of Model Maintenance

- Once deployed, ML models require ongoing maintenance to ensure they continue to perform effectively. This includes retraining models as new data becomes available, adjusting for changes in the network environment, and handling evolving attack techniques.
- Without regular updates and fine-tuning, the effectiveness of an ML model can degrade over time, leaving security gaps.

5. Use Cases of Real-Time ML Monitoring in Cybersecurity

1. Intrusion Detection Systems (IDS)

ML can be integrated into IDS platforms to improve the detection of anomalies in network traffic, helping to identify potential intrusions or suspicious activity faster than traditional signature-based methods.

2. User and Entity Behavior Analytics (UEBA)

ML can analyze the behavior of users and devices across the network, detecting anomalous actions that may indicate insider threats, compromised accounts, or privilege escalation attempts.

3. Endpoint Security

On endpoints, ML algorithms can monitor processes, file behavior, and interactions to detect potential malware, ransomware, or fileless attacks. By recognizing abnormal behavior patterns, ML can detect threats before they spread.

4. Phishing Detection

ML algorithms can analyze email traffic, URLs, and web content in real-time to detect phishing attempts, often identifying fraudulent communications that might bypass traditional filters.

Real-time monitoring powered by machine learning is a game-changer in modern cybersecurity. By enabling continuous learning and quick adaptation to new threats, ML algorithms provide the speed, accuracy, and scalability needed to detect and respond to attacks in real-time. Despite some challenges, such as the need for large datasets and computational resources, the benefits of AI-driven real-time monitoring far outweigh the limitations. As cyber threats continue to evolve, integrating ML into security systems will be critical for organizations aiming to stay ahead of adversaries and protect their digital assets effectively.

4.4 Case Studies: AI-Powered IDS in Action

In recent years, organizations have increasingly adopted AI-powered Intrusion Detection Systems (IDS) to enhance their cybersecurity defenses. By integrating machine learning (ML) and artificial intelligence (AI) into IDS, companies can detect and respond to threats in real time, uncover sophisticated attack patterns, and adapt to new, unknown threats more efficiently than traditional signature-based systems. This section explores several case studies that highlight how AI-powered IDS have been successfully deployed in real-world environments to improve cybersecurity outcomes.

1. Case Study 1: Financial Institution – Detecting Insider Threats with AI

Background:

A large financial institution was experiencing an uptick in suspicious internal activities, including unauthorized access to sensitive data by employees and unusual transaction patterns. Traditional signature-based IDS systems were ineffective at detecting insider threats, as they relied on known attack signatures and could not detect the nuanced behavioral patterns of trusted users who had legitimate access to the network.

AI-Powered IDS Solution:

The institution decided to integrate an AI-powered IDS system that utilized Machine Learning (ML) algorithms, specifically User and Entity Behavior Analytics (UEBA), to monitor user actions across the network. The system was trained to learn the typical behavior of employees based on factors such as login times, data access patterns, file transfers, and communication behaviors. Using this baseline, the IDS could detect anomalies that deviated from established norms.

Implementation:

The AI-powered IDS was configured to flag any behavior that appeared abnormal, even if it came from trusted internal users. For example, if an employee attempted to access a database they had no reason to interact with, or if they downloaded large amounts of sensitive data outside of business hours, the system would trigger an alert.

Outcome:

- **Early Detection of Insider Threats**: The AI-powered IDS was able to identify suspicious user activity much earlier than the institution's previous systems. For example, the system flagged an employee who was accessing data they were not authorized to view, helping the security team intervene before any sensitive information was leaked or exfiltrated.
- **Reduced False Positives**: By learning each user's behavior, the AI-powered system significantly reduced false positives compared to traditional methods. Security analysts no longer had to sift through mountains of irrelevant alerts, allowing them to focus on genuine threats.
- **Enhanced Response Time**: The real-time anomaly detection capabilities allowed the institution to respond more quickly to potential insider threats, preventing a major data breach.

2. Case Study 2: E-Commerce Platform – Detecting DDoS Attacks with AI

Background:

A rapidly growing e-commerce platform faced increasing threats from Distributed Denial-of-Service (DDoS) attacks. The platform's website and services would often become unresponsive during peak shopping seasons, causing significant revenue loss and customer dissatisfaction. The traditional signature-based IDS they employed could detect some DDoS attacks, but it struggled with sophisticated, low-and-slow attacks that were difficult to identify with predefined patterns.

AI-Powered IDS Solution:

The e-commerce platform integrated an AI-powered IDS that utilized anomaly detection algorithms to identify unusual traffic patterns indicative of a DDoS attack. The system monitored network traffic in real time and compared it to normal patterns based on historical traffic data. The AI model was trained to recognize subtle shifts in traffic volume, request patterns, and user behavior that could signal a potential attack.

Implementation:

The AI system was designed to automatically scale up detection when an attack was suspected. It used machine learning-based clustering algorithms to identify clusters of abnormal traffic behaviors. For instance, the system could identify when a large number of requests were coming from a single IP address or when requests were unusually slow and steady, which are common characteristics of DDoS attacks.

Outcome:

- **Early Detection and Mitigation**: The AI-powered IDS was able to identify the early signs of a DDoS attack much faster than the signature-based system. It detected the first signs of an attack when traffic patterns began to deviate from typical usage, allowing the security team to take preventive actions such as rerouting traffic or applying rate limiting.
- **Reduced Service Downtime**: By providing early alerts, the AI system helped the platform mitigate attacks before they caused significant downtime. This reduced the number of incidents during peak sales periods, minimizing revenue loss.
- **Adaptive Defense**: The system continuously learned and adapted to changes in legitimate traffic, making it increasingly effective at distinguishing between real attacks and regular traffic over time.

3. Case Study 3: Healthcare Organization – Detecting Ransomware with AI

Background:

A major healthcare organization was facing a growing threat from ransomware attacks. These attacks were particularly dangerous as they targeted patient data and critical healthcare systems, with the potential to disrupt operations and compromise sensitive medical records. Traditional IDS could not keep up with the new, evolving tactics used by cybercriminals to encrypt files and demand ransom payments.

AI-Powered IDS Solution:

The healthcare provider deployed an AI-powered IDS that utilized deep learning algorithms to analyze file and network behaviors for signs of ransomware activity. The system was configured to detect unusual encryption patterns, such as rapid file modifications, attempts to encrypt files across multiple endpoints, or the use of known encryption tools by malware. The AI model was trained on millions of file operations and interactions within the network to detect subtle, often hidden, signs of ransomware infection.

Implementation:

The AI system operated in real time, continuously monitoring the network and endpoint devices. When it detected a spike in encryption activity or recognized a pattern consistent with ransomware behavior, it immediately triggered alerts. It also automatically isolated affected devices to prevent further spread of the ransomware, while notifying the security team of the ongoing attack.

Outcome:

- **Rapid Identification of Ransomware**: The AI-powered IDS identified a ransomware attack in progress within minutes of infection, much faster than the organization's traditional antivirus and IDS systems. The system's ability to recognize encryption behavior allowed the security team to intervene before the ransomware could fully encrypt critical files.
- **Containment and Mitigation**: The AI-driven system autonomously isolated affected devices, preventing lateral movement and reducing the overall damage caused by the attack. This automated response helped contain the ransomware infection before it could spread across the network.
- **Reduced Impact on Operations**: By detecting and responding to the ransomware attack so quickly, the healthcare provider was able to maintain business continuity and avoid a significant disruption to patient care.

4. Case Study 4: Global Technology Firm – Enhancing Threat Detection in Cloud Environments

Background:

A global technology firm with a significant presence in the cloud was facing difficulties in securing its multi-cloud infrastructure. Traditional IDS solutions were not able to monitor the diverse cloud environments effectively. Additionally, the company needed a solution capable of scaling to match the increasing volume of cloud-based traffic and complex threat vectors in the cloud.

AI-Powered IDS Solution:

The firm implemented an AI-powered IDS that utilized a combination of machine learning and behavioral analytics to monitor cloud traffic. The solution was specifically designed to detect malicious activities in cloud environments by analyzing patterns such as unusual access requests, unauthorized data transfers, and potential misconfigurations that could lead to security vulnerabilities.

Implementation:

The system integrated with the firm's cloud infrastructure to continuously analyze traffic, identify risky behaviors, and ensure that only authorized users had access to critical cloud resources. The AI model was trained to recognize the unique behavioral patterns of cloud applications, users, and devices to detect potential misuse or external threats.

Outcome:

- **Real-Time Threat Detection**: The AI-powered IDS allowed the technology firm to quickly detect and respond to potential security incidents in the cloud. It could identify unauthorized access attempts or abnormal data transfer activities in real time.
- **Scalability**: As the firm expanded its cloud footprint, the AI-powered IDS scaled seamlessly, adapting to the increased volume of traffic without performance degradation. This flexibility was crucial for maintaining security as the company continued to adopt new cloud services.
- **Improved Security Posture**: By automating threat detection and response in the cloud, the firm improved its overall security posture, reducing the time it took to identify and mitigate threats across its distributed infrastructure.

AI-powered IDS solutions have proven to be highly effective in real-world cybersecurity applications, offering enhanced detection capabilities, reduced false positives, and faster response times compared to traditional systems. From insider threats and DDoS attacks to ransomware and cloud security, organizations across various industries are leveraging

AI to protect their digital assets and critical infrastructure. These case studies demonstrate the practical benefits of incorporating AI into cybersecurity strategies, providing a proactive and adaptive defense against the ever-evolving threat landscape. As AI technology continues to evolve, its integration into IDS systems will only become more crucial for keeping organizations secure in the face of increasingly sophisticated cyber threats.

4.5 Overcoming False Positives and Model Tuning

One of the major challenges in the implementation of AI-powered Intrusion Detection Systems (IDS) is dealing with false positives—alerts that indicate a potential security threat, but upon further investigation, turn out to be benign. False positives can overwhelm security teams, wasting time, resources, and ultimately diluting the effectiveness of an IDS system. In the context of machine learning and artificial intelligence (AI) in cybersecurity, fine-tuning the detection model to minimize false positives while maintaining the ability to detect real threats is an ongoing challenge. This section explores how AI-powered IDS systems can be optimized to reduce false positives and achieve the ideal balance between sensitivity and accuracy, as well as the techniques and strategies involved in model tuning to improve performance.

1. The Problem of False Positives in AI-Driven IDS

False positives occur when an IDS flags an event as malicious or suspicious when it is, in fact, legitimate behavior. This can have serious consequences:

- **Wasted Resources**: Security teams must spend time investigating these alerts, leading to inefficiencies and a decrease in the overall productivity of cybersecurity staff.
- **Alert Fatigue**: Constant false alarms may lead to alert fatigue, where analysts become desensitized to warnings, increasing the risk of overlooking genuine threats.
- **Operational Disruption**: In some cases, excessive false positives can lead to unnecessary disruptions, such as blocking legitimate network traffic or access to services, which may hinder business operations.

In AI-driven IDS systems, which rely on machine learning to detect anomalous patterns, this issue is particularly prominent. While machine learning models have the ability to detect complex attack vectors, they also have the capacity to misinterpret normal behavior as an attack, especially in environments where patterns of user behavior, network traffic, or system processes are not fully understood by the model.

Key Factors Contributing to False Positives:

- **Over-sensitivity to Anomalies**: ML models might be too sensitive and flag any deviation from established patterns, even if it's due to a harmless, routine change in behavior.
- **Lack of Contextual Awareness**: Many models struggle to incorporate context into their analysis, leading to alerts triggered by patterns that are anomalous in isolation but normal within a specific operational context.
- **Insufficient Training Data**: If the model is trained on an incomplete or biased dataset, it may learn patterns that do not accurately reflect the full range of network or user behaviors, resulting in misclassifications.

2. Reducing False Positives Through Effective Model Tuning

The key to overcoming false positives is model tuning—a process where machine learning models are adjusted to improve performance without sacrificing detection accuracy. There are several techniques and strategies for fine-tuning AI-powered IDS systems to achieve the optimal balance between sensitivity and specificity.

1. Hyperparameter Tuning

Hyperparameters are the parameters of a machine learning algorithm that are set before the training process begins (e.g., learning rate, regularization strength, number of layers in a neural network). The tuning of these hyperparameters can significantly affect the model's performance and its propensity to generate false positives.

- **Objective**: The goal is to adjust the hyperparameters to avoid overfitting (which can increase false positives) or underfitting (which can decrease the model's ability to detect real threats).
- **Approach**: Common techniques for hyperparameter tuning include grid search, where the model is tested with a predefined set of hyperparameters, and random search, where the algorithm explores a larger, more diverse set of hyperparameters.
- **Effect**: Proper hyperparameter tuning can help reduce the model's sensitivity to benign anomalies while maintaining its ability to detect novel threats.

2. Model Complexity Adjustment

Complex models (e.g., deep neural networks) have the potential to capture intricate patterns, but they are also more likely to overfit the training data, resulting in more false positives. In contrast, simpler models may not capture enough complexity, leading to underfitting and missed threats.

- **Objective**: Striking the right balance in model complexity is crucial. Using simpler models may lower the false positive rate but could reduce the system's ability to detect sophisticated attacks. Conversely, more complex models might be more sensitive but risk overfitting.
- **Approach**: Techniques like regularization (e.g., L2 regularization) and dropout (in neural networks) can be applied to reduce overfitting. These methods force the model to generalize better by penalizing overly complex or highly specialized models.

3. Refining Feature Engineering

The performance of a machine learning model heavily depends on the features used for training. Feature engineering is the process of selecting and transforming the data inputs to the model to improve its predictive power. In cybersecurity, this might involve including network traffic data, user behavior patterns, or application logs.

- **Objective**: To improve the model's ability to discern between legitimate and malicious behavior.
- **Approach**: Experts in the field of cybersecurity can help refine features that better represent attack behaviors while eliminating noise from normal activities. This can include aggregating data from multiple sources, normalizing values, or using domain knowledge to create more accurate features.
- **Effect**: High-quality features can make it easier for the model to identify true threats while reducing the number of benign patterns flagged as attacks.

4. Ensemble Methods

An ensemble approach combines multiple models to improve performance by leveraging the strengths of each individual model. In the context of AI-powered IDS, ensemble methods can be used to create a more robust detection system that is less prone to false positives.

- **Objective**: Reduce the likelihood of misclassifications by combining different model types to offer a more holistic view of the data.

- **Approach**: Common ensemble techniques include bagging (e.g., Random Forests), where multiple instances of a model are trained on different subsets of the data, and boosting (e.g., AdaBoost), where weak learners are combined to form a stronger overall model.
- **Effect**: By combining models with different strengths, ensemble methods can provide more reliable threat detection with fewer false alarms.

5. Continuous Learning and Model Updates

Cybersecurity threats evolve constantly, so the detection models must be updated regularly to keep up with emerging attack methods. Static models that were trained months or years ago may no longer be effective at recognizing new threats or at adapting to shifts in normal behavior.

- **Objective**: Continuously improve the model's performance by retraining it with new data and updating its parameters over time.
- **Approach**: Implementing online learning or incremental learning allows the model to update continuously as new data comes in, rather than requiring a complete retraining of the model. Additionally, regular updates using feedback loops from security analysts can help the model improve over time, especially when false positives are manually corrected.
- **Effect**: Keeping the model up-to-date ensures that it stays relevant in the face of evolving threats while reducing the likelihood of both false positives and missed attacks.

3. Balancing Sensitivity and Specificity

A key aspect of tuning an AI-powered IDS system is finding the right balance between sensitivity (true positive rate) and specificity (true negative rate). High sensitivity means the model is good at detecting real threats but may also flag more benign activities as suspicious, leading to false positives. High specificity, on the other hand, means the model will miss fewer legitimate activities but might overlook some actual threats.

To achieve the optimal balance:

- **Precision-Recall Tradeoff**: Adjusting thresholds for alerts allows security teams to decide on acceptable levels of false positives and false negatives. Lowering the threshold for alerts increases sensitivity but also increases false positives.
- **Receiver Operating Characteristic (ROC) Curve**: The ROC curve can be used to assess the performance of the IDS model by plotting the true positive rate

against the false positive rate. By adjusting the decision threshold, organizations can find an optimal point on the curve that minimizes false positives while maintaining high detection accuracy.

Reducing false positives and fine-tuning machine learning models are critical to the success of AI-powered IDS systems. False positives, if left unchecked, can overwhelm security teams and diminish the effectiveness of detection systems. However, through careful model tuning, including hyperparameter adjustments, ensemble methods, feature engineering, and continuous learning, organizations can significantly reduce false positives without compromising the ability to detect real threats. Ultimately, the goal is to create an IDS system that is both highly accurate and adaptive to the constantly changing cybersecurity landscape, ensuring that AI models continue to provide value in protecting against increasingly sophisticated cyber threats.

5. Automating Threat Intelligence with AI

In the battle against cyber threats, timely and actionable intelligence is key—but manually gathering and analyzing threat data is both time-consuming and prone to human error. This chapter examines how AI automates the process of collecting, correlating, and interpreting threat intelligence, enabling faster and more precise decision-making. Readers will explore the use of AI in aggregating data from diverse sources, detecting emerging vulnerabilities, and generating predictive insights to anticipate potential attacks. By automating threat intelligence, organizations can stay one step ahead of adversaries and build proactive defense strategies.

5.1 Gathering Threat Data from Global Sources

In the fight against cyber threats, having access to up-to-date, relevant, and comprehensive threat data is essential. Cybersecurity experts and organizations need continuous access to a wide range of threat intelligence to stay ahead of adversaries and defend against emerging risks. One of the most effective ways to gather this data is by tapping into global threat intelligence sources. This section delves into the importance of gathering threat data from global sources, the different types of threat intelligence available, and the methods for collecting, aggregating, and utilizing this data to enhance cybersecurity defenses.

1. The Importance of Global Threat Data

As cyber threats evolve, organizations must adapt quickly to new tactics, techniques, and procedures (TTPs) used by cybercriminals, hackers, and state-sponsored actors. Global threat data plays a crucial role in helping organizations:

- **Identify emerging threats**: By gathering data from around the world, organizations can spot new attack patterns, malware, and vulnerabilities before they spread to their own networks.
- **Understand attack vectors**: Threat data provides insights into the most common ways attacks are launched, helping security teams focus on preventing those attack vectors.
- **Improve proactive defenses**: With real-time threat data, organizations can adjust their security measures to defend against the latest tactics used by attackers.

- **Enhance collaboration**: Sharing threat data between organizations and industries allows for collective defense, increasing the overall resilience of the cybersecurity ecosystem.

Global threat data can come from a variety of sources, including government agencies, private companies, academic research, and international collaborations. It helps organizations build a comprehensive view of the threat landscape, allowing them to stay ahead of increasingly sophisticated adversaries.

2. Types of Threat Intelligence Data

Threat intelligence comes in many forms, each serving a specific purpose in the cybersecurity ecosystem. Broadly, threat intelligence can be categorized into several types, each with different levels of detail and scope:

1. Strategic Threat Intelligence

- **Purpose**: Provides high-level insights into global trends, emerging threats, and geopolitical risks. It is often used by senior leadership to understand the broader cybersecurity landscape and to inform long-term security planning.
- **Sources**: Global news outlets, governmental agencies (e.g., US-CERT, Europol), and cybersecurity firms.
- **Example**: Reports on nation-state cyber activity, emerging threats like ransomware-as-a-service, and analysis of global attack trends.

2. Tactical Threat Intelligence

- **Purpose**: Focuses on the tactics, techniques, and procedures (TTPs) used by cybercriminals and attackers. This data helps security teams understand how threats are executed and how to defend against them.
- **Sources**: Threat intelligence sharing platforms, open-source intelligence (OSINT) tools, security vendors, and industry collaborations.
- **Example**: Information about the latest phishing techniques, malware delivery methods, or attack infrastructure used by threat actors.

3. Operational Threat Intelligence

- **Purpose**: Provides actionable data about ongoing attacks, such as indicators of compromise (IOCs), which are essential for immediate defense actions.

- **Sources**: Real-time threat data from security monitoring tools, threat intelligence feeds, and incident response reports.
- **Example**: A list of IOCs related to a specific malware campaign, such as malicious IP addresses, URLs, and file hashes.

4. Tactical and Technical Indicators (TTPs and IOCs)

- **Purpose**: Provides technical information related to attacks in progress. These indicators, such as malware signatures, IP addresses, and attack patterns, can be used to detect and block cyberattacks.
- **Sources**: Automated threat feeds, security vendors (such as FireEye, CrowdStrike), government threat-sharing platforms (e.g., FS-ISAC), and dark web monitoring services.
- **Example**: An IOC that identifies a specific version of malware currently targeting financial institutions globally.

3. Global Sources of Threat Data

The most effective threat intelligence comes from a wide range of global sources, each providing unique and valuable information. Some of the most critical global sources include:

1. Government Agencies and Cybersecurity Organizations

Governments and international organizations often share critical threat intelligence related to national security risks, cybercrime, and attacks on critical infrastructure. These entities provide information about high-level threats, state-sponsored cyber actors, and large-scale attack campaigns.

- **Examples**: US-CERT (United States Computer Emergency Readiness Team), NCSC (National Cyber Security Centre, UK), Europol, and ENISA (European Union Agency for Cybersecurity).
- **Contribution**: These organizations often issue warnings, bulletins, and advisories that provide information on specific vulnerabilities, active threats, and mitigation measures.

2. Information Sharing and Analysis Centers (ISACs)

ISACs are sector-specific organizations designed to facilitate the sharing of cybersecurity data among businesses within the same industry. They allow organizations to share detailed threat data anonymously and securely, enabling more robust defense strategies across sectors.

- **Examples**: Financial Services ISAC (FS-ISAC), Health ISAC, Energy ISAC, and Industrial Control Systems ISAC (ICS-ISAC).
- **Contribution**: These centers provide actionable intelligence, share vulnerabilities, and help organizations monitor industry-specific threats.

3. Threat Intelligence Feeds and Vendors

Cybersecurity vendors often provide paid or open-source threat intelligence feeds that deliver real-time information about known threats. These feeds provide technical details about malware, attack infrastructure, and indicators of compromise (IOCs) that can be used for immediate detection and mitigation.

- **Examples**: FireEye, CrowdStrike, IBM X-Force, and Palo Alto Networks.
- **Contribution**: These vendors often offer IOCs, TTPs, and other actionable intelligence that can be integrated into an organization's security operations.

4. Open Source Intelligence (OSINT)

Open-source intelligence is gathered from publicly available sources, including online forums, social media platforms, and deep and dark web marketplaces. OSINT tools and platforms allow organizations to monitor threat actor discussions, exploit kits, and leaked data.

- **Examples**: Shodan, Have I Been Pwned, and Dark Web monitoring tools.
- **Contribution**: OSINT can reveal threat actor tactics, ongoing campaigns, and exposed sensitive data, offering valuable insights into potential vulnerabilities.

5. Academic and Research Institutions

Academic and research institutions often contribute to the global cybersecurity landscape by conducting studies, publishing reports, and collaborating with governments and industries. Their research provides insights into emerging attack methodologies and the underlying technological trends driving cybersecurity risks.

- **Examples**: CERTs (Computer Emergency Response Teams) affiliated with universities, MITRE ATT&CK Framework, and academic papers on new threat vectors.

- **Contribution**: Research institutions provide early warning signs about new attack vectors, emerging malware types, and the evolving tactics used by cyber adversaries.

4. Techniques for Gathering and Aggregating Global Threat Data

Once organizations identify key sources of global threat data, it is important to have effective methods for gathering, aggregating, and processing this information.

1. Threat Intelligence Feeds

Integrating multiple threat intelligence feeds into a centralized system allows organizations to aggregate data from a wide variety of sources. Feeds are often delivered in standardized formats such as STIX (Structured Threat Information Expression) and TAXII (Trusted Automated Exchange of Indicator Information), which allow for easy integration with existing security systems like SIEMs (Security Information and Event Management) and firewalls.

2. Automated Threat Collection Tools

Automated tools such as web scrapers, crawlers, and API integrations can be used to gather real-time data from open-source platforms, threat intelligence sharing platforms, and even deep/dark web sources. These tools continuously scan for new IOCs, malware hashes, and attack patterns, helping organizations stay updated on the latest threats.

3. Collaboration and Sharing Networks

Collaborating with other organizations, industry groups, and government agencies allows for faster data exchange and collective defense. Platforms like MISP (Malware Information Sharing Platform & Threat Sharing), ThreatConnect, and AlienVault OTX (Open Threat Exchange) provide repositories of shared threat data and allow organizations to contribute information on emerging threats.

Gathering and utilizing threat data from global sources is crucial for organizations aiming to defend themselves against the growing number and sophistication of cyber threats. By leveraging multiple types of threat intelligence—from high-level strategic insights to real-time operational data—organizations can stay ahead of attackers, adapt to new risks, and bolster their overall cybersecurity posture. Accessing and integrating global threat intelligence helps cybersecurity teams to anticipate potential threats, improve incident response, and enhance their defenses against both known and emerging attacks.

5.2 AI Techniques for Analyzing Threat Feeds

In the context of cybersecurity, threat feeds play a crucial role in identifying and mitigating potential threats. As threat actors become more sophisticated, analyzing threat feeds with traditional methods alone is not sufficient. Artificial Intelligence (AI) and Machine Learning (ML) techniques have revolutionized the ability to process vast amounts of threat data, identify patterns, detect anomalies, and quickly adapt to evolving threats. This section explores various AI techniques that can be applied to analyze threat feeds, enabling cybersecurity professionals to make informed decisions about threat response and mitigation.

1. The Challenge of Analyzing Threat Feeds

Threat feeds contain data from multiple sources, including logs, network traffic, web traffic, malware hashes, IP addresses, domain names, and other security events. These feeds are often massive, noisy, and contain a diverse range of data types. Without advanced analytical techniques, it can be difficult to accurately sift through this data to find actionable insights. Traditional rule-based approaches or manual analysis fall short in this high-volume, high-velocity environment, making AI an ideal tool to augment human efforts and automate the analysis process.

2. AI Techniques for Threat Feed Analysis

1. Natural Language Processing (NLP) in Threat Intelligence

NLP techniques can help process textual data from threat feeds, such as reports, blog posts, and security advisories. By extracting entities like key terms, threat actor names, code vulnerabilities, or attack techniques, NLP can help analysts quickly understand the context and relevance of the data.

- **Application**: NLP can be used to process threat actor descriptions, code analysis, or domain registration data, allowing cybersecurity teams to extract relevant patterns and behaviors.
- **Benefits**: NLP helps bridge the gap between structured data (e.g., IP addresses, hashes) and unstructured data (e.g., attack reports, phishing emails), allowing threat analysts to connect the dots between disparate data sources.

2. Machine Learning Clustering Algorithms

Clustering algorithms, such as k-means or DBSCAN (Density-Based Spatial Clustering of Applications with Noise), can be used to group similar patterns and behaviors in threat feeds. By clustering related data points (e.g., IP addresses, URLs, domains, network flows), analysts can detect common attack patterns, campaigns, or threat actors.

- **Application**: Machine learning clustering algorithms can identify and group related entities in threat feeds, enabling analysts to spot persistent campaigns or distributed attacks with multiple entry points.
- **Benefits**: This helps analysts to prioritize resources based on common characteristics, trends, or attack vectors, allowing the security team to respond more effectively to evolving threats.

3. Anomaly Detection Using AI Techniques

Anomaly detection algorithms like Isolation Forest, One-Class SVM (Support Vector Machine), or Autoencoders can identify outliers in threat feeds. These algorithms are particularly useful for detecting unknown or zero-day threats that may not fit into existing threat patterns.

- **Application**: By processing threat data from logs, network traffic, and endpoint data, anomaly detection algorithms can identify unusual behaviors that may be indicative of malicious activity.
- **Benefits**: They help detect anomalies that fall outside the bounds of regular operations, allowing security teams to prioritize incidents that require immediate investigation.

4. Temporal Analysis with Time Series Forecasting

Time series forecasting algorithms like LSTM (Long Short-Term Memory) networks or ARIMA (AutoRegressive Integrated Moving Average) models can analyze trends over time, such as the frequency of certain malicious domains or IP addresses appearing in threat feeds.

- **Application**: By forecasting future patterns and trends in threat feeds, cybersecurity teams can anticipate potential spikes in malicious activity and proactively take countermeasures.
- **Benefits**: Temporal analysis enables teams to understand past behavior and predict patterns, thereby improving their ability to prevent future attacks.

5. Graph Analytics for Threat Intelligence

Graph analytics techniques can be used to understand the relationships between entities in threat data, such as IP addresses, domains, user accounts, and malware samples. By mapping these relationships, analysts can build a more comprehensive understanding of the cyber threat landscape.

- **Application**: For example, if a domain name is linked to various IP addresses and users, graph analytics can help reveal connections between malicious behaviors and threat actors.
- **Benefits**: It allows security teams to uncover complex relationships between entities in threat feeds, revealing hidden connections that might not be immediately apparent, enabling a more nuanced understanding of threat activity.

6. Deep Learning for Threat Feed Analysis

Deep learning models like Convolutional Neural Networks (CNNs) and Recurrent Neural Networks (RNNs) can process highly complex data types, such as images of malware, raw traffic data, or encrypted payloads. These models are capable of discovering intricate patterns that traditional techniques might miss.

- **Application**: Deep learning can be used to analyze raw binary data from malware samples, encrypted communication traffic, and images of phishing sites.
- **Benefits**: Deep learning enables analysts to detect threats in complex, highly obfuscated data that cannot be easily decoded by traditional methods. This helps detect sophisticated attacks like fileless malware, evasive encryption, and other novel techniques used by cybercriminals.

7. Reinforcement Learning in Cyber Defense

While less common in threat analysis, reinforcement learning can be applied to dynamic cyber defense strategies. It can help models adapt to changing conditions by learning from past interactions with cyber threats and refining response strategies based on observed behaviors.

- **Application**: Reinforcement learning can optimize automated responses to detected threats, such as adjusting detection thresholds or refining IDS rules.
- **Benefits**: By continuously adapting to evolving threats, reinforcement learning-based models can improve their effectiveness and reduce false positives over time.

8. Combining Multiple AI Techniques

One of the most powerful uses of AI for threat feed analysis is combining multiple techniques. For example, using NLP to extract data from threat reports, then applying clustering and anomaly detection to group patterns and behaviors, can reveal complex relationships between threats and adversary tactics.

- **Benefits**: Combining AI techniques allows security teams to leverage complementary strengths, providing a more comprehensive view of the threat landscape and enhancing their ability to detect and respond to cyber threats.

3. Tools and Platforms for AI-Based Threat Feed Analysis

There are various tools and platforms that offer AI techniques for analyzing threat feeds, enabling cybersecurity teams to process and analyze data at scale. Some popular options include:

- **Elastic Security (formerly known as Elasticsearch SIEM):** Uses Elasticsearch, Logstash, and Kibana to provide real-time threat analysis and threat feed analysis.
- **Splunk**: Offers AI-driven threat intelligence and anomaly detection capabilities using data from threat feeds.
- **IBM QRadar and Watson for XDR (Extended Detection and Response):** Combines AI-driven threat intelligence, behavior analysis, and anomaly detection to provide comprehensive threat analysis and incident response.
- **CrowdStrike Falcon**: An endpoint detection and response (EDR) solution that uses AI to analyze endpoint data, identify threats, and prioritize alerts.
- **MISP (Malware Information Sharing Platform):** An open-source threat intelligence platform for collecting, sharing, and correlating data on threats and incidents across organizations.

4. Real-World Use Cases of AI in Analyzing Threat Feeds

- **Detecting Zero-Day Exploits**: By analyzing patterns in threat feeds using machine learning, organizations can detect zero-day exploits before they are formally reported. For example, if unusual behavior in threat data matches previously unknown patterns, AI models can alert security teams to investigate further.
- **Uncovering Advanced Persistent Threats (APTs):** Using graph analytics and clustering, AI can help analysts piece together disparate data points across threat

feeds to uncover long-term APT campaigns. By identifying overlapping behaviors and connections between entities, analysts can build a more complete picture of threat actors' tactics, techniques, and procedures.

- **Automating Response to Repetitive Threats**: AI models can learn patterns from repeated threats (e.g., specific phishing emails or attack campaigns) and automatically generate rules to block similar incidents in the future. This reduces the need for human intervention in responding to common, repetitive threats.

AI techniques for analyzing threat feeds are transforming how cybersecurity professionals detect, analyze, and respond to cyber threats. By leveraging AI techniques such as NLP, clustering, anomaly detection, graph analytics, and deep learning, organizations can process complex data types, understand intricate patterns, and respond more rapidly to threats. As cyber threats continue to grow in sophistication, AI-based threat analysis is becoming indispensable for maintaining a proactive and effective cybersecurity posture. The combination of human expertise and AI-driven analysis provides security teams with a powerful toolset to identify, understand, and mitigate cyber threats more effectively and efficiently.

5.3 Automating Threat Hunting with Machine Learning

In the ever-evolving landscape of cybersecurity, threat hunting has become a proactive strategy to identify and neutralize potential cyber threats before they can cause significant damage. Traditional threat hunting often requires skilled human analysts to sift through vast amounts of data, hunting for signs of compromise, anomalies, or unknown threats. However, as cyber threats become more sophisticated and the volume of data grows exponentially, human-driven threat hunting is increasingly inefficient and time-consuming. This is where machine learning (ML) comes into play, automating and enhancing the threat hunting process.

Machine learning has emerged as a powerful tool in cybersecurity, enabling faster, more efficient, and more accurate identification of cyber threats. By leveraging ML algorithms, organizations can automate many aspects of the threat hunting process, reducing the manual effort involved and increasing the speed at which threats are identified. This section explores how machine learning can be used to automate threat hunting, the benefits it offers, and the key challenges involved in integrating machine learning into threat hunting workflows.

1. The Evolution of Threat Hunting

Threat hunting traditionally involved analysts manually searching for signs of hidden threats within an organization's systems. This process included:

- **Log analysis**: Sifting through system logs to identify anomalies.
- **Signature-based detection**: Searching for known patterns of malicious behavior.
- **Alert triage**: Reviewing and prioritizing alerts from security tools like intrusion detection systems (IDS) and firewalls.

While effective, traditional threat hunting methods often miss emerging threats, particularly those that have not been previously encountered or that are disguised through novel techniques. Manual hunting is also labor-intensive, requiring experts to analyze massive datasets without automation tools to highlight meaningful patterns. As the scale of networks, systems, and data increases, human threat hunters face challenges in keeping up with the sheer volume and complexity of potential attacks.

Machine learning offers a way to enhance and automate many aspects of threat hunting, helping security teams identify potential threats in real-time and detect sophisticated attacks that might otherwise evade traditional methods.

2. Key Machine Learning Techniques for Automating Threat Hunting

To effectively automate the threat hunting process, machine learning employs several key techniques that allow algorithms to identify and classify suspicious activity, detect anomalies, and predict future attack behaviors. The main techniques that support automated threat hunting include:

1. Supervised Learning

Supervised learning involves training a model using labeled data—where the outcome (e.g., "malicious" or "benign") is known. The model learns from this historical data and is then able to classify new, unseen data based on its learned patterns. In the context of threat hunting, supervised learning can be used to:

Classify network traffic as either benign or malicious, based on features like IP addresses, protocols, and payloads.

Detect malware by analyzing known malware signatures and distinguishing between normal and abnormal system behaviors.

Examples: Decision Trees, Random Forests, Support Vector Machines (SVM), and Naive Bayes algorithms are often used for supervised learning in cybersecurity.

2. Unsupervised Learning

Unsupervised learning does not require labeled data, making it particularly useful when hunting for previously unknown or zero-day threats. Instead, the machine learning algorithm groups data into clusters based on similarities, enabling the identification of anomalous patterns that might indicate an attack. Unsupervised learning can be used to:

Detect anomalies in network traffic, system behavior, or user actions.

Identify zero-day attacks that don't match known threat patterns but deviate from normal behavior.

Examples: Clustering algorithms such as k-means, DBSCAN (Density-Based Spatial Clustering of Applications with Noise), and Hierarchical Clustering are commonly used in unsupervised learning for threat detection.

3. Reinforcement Learning

Reinforcement learning involves training an agent to make a sequence of decisions by rewarding or penalizing it for specific actions. This approach is particularly effective in real-time threat hunting, where the model learns to respond to new and evolving threats by trial and error. In cybersecurity, reinforcement learning can be used to:

Optimize threat response strategies, where the system improves its defensive tactics based on past experiences.

Adapt to new attack techniques by adjusting to changes in adversarial behavior and identifying the best mitigation strategies over time.

Examples: Q-learning and Deep Q-Networks (DQNs) are reinforcement learning techniques used in autonomous decision-making for cybersecurity tasks.

4. Deep Learning

Deep learning, a subset of machine learning, involves using neural networks with many layers to automatically extract features from raw data. This approach is particularly effective in automating the detection of complex patterns and high-dimensional data, such as network traffic logs or endpoint data. Deep learning techniques can be used in threat hunting to:

Detect advanced threats, including fileless malware, which is harder to detect with traditional methods.

Analyze large-scale datasets, such as network traffic, in real-time, to identify novel attack behaviors or anomalies.

Examples: Convolutional Neural Networks (CNNs), Recurrent Neural Networks (RNNs), and Long Short-Term Memory (LSTM) networks are common deep learning algorithms applied to threat hunting.

3. Benefits of Automating Threat Hunting with Machine Learning

Machine learning provides several key advantages for automating threat hunting, enabling organizations to respond more quickly and effectively to cyber threats. Some of the key benefits include:

1. Increased Efficiency and Speed

Machine learning models can process and analyze vast amounts of data in a fraction of the time it would take a human analyst. By automating the collection, analysis, and triage of threat data, ML systems can quickly identify patterns or anomalies that may indicate malicious activity. This enables security teams to detect threats in real-time and respond to incidents more rapidly.

2. Improved Accuracy and Reduced Human Error

Machine learning models, when properly trained, can identify suspicious activities with greater accuracy than humans. By continuously learning from new data, ML models can reduce the risk of false positives and false negatives, improving the precision of threat detection. This reduces the workload for security teams, who no longer need to manually review every alert.

3. Proactive Threat Detection

ML models can help organizations move from a reactive security posture to a proactive one. By analyzing patterns and trends across threat feeds, logs, and historical data, machine learning can predict emerging threats before they materialize, allowing security teams to take preemptive actions to prevent attacks.

4. Identifying Sophisticated Attacks

Machine learning excels in detecting complex and sophisticated attacks, such as zero-day exploits, fileless malware, and advanced persistent threats (APTs), that might bypass traditional signature-based detection methods. By learning from historical data and continuously adapting, machine learning models are better equipped to detect evolving attack techniques.

4. Challenges in Implementing Machine Learning for Threat Hunting

While machine learning offers numerous advantages for threat hunting, several challenges must be addressed to ensure its successful implementation:

1. Data Quality and Quantity

For machine learning models to be effective, they need large volumes of high-quality data for training. Inconsistent or incomplete data can lead to inaccurate models and poor detection performance. Organizations must ensure they have access to comprehensive, clean, and relevant datasets for effective model training.

2. Model Overfitting

Overfitting occurs when a machine learning model becomes too tailored to the training data, causing it to perform poorly on unseen data. In threat hunting, this could mean that a model may not generalize well to new or evolving attack techniques. Regular model evaluation and retraining are necessary to ensure the model continues to perform well over time.

3. Interpretability of Results

Machine learning models, especially deep learning models, can sometimes act as "black boxes," making it difficult for human analysts to understand how a particular decision was made. This lack of interpretability can be a challenge in a cybersecurity environment, where understanding the reasoning behind detection is crucial for response and investigation.

4. Integration with Existing Security Infrastructure

Integrating machine learning-based threat hunting tools with existing security infrastructure, such as Security Information and Event Management (SIEM) systems, endpoint detection systems, and intrusion detection/prevention systems (IDS/IPS), can be complex. Ensuring seamless communication and data flow between various security tools is essential for automated threat hunting to be effective.

Automating threat hunting with machine learning offers significant benefits, including increased efficiency, improved detection accuracy, and the ability to proactively identify and mitigate sophisticated threats. By leveraging supervised, unsupervised, reinforcement learning, and deep learning techniques, organizations can enhance their cybersecurity posture and better defend against modern cyber threats. However, to fully realize the potential of machine learning in threat hunting, organizations must address challenges related to data quality, model generalization, interpretability, and integration with existing tools. When implemented correctly, machine learning-powered threat hunting can become a critical component of a proactive cybersecurity strategy, helping organizations stay ahead of evolving threats and enhancing overall resilience.

5.4 Predictive Threat Modeling and Risk Scoring

In the complex and rapidly evolving landscape of cybersecurity, organizations face an increasing number of threats that can potentially impact their operations, financial standing, and reputation. As cyber threats grow more sophisticated, it's no longer sufficient to rely on traditional defense mechanisms that focus on detecting known threats or reacting after an attack occurs. To stay ahead of adversaries, businesses need proactive, predictive approaches to identify potential threats and evaluate risks before they materialize. Predictive threat modeling and risk scoring, powered by advanced machine learning (ML) techniques, have emerged as critical tools in this proactive defense strategy. These approaches enable organizations to anticipate, model, and assess cybersecurity risks, making it easier to allocate resources and take preventative actions.

This section explores the role of predictive threat modeling and risk scoring in cybersecurity, how machine learning enhances these practices, and how organizations can use them to improve their security posture.

1. The Need for Predictive Threat Modeling

Traditional threat detection systems often rely on reactive approaches, such as signature-based detection and real-time monitoring of network traffic, logs, and endpoints. While these methods are essential for detecting known threats, they fall short when it comes to uncovering previously unseen attacks or advanced persistent threats (APTs) that employ novel techniques.

Predictive threat modeling is an approach that moves away from this reactive mindset and anticipates future cyber threats by simulating potential attack vectors. By understanding how an attacker might exploit vulnerabilities in the system, organizations can predict attack scenarios and assess their potential impact. Predictive threat models help businesses prioritize resources and focus on areas with the highest potential for attack, enabling them to proactively defend against threats before they can cause harm.

2. Key Components of Predictive Threat Modeling

Predictive threat modeling involves the use of advanced analytics and machine learning algorithms to build models that can simulate and predict future attack scenarios. The key components of predictive threat modeling include:

1. Data Collection and Integration

For predictive models to be effective, organizations must gather large amounts of data from various sources. These data sources include:

- **Historical attack data**: Past cyberattacks provide valuable information about attack methods, targets, and the success or failure of defensive measures.
- **Threat intelligence feeds**: External data from threat intelligence providers offer real-time insights into emerging attack trends and tactics used by cybercriminals.
- **Internal system and network data**: This includes logs from firewalls, intrusion detection systems (IDS), endpoint data, and more. By analyzing this data, organizations can identify vulnerabilities and patterns that may suggest areas of weakness.

2. Risk Assessment Models

Risk assessment is a critical aspect of predictive threat modeling. By analyzing the likelihood and potential impact of various attack scenarios, organizations can prioritize their resources to mitigate the most significant risks. A variety of machine learning techniques can be applied to risk assessment, including:

- **Statistical models**: These models analyze historical data to estimate the probability of various types of cyber threats occurring in the future.
- **Bayesian networks**: Bayesian models can quantify uncertainty by calculating the probability of different outcomes, helping organizations assess risk more accurately.
- **Monte Carlo simulations**: These techniques simulate different attack scenarios under varying conditions to model potential threats and their outcomes, providing insights into risk likelihood and impact.

3. Attack Surface and Vulnerability Analysis

Predictive threat modeling focuses heavily on assessing the attack surface—the sum total of all the potential points where an attacker could attempt to gain unauthorized access. By identifying and evaluating weaknesses in this attack surface, predictive models can simulate which vulnerabilities are most likely to be exploited.

Machine learning algorithms can be used to:

- **Analyze vulnerability scans**: ML models can analyze vulnerability scan results and historical data on exploited vulnerabilities to determine which flaws are most likely to be targeted.
- **Map attack paths**: Attackers often follow specific paths when exploiting vulnerabilities. Machine learning models can map out these attack paths to predict potential routes and determine where security controls are most needed.

3. Machine Learning's Role in Predictive Threat Modeling

Machine learning plays a crucial role in predictive threat modeling by helping organizations analyze large datasets, identify patterns, and make predictions about potential future threats. Below are some of the key ML techniques used in predictive modeling:

1. Supervised Learning for Pattern Recognition

Supervised learning techniques involve training a model using labeled datasets, where the outcomes (e.g., successful or unsuccessful attacks) are known. The model learns to recognize patterns in the data and apply them to new, unseen data. In predictive threat modeling, supervised learning can be used to:

- **Identify recurring attack patterns**: By analyzing historical attack data, supervised learning models can identify patterns or tactics used by threat actors, such as phishing attacks, DDoS (Distributed Denial of Service), or social engineering tactics.
- **Predict potential attack vectors**: By training on past data, supervised models can predict which attack methods are most likely to be used against specific systems or organizations.

2. Unsupervised Learning for Anomaly Detection

Unsupervised learning, on the other hand, involves identifying patterns in data without relying on labeled outcomes. This technique is particularly useful for detecting unknown threats or attacks that do not match known patterns. In predictive threat modeling, unsupervised learning can:

- **Detect emerging threats**: By analyzing large datasets of network traffic, logs, and other security data, unsupervised learning algorithms can detect anomalies that might indicate an unknown or evolving threat.
- **Identify zero-day vulnerabilities**: These attacks, which exploit previously unknown vulnerabilities, are often difficult to detect with traditional methods. Unsupervised learning can help identify unusual behaviors or anomalies that could signal such threats.

3. Ensemble Learning for Improved Prediction Accuracy

Ensemble learning involves combining multiple machine learning models to improve prediction accuracy and reduce the risk of error. In predictive threat modeling, ensemble techniques can be used to combine various models, such as decision trees, random forests, and gradient boosting, to increase the robustness of the threat predictions.

Ensemble methods can:

- **Combine predictions from different models**: This provides a more comprehensive and accurate prediction by using the strengths of various models.
- **Minimize false positives**: By combining multiple models, ensemble learning helps ensure that the threat predictions made are not only accurate but also reliable.

4. Risk Scoring in Predictive Threat Modeling

Risk scoring involves quantifying the potential impact of a given threat by evaluating its likelihood and potential consequences. Machine learning can significantly enhance risk scoring by automating the process and providing more accurate predictions. Some key elements of ML-driven risk scoring include:

1. Risk Calculation Models

ML models can integrate historical data, threat intelligence feeds, and real-time monitoring to generate dynamic risk scores for assets, users, or systems within the network. These scores indicate the likelihood and severity of a security breach, helping organizations prioritize which threats to address first.

Example: If a particular asset (e.g., a server or endpoint) is exposed to known vulnerabilities, has unpatched software, and is accessed by high-risk users, it may be assigned a higher risk score, indicating that it is more likely to be targeted in an attack.

2. Continuous Monitoring and Adjustments

Unlike traditional risk scoring systems, which might rely on static data, ML-driven risk scoring systems can continuously adjust based on changing circumstances. For example, if new vulnerabilities or threats are identified, the risk score for affected systems can be updated in real-time to reflect the new level of exposure.

Example: A critical database that was previously deemed low-risk might suddenly have its risk score increased if it starts exhibiting suspicious activity or if an attacker is detected scanning it for weaknesses.

3. Prioritizing Remediation Efforts

Risk scoring helps organizations prioritize their remediation efforts by providing a clear, data-driven ranking of vulnerabilities and threats. Assets or systems with high-risk scores should be addressed first to reduce the chance of an attack.

5. Benefits of Predictive Threat Modeling and Risk Scoring

Predictive threat modeling and risk scoring provide several critical benefits to organizations seeking to strengthen their cybersecurity posture:

- **Proactive Defense**: By predicting potential attack scenarios and identifying vulnerabilities before they are exploited, organizations can take preventive measures and mitigate risks early.
- **Informed Decision Making**: Risk scoring helps security teams make data-driven decisions about where to allocate resources, which systems to harden, and which threats to prioritize.
- **Improved Resource Allocation**: With risk scoring and predictive models in place, security teams can optimize their resources by focusing on the most critical assets and vulnerabilities.
- **Enhanced Threat Awareness**: Predictive models give security teams a broader view of the threat landscape, enabling them to better understand emerging attack vectors and the tactics of threat actors.

6. Challenges and Considerations

While predictive threat modeling and risk scoring offer significant benefits, organizations must consider several challenges:

- **Data Quality**: Predictive models require high-quality, accurate data to generate reliable predictions. Inaccurate or incomplete data can lead to false predictions.
- **Model Accuracy**: Developing accurate models requires extensive training and fine-tuning. Incorrect or biased models can lead to ineffective threat predictions.
- **Real-Time Implementation**: Predictive threat models must be capable of handling real-time data to provide timely alerts and responses.

Predictive threat modeling and risk scoring are transformative practices that enable organizations to anticipate and prepare for potential cyberattacks. By using machine learning techniques to model attack scenarios, evaluate vulnerabilities, and assign risk scores, organizations can proactively defend against emerging threats. These predictive approaches, when integrated with existing security measures, help security teams prioritize actions, allocate resources effectively, and reduce the likelihood of successful attacks. While challenges remain, the combination of machine learning and predictive threat modeling is crucial for staying ahead of ever-evolving cyber adversaries.

5.5 Building AI-Powered Threat Intelligence Platforms

In today's interconnected digital world, organizations face an ever-growing and constantly evolving range of cybersecurity threats. The sheer volume of data and complexity of modern attacks have made traditional defense mechanisms, like signature-based systems, insufficient. To keep up with these threats, organizations must embrace more advanced, data-driven approaches to cybersecurity. AI-powered threat intelligence platforms (TIPs) are emerging as a critical tool for proactively identifying, analyzing, and responding to cyber threats in real time. These platforms harness the power of artificial intelligence (AI) and machine learning (ML) to automate the collection, analysis, and dissemination of threat intelligence, helping organizations stay ahead of adversaries and make more informed decisions about their cybersecurity strategies.

This section delves into the process of building AI-powered threat intelligence platforms, the technologies and techniques involved, and how they can transform cybersecurity operations.

1. The Need for AI-Powered Threat Intelligence Platforms

Cybersecurity threats are no longer limited to traditional forms like viruses or worms. Today's attacks range from advanced persistent threats (APTs) to ransomware, phishing, and insider threats, all of which are becoming more sophisticated and difficult to detect. The growing complexity of these attacks, combined with the massive amount of security data generated by modern IT environments, has created a need for more advanced tools to manage and respond to threats.

Traditional threat intelligence platforms (TIPs) rely heavily on human analysts to manually sift through security data, identify emerging trends, and make decisions. While these platforms provide valuable insight, they are often too slow to keep pace with the dynamic and rapidly evolving threat landscape. AI-powered TIPs, on the other hand, automate much of this process, enabling organizations to collect, process, and act on threat intelligence at machine speed. This results in faster, more accurate detection of emerging threats and the ability to respond proactively before an attack escalates.

2. Key Components of an AI-Powered Threat Intelligence Platform

Building an effective AI-powered threat intelligence platform involves integrating several components, including data collection, processing, analysis, and dissemination. Here are the key components involved in creating such a platform:

1. Data Collection and Aggregation

The first step in building an AI-powered TIP is gathering data from a variety of sources. The more diverse the data sources, the more accurate and comprehensive the threat intelligence will be. Common data sources include:

- **Internal Logs**: Logs from firewalls, intrusion detection systems (IDS), antivirus software, endpoint security, and other network monitoring tools.
- **External Threat Feeds**: Data from external threat intelligence providers, which offer information on emerging attack trends, known malware hashes, IP addresses associated with attackers, and more.
- **Open-Source Intelligence (OSINT):** Publicly available sources, such as forums, social media, and blogs, where threat actors often communicate or leak information about upcoming attacks.
- **Dark Web Intelligence**: Information gathered from dark web forums and marketplaces where cybercriminals trade tools and tactics.

AI algorithms are used to aggregate and standardize this data from various sources, ensuring that it is ready for analysis. By combining data from internal and external sources, organizations gain a holistic view of the threat landscape, allowing them to identify both internal vulnerabilities and external threats.

2. Data Processing and Normalization

Once data is collected, it must be processed and normalized. Raw data from different sources often comes in various formats, making it difficult to analyze. AI-powered platforms utilize data preprocessing techniques to clean, structure, and normalize this data so that it can be easily understood by machine learning algorithms. This step is essential to ensure that the platform can generate actionable insights from the data, such as identifying malicious IP addresses or detecting unusual activity patterns.

3. Machine Learning for Threat Analysis

Machine learning is the heart of AI-powered TIPs. The platform uses ML algorithms to analyze the collected data and detect patterns indicative of potential cyber threats. There are several techniques used in threat analysis:

- **Clustering and Classification**: Machine learning models are trained to classify incoming data as either benign or malicious. They can also be used to cluster similar threats based on attributes such as IP address, domain names, file hashes, or attack patterns. This helps identify new variants of known attacks or entirely new types of threats.
- **Anomaly Detection**: ML algorithms can detect anomalous behavior by comparing new data against a baseline of "normal" activity. For example, if a user suddenly

logs in from an unfamiliar location or performs actions outside their usual behavior, the system can flag it as potentially suspicious.

- **Predictive Modeling**: AI-powered TIPs can use predictive models to forecast future attack trends. By analyzing historical attack data, these models can identify patterns that may indicate an emerging threat, allowing organizations to take preventive measures before a breach occurs.

AI-based threat analysis can process data at much faster speeds than human analysts, enabling the platform to detect and respond to threats in real-time.

4. Threat Intelligence Correlation

AI-powered TIPs can correlate data from multiple sources to build a more comprehensive understanding of a threat. For example, if an organization detects an incoming spear-phishing attack, the system might correlate this with data from external threat intelligence feeds indicating that the attacker's IP address has been linked to previous APT activity. By correlating threat data across multiple platforms, AI-powered systems can provide more accurate and contextual insights, helping organizations identify high-priority threats faster.

5. Automation of Response and Workflow

Once a threat is detected and analyzed, AI-powered platforms can automate certain response actions. For example:

- **Automated Alerts**: When a potential threat is identified, the system can automatically trigger an alert and notify relevant stakeholders (e.g., security operations center (SOC) teams or incident response teams).
- **Blocking Malicious Traffic**: In some cases, the system can automatically block traffic from malicious IP addresses or quarantine infected endpoints based on predefined rules.
- **Intelligent Playbooks**: The platform can trigger predefined response playbooks based on the nature of the threat. For example, if a ransomware attack is detected, the system can automatically isolate affected systems, alert security teams, and initiate backup restoration processes.

Automation speeds up the response time and ensures that the appropriate actions are taken promptly, minimizing the damage caused by attacks.

6. Visualization and Reporting

AI-powered TIPs often feature visualization tools that provide security teams with an intuitive, real-time view of the threat landscape. These dashboards allow analysts to quickly understand the scope and severity of a threat, track ongoing incidents, and assess risk levels. Reporting features also allow for generating detailed reports that provide insights into the effectiveness of threat mitigation strategies, compliance with regulations, and overall security posture.

3. Technologies Enabling AI-Powered Threat Intelligence Platforms

Several technologies are crucial for building AI-powered TIPs. These include:

1. Natural Language Processing (NLP)

NLP is used to analyze and extract meaningful insights from unstructured data sources like threat reports, social media, and dark web activity. By using NLP, the platform can identify discussions or mentions of upcoming attacks, new malware, or vulnerabilities, providing early warnings of potential threats.

2. Big Data Analytics

AI-powered TIPs rely on big data technologies to process and analyze large volumes of security data in real-time. By leveraging distributed computing platforms like Hadoop or Spark, organizations can handle the massive amounts of data generated by security systems and external threat intelligence sources.

3. Cloud Computing

Cloud computing enables scalability and flexibility, allowing organizations to process and store vast amounts of threat intelligence data without the limitations of on-premise infrastructure. Cloud-based AI-powered TIPs can scale dynamically to accommodate increased data volumes and provide continuous threat analysis.

4. Benefits of AI-Powered Threat Intelligence Platforms

1. Real-Time Threat Detection

AI-powered TIPs enable organizations to detect and respond to cyber threats in real-time. By continuously analyzing data and identifying anomalies, these platforms can quickly identify emerging threats and reduce the time between detection and response.

2. Improved Accuracy and Reduced False Positives

Machine learning models continuously learn from new data, improving their accuracy over time. This reduces the number of false positives and ensures that security teams focus on the most critical threats, improving the efficiency of threat detection and response.

3. Enhanced Decision-Making

AI-powered TIPs provide security teams with actionable intelligence that helps them make more informed decisions. The platform's ability to correlate data from multiple sources ensures that the information security teams receive is comprehensive and contextually relevant.

4. Proactive Defense

By predicting future attack trends and identifying vulnerabilities before they are exploited, AI-powered TIPs help organizations move from a reactive defense posture to a proactive one. Predictive capabilities enable organizations to take preventive action and mitigate risks before an attack occurs.

5. Challenges in Building AI-Powered Threat Intelligence Platforms

While AI-powered threat intelligence platforms offer numerous benefits, there are challenges involved in their development and implementation:

- **Data Quality**: AI models require high-quality data to generate accurate predictions. Inaccurate or incomplete data can lead to false conclusions and missed threats.
- **Integration with Existing Systems**: Integrating AI-powered TIPs with existing cybersecurity infrastructure, such as firewalls, SIEMs, and IDS/IPS, can be complex and time-consuming.
- **Model Training and Maintenance**: AI models need to be regularly retrained and fine-tuned to keep up with evolving threats. This requires ongoing monitoring and maintenance.

AI-powered threat intelligence platforms are transforming the way organizations approach cybersecurity. By leveraging machine learning, natural language processing, and big data analytics, these platforms provide real-time, actionable intelligence that enables organizations to detect, analyze, and respond to threats more effectively. With the ability to correlate data from multiple sources, predict emerging threats, and automate response actions, AI-powered TIPs are essential tools for any organization looking to stay ahead of the increasingly sophisticated cyber threat landscape. However, building and maintaining these platforms requires careful planning, data management, and continuous refinement to ensure their effectiveness.

6. Behavioral Analytics and User Anomaly Detection

Traditional cybersecurity measures often focus on static defenses, but modern threats, particularly insider threats, require more dynamic approaches. This chapter explores how AI-driven behavioral analytics and user anomaly detection are transforming the way organizations detect malicious activity. By analyzing patterns in user behavior—such as login times, access frequency, and data usage—AI systems can identify deviations that may indicate compromised accounts or insider threats. Readers will learn how these advanced techniques offer a proactive approach to security, providing real-time alerts and the ability to respond swiftly to suspicious behavior before it leads to a breach.

6.1 Profiling User Behavior with AI

In the modern cybersecurity landscape, one of the most powerful approaches to detecting anomalies and potential threats is through user behavior profiling. This technique involves continuously monitoring and analyzing user activities across an organization's network and systems to establish a baseline of normal behavior. Once this baseline is established, artificial intelligence (AI) can then be employed to identify deviations from this norm—deviations that may indicate security breaches, data theft, or malicious activities.

User behavior profiling with AI leverages machine learning (ML) algorithms and data analytics to identify patterns in how users interact with systems, applications, and data. This enables organizations to detect unusual activities that could signify threats such as insider attacks, compromised accounts, or credential abuse. By moving beyond traditional methods, such as relying on signature-based detection, AI-powered profiling allows security systems to continuously adapt and learn from new patterns of user behavior, enhancing detection accuracy and reducing the risk of false positives.

1. The Need for User Behavior Profiling

Traditional cybersecurity measures, such as firewalls, antivirus software, and intrusion detection systems (IDS), are largely effective at defending against known threats but are less efficient when it comes to detecting more sophisticated, adaptive, and internal threats. Attackers increasingly bypass perimeter defenses, either through external means or by exploiting insider threats, making it crucial for organizations to take a more proactive approach to identifying unusual activities.

User behavior profiling addresses this need by focusing on the actions of individual users within a network. Every user within an organization has a set of typical behaviors based on their job role, work patterns, and interactions with systems and data. AI-powered profiling systems track these behaviors and establish a "normal" baseline for each user, allowing the system to flag any behavior that deviates from this baseline.

For example, if a user who typically accesses only a limited set of files suddenly downloads a large volume of sensitive data, or if a user accesses systems outside their normal working hours or from a geographic location they don't typically work from, these are significant behavioral anomalies that could suggest malicious activity.

2. How AI Profiles User Behavior

AI profiling of user behavior is typically powered by machine learning algorithms that analyze massive volumes of data from various sources, including network logs, application logs, system interactions, and more. The steps in this process can be broken down into several key phases:

1. Data Collection

The first step in profiling user behavior is collecting data on user activities. This data can include:

- **Login times and locations**: Where and when a user logs in or accesses the system.
- **File and data access patterns**: What files or databases a user interacts with, how frequently, and from which devices.
- **Application usage**: Which applications a user typically uses, how often, and for how long.
- **Network behavior**: The websites, IP addresses, or servers a user connects to.
- **Communication patterns**: Email, chat, and collaboration tool usage, including who the user communicates with and the frequency of those interactions.

2. Baseline Behavior Modeling

Once the data is collected, AI algorithms begin the process of modeling normal user behavior. This is done by employing machine learning techniques, such as clustering or unsupervised learning, to analyze the user's interactions over time. Through this analysis, the system builds a baseline or profile of what constitutes "normal" behavior for each user. The model takes into account factors such as:

- **Historical behavior**: The user's typical actions based on past behavior.
- **Time-based patterns**: Common activity patterns, like working hours and periods of inactivity.
- **Role-based behavior**: Expected behaviors aligned with the user's job role or department, such as what data they are permitted to access or what systems they typically use.

3. Anomaly Detection and Identification

Once a baseline is established, the AI system continuously monitors the user's activities in real time. If any activity deviates from the established baseline, the system flags it as an anomaly. AI algorithms use anomaly detection techniques to identify significant deviations from the user's normal behavior. Some of the common anomaly detection methods include:

- **Threshold-based detection**: If a user's activity exceeds a pre-defined threshold (e.g., accessing a certain number of files or login attempts in a given time), it is flagged for review.
- **Statistical analysis**: By evaluating a user's behavior in relation to their historical patterns and comparing it with statistical norms, AI can detect outliers that might signify a potential threat.
- **Clustering**: AI can group similar user behaviors together, helping to detect when a user's activities do not fit into their typical cluster, signaling a potential issue.

4. Continuous Learning and Adaptation

AI-powered user behavior profiling systems continuously evolve as more data becomes available. Unlike traditional systems that rely on static rules, AI systems improve over time by learning from new patterns and adapting to changes in user behavior. For example, if a user's working hours shift due to a change in their role or work habits, the system will update the user's profile to reflect this change.

Moreover, AI platforms can perform incremental learning, where they gradually adjust their models as new behaviors and patterns emerge, ensuring that the system remains effective in detecting threats even as users' legitimate activities evolve.

3. Benefits of AI-Based User Behavior Profiling

User behavior profiling with AI offers several significant advantages over traditional security measures:

1. Detection of Insider Threats

AI-based profiling is highly effective at detecting insider threats. These threats may originate from disgruntled employees, contractors, or compromised accounts. Since the system is monitoring user behavior in real time, it can detect subtle changes in activity that indicate malicious intent, such as unauthorized data access, attempts to elevate privileges, or unusual login locations.

2. Early Detection of Compromised Accounts

One of the most common entry points for attackers is compromised user credentials. By profiling user behavior, AI systems can detect when a user account has been hijacked. For instance, if an attacker uses a legitimate user's credentials to perform suspicious activities (e.g., accessing sensitive files or systems), the AI system will recognize the behavior as an anomaly and trigger an alert.

3. Reduced False Positives

Traditional intrusion detection systems (IDS) often rely on signature-based methods, which can produce a high number of false positives—alerts triggered by harmless activities that resemble attack patterns. AI-driven user behavior profiling significantly reduces false positives because it tailors its detection to the specific behavior of each user, leading to more accurate alerts.

4. Better Incident Response and Prioritization

Behavior profiling allows security teams to prioritize incidents based on the severity and context of the anomaly. If a user's behavior deviates significantly from the baseline in a critical way—such as accessing sensitive data or initiating unusual network traffic—the security team can immediately focus on investigating and mitigating the threat, reducing the time to response.

5. Adaptive and Scalable Security

As organizations grow, so does the complexity of their security needs. AI-powered systems can scale with the organization's growth, adapting to new users, devices, and behavior patterns without the need for manual intervention. This flexibility ensures that organizations can maintain effective security as they expand.

4. Challenges and Considerations

While AI-driven user behavior profiling offers many benefits, there are also challenges and considerations that organizations must address:

1. Privacy Concerns

User behavior profiling can raise privacy concerns, as it involves the monitoring of individuals' activities. Organizations must be transparent about what data is being collected, how it is used, and how employees' privacy is protected. Balancing security with privacy rights is critical to avoid legal or ethical violations.

2. Data Overload

Organizations may be overwhelmed with the volume of data generated by user behavior monitoring. Efficient data storage, management, and processing systems are necessary to handle the large amounts of information collected without causing delays or performance issues.

3. False Positives and Model Accuracy

While AI-based systems are generally more accurate than traditional methods, they are not immune to false positives. For instance, a user might perform an activity that is legitimate but rare, which the system may incorrectly flag as anomalous. Continuous model tuning and updates are required to minimize these instances.

Profiling user behavior with AI is a powerful and dynamic approach to enhancing cybersecurity. By continuously monitoring and analyzing user activities, AI-powered systems can quickly identify anomalies that may indicate a security breach or malicious activity. The ability to detect insider threats, compromised accounts, and abnormal behaviors in real-time provides organizations with the tools they need to safeguard sensitive data and networks. While challenges such as privacy concerns and data management exist, the benefits of AI-based user behavior profiling make it an invaluable tool in the ongoing fight against cybercrime.

6.2 Detecting Insider Threats through Behavioral Patterns

Insider threats represent one of the most dangerous and insidious risks to an organization's cybersecurity. Unlike external attackers who need to breach a company's defenses to gain access, insiders already have trusted access to systems, data, and networks. This access makes it easier for malicious insiders, or compromised legitimate users, to exploit their privileges and cause harm, often without detection for extended periods. Behavioral analytics powered by artificial intelligence (AI) has emerged as a vital tool for detecting and preventing insider threats by analyzing patterns of user behavior to identify anomalies that might indicate malicious actions.

Detecting insider threats through behavioral patterns involves monitoring the activities of users to establish a baseline of normal behavior and then identifying deviations from this baseline that could signal potential security risks. AI models are particularly suited for this task as they can analyze massive datasets, recognize subtle trends in behavior, and make real-time predictions based on historical patterns, making it possible to spot insider threats before they escalate into significant breaches.

1. The Insider Threat Problem

An insider threat is any threat to an organization's data or systems that originates from someone within the organization, such as an employee, contractor, business partner, or other trusted entities. Insiders can exploit their access to systems in several ways, including:

- **Malicious intent**: Employees or contractors who intentionally misuse their access to steal sensitive information, disrupt business operations, or harm the organization's reputation.
- **Accidental actions**: Employees who inadvertently make mistakes that result in security breaches, such as sending sensitive information to the wrong recipient or falling victim to phishing scams.
- **Compromised accounts**: External attackers who gain access to an organization's systems by stealing or compromising the credentials of an insider.

What makes insider threats particularly difficult to detect is the legitimate access insiders have, which often bypasses traditional perimeter security defenses like firewalls and intrusion detection systems. Furthermore, insiders are often familiar with security protocols, making it easier for them to evade detection and cover their tracks. For these reasons, detecting insider threats requires more than just a perimeter defense—it requires a sophisticated, internal monitoring solution that can continuously analyze user behavior and identify any deviations from normal activities.

2. Profiling Normal User Behavior

The foundation of detecting insider threats through AI-driven behavioral analytics lies in the ability to establish a clear understanding of "normal" user behavior. This is typically achieved through a combination of data collection and machine learning (ML). By continuously tracking a user's activities over time, AI models can create a behavioral profile for each individual, capturing details such as:

- **Login and access patterns**: When and where a user logs in, what systems or applications they typically access, and the frequency of their interactions.
- **Data access patterns**: The types of files or databases a user typically interacts with, how often they access them, and the actions they perform (e.g., read, write, delete).
- **File and data transfers**: Whether the user uploads, downloads, or shares sensitive data and how often.
- **Work hours and location**: The typical times and locations from which a user accesses the network.

By monitoring these behaviors, AI systems can build a detailed, individualized baseline profile for each user. For example, if a marketing employee typically works between 9 a.m. and 5 p.m., accesses a few specific files related to customer data, and communicates primarily with the marketing team, this creates a "normal" behavioral baseline.

3. Identifying Deviations and Anomalies

Once a baseline is established, AI-powered systems can continuously monitor users in real-time and compare their current behavior to their profile. Any deviation from the norm that falls outside of predefined thresholds or expected patterns is flagged as an anomaly. These deviations may be indicative of potential insider threats.

Some examples of behavioral anomalies that may signal an insider threat include:

- **Unusual access patterns**: If a user accesses files or systems they do not typically interact with (such as sensitive financial data by an employee in the marketing department), this could indicate an attempt to steal or misuse sensitive information.

- **Excessive data transfers**: Large-scale data downloads or uploads, especially for users who do not typically engage in such activity, may suggest that an insider is attempting to exfiltrate data.
- **After-hours activity**: A user logging in outside their regular working hours or from an unfamiliar location may be a sign of an account compromise or an insider conducting unauthorized activities.
- **Access to restricted data**: When a user accesses data that is beyond their job role or clearance level, this behavior could indicate that they are attempting to gather information for malicious purposes.
- **Unusual communication behavior**: Significant changes in how a user communicates (e.g., reaching out to individuals outside their usual workgroup, or sending large volumes of emails) might point to an insider attempting to share sensitive data.

By analyzing these and other anomalous activities, AI systems can spot potential threats in real-time, allowing security teams to act quickly before significant damage is done.

4. Machine Learning Models for Insider Threat Detection

AI-driven insider threat detection relies on various machine learning techniques to analyze and interpret user behavior patterns. Some of the most common ML models used in this process include:

1. Unsupervised Learning

Unsupervised learning algorithms are often employed in anomaly detection because they can identify outliers in behavior without the need for labeled data. These models learn from the data itself and can detect unusual activities that deviate from established norms. Examples of unsupervised learning methods include:

- **Clustering algorithms**: These group users or activities into clusters based on similar behaviors. Any activity that doesn't fit into any of the predefined clusters is flagged as anomalous.
- **Isolation Forests**: This technique isolates anomalies by randomly selecting features and splitting the data into smaller sections, making it easier to detect outliers.

2. Supervised Learning

Supervised learning models can also be used when labeled data is available, particularly in cases where known threats are already identified. These models can be trained using historical data on insider incidents, teaching the algorithm to recognize the patterns of malicious behavior. Techniques like decision trees, support vector machines (SVMs), and random forests are often used for this purpose.

3. Deep Learning

Deep learning models, specifically recurrent neural networks (RNNs) or long short-term memory networks (LSTMs), are particularly useful for time-series analysis. These models can detect anomalies in user behavior over time, such as changes in how a user typically accesses data or interacts with applications. Deep learning models are highly effective for identifying complex patterns and subtle deviations from the norm.

5. Real-Time Threat Detection and Incident Response

The true value of AI-powered behavioral analytics lies in its ability to detect insider threats in real time and trigger automated responses. When anomalous behavior is identified, the system can take several actions to mitigate potential risks, including:

- **Alerting security teams**: Security teams are notified immediately so that they can investigate the anomaly and assess the situation.
- **Automated containment**: In certain scenarios, the system can automatically block the user's access to sensitive systems or data to prevent further damage. For example, if an employee begins downloading sensitive information at an unusual rate, the system might automatically revoke their access to prevent data exfiltration.
- **Further investigation**: Security analysts can investigate the flagged behaviors by reviewing logs, conducting interviews, and assessing the context of the detected anomaly.

By incorporating real-time analysis and response, organizations can dramatically reduce the time between detecting insider threats and mitigating them, minimizing the potential for data breaches, financial loss, or reputational damage.

6. Challenges and Considerations

Despite the powerful capabilities of AI-based behavioral analysis, there are several challenges to overcome:

1. Privacy and Ethical Concerns

Monitoring user behavior raises significant privacy issues, especially when it comes to the ethical implications of tracking employees' actions. Organizations must balance the need for security with employees' rights to privacy, ensuring that monitoring practices are transparent and compliant with laws and regulations (such as GDPR or HIPAA).

2. False Positives

AI-based behavioral profiling systems are not foolproof. There is always the risk of false positives, where legitimate actions are mistakenly flagged as malicious. This can lead to unnecessary investigations or disruptions to business operations. Fine-tuning models and continuously improving algorithms can help minimize these false alarms.

3. Data Quality and Volume

The effectiveness of behavioral profiling depends heavily on the quality and volume of data collected. Inaccurate or incomplete data can lead to misinterpretations, while large volumes of data can create performance bottlenecks. Ensuring that data is accurate, comprehensive, and managed effectively is essential for reliable detection.

AI-driven behavioral analysis is a transformative approach to detecting insider threats. By profiling normal user behavior and flagging deviations, AI systems can identify potential threats more accurately and efficiently than traditional security tools. These systems allow organizations to proactively detect malicious actions, protect sensitive data, and respond swiftly to potential breaches. As insider threats continue to evolve, AI-powered solutions will remain an essential component of any robust cybersecurity strategy.

6.3 Identifying Compromised Accounts in Real Time

In the age of digital transformation, account compromises are among the most common and dangerous forms of cyberattack. Cybercriminals often target user accounts to gain unauthorized access to sensitive data, execute fraudulent transactions, or manipulate systems. Since many cyberattacks, such as phishing, credential stuffing, or brute force attacks, rely on gaining access to legitimate user accounts, identifying compromised accounts quickly is crucial for minimizing damage and preventing further exploitation. Real-time detection of compromised accounts using artificial intelligence (AI) and machine learning (ML) is increasingly becoming an essential component of modern cybersecurity strategies.

Real-time detection involves continuously monitoring user accounts for suspicious behavior and promptly identifying when an account has been compromised. AI and ML models enable dynamic analysis of user activities, applying advanced algorithms to recognize patterns, and flagging deviations that could indicate unauthorized access. In this section, we explore the importance of identifying compromised accounts, how AI helps in real-time detection, and best practices for mitigating the risks associated with account compromise.

1. The Challenge of Identifying Compromised Accounts

Compromised accounts are often challenging to detect because attackers typically seek to mimic the legitimate behavior of users. Once a cybercriminal gains access to a user's credentials, they can bypass many traditional security measures that rely on perimeter defense, such as firewalls or intrusion detection systems. The attacker might continue to use the account in a manner similar to the legitimate user, making it hard for security systems to detect the intrusion. For example, a hacker might log in at the same times and from the same locations the user typically uses, limiting the effectiveness of static detection systems.

Compromised accounts can be used in various malicious ways, such as:

- Exfiltrating sensitive data (e.g., financial information, intellectual property)
- Executing fraudulent actions (e.g., making unauthorized payments, transferring funds)
- Performing lateral movement within the network to gain access to other systems or data
- Spreading malware or ransomware across the network

Detecting compromised accounts requires advanced, continuous monitoring techniques that go beyond simple password checks or login authentication systems. AI-powered real-time detection systems use advanced algorithms to analyze behavior across multiple parameters, such as login times, locations, and activity patterns, and flag anomalies that may indicate unauthorized access.

2. How AI Detects Compromised Accounts in Real Time

AI-driven systems detect compromised accounts by continuously monitoring user activities, comparing them against established baselines of normal behavior. Here's how this process typically works:

1. Behavioral Analytics and Baseline Creation

AI systems first establish a baseline profile of normal user behavior. This is done by collecting data on user activities over a period of time and identifying patterns such as:

- **Typical login times**: The usual hours a user logs into their account.
- **Accessed resources**: The specific files, applications, and systems the user regularly interacts with.
- **Geographic location**: The physical locations from which the user typically accesses the system.
- **Devices used**: The type of devices the user generally uses to log in (e.g., desktop, laptop, mobile).
- **Patterns of data access**: How often the user accesses particular types of data or performs certain actions (e.g., editing files, making transfers).

AI models, often leveraging unsupervised machine learning algorithms, can create a profile of these behaviors and establish what is "normal" for each user. This profile is then used as a reference point for detecting anomalies.

2. Real-Time Monitoring and Detection of Deviations

Once the baseline is established, AI systems continuously monitor user activities. When an action deviates from the established baseline, it is flagged as an anomaly. Common signs of a compromised account include:

- **Unusual login times or locations**: If a user logs in from an unexpected geographic location or at unusual times (e.g., during the middle of the night or from an IP address in a different country), it could suggest that the account has been compromised.
- **Unusual device usage**: A login attempt from a device that the user does not typically use could be a red flag. This includes mobile devices or browsers not previously associated with the user's account.
- **Large-scale data access or downloads**: If a user typically accesses only a small set of files or data, but suddenly begins downloading large amounts of sensitive data, it could indicate an attacker exfiltrating information.
- **Multiple failed login attempts or unusual authentication patterns**: Failed login attempts followed by successful login can indicate a brute-force attack, where an attacker is trying to guess or crack the user's password.

These anomalies are detected in real-time by AI systems that continuously assess user activity. Upon detection of suspicious behavior, the system immediately triggers alerts for security teams to investigate further.

3. Correlation with Threat Intelligence and External Data

AI systems can also correlate internal data with external threat intelligence feeds to enhance real-time detection. By integrating threat intelligence, AI systems can better detect known attack tactics, such as:

- IP addresses associated with known malicious activity (e.g., botnets, VPN services used by attackers)
- Blacklisted devices or compromised external accounts (e.g., credentials leaked on the dark web)
- **Credential stuffing attacks**: When attackers attempt to use stolen credentials to gain access to other services.

By combining internal user behavior data with external threat intelligence, AI systems can strengthen their detection capabilities, even identifying compromised accounts from sources outside the organization's network.

3. Machine Learning Techniques for Real-Time Detection

AI and machine learning algorithms play a critical role in the detection and identification of compromised accounts. Some common machine learning techniques used for real-time account compromise detection include:

1. Anomaly Detection

Anomaly detection algorithms, particularly unsupervised learning models, are well-suited to identifying deviations in user behavior. By recognizing unusual activities in real-time, these models can flag potential account compromises without needing to rely on pre-programmed rules. Examples of anomaly detection techniques include:

- **Clustering algorithms**: Group similar behaviors and detect outliers.
- **Isolation forests**: Identify data points that are far from the normal data distribution.
- **Principal component analysis (PCA):** Reduce dimensionality and find patterns in complex, high-dimensional data.

2. Supervised Learning

Supervised learning models can be trained on labeled datasets, where instances of both normal and compromised accounts are identified. These models learn to recognize patterns that distinguish legitimate activity from malicious activity. Techniques such as decision trees, support vector machines (SVMs), and random forests are often used to classify behaviors as normal or suspicious based on past data.

3. Deep Learning

For more complex scenarios, deep learning techniques, such as recurrent neural networks (RNNs) or long short-term memory networks (LSTMs), can be applied to detect temporal anomalies in user behavior. Deep learning models are capable of recognizing long-term dependencies in user activity, which allows them to detect subtle, yet significant deviations over time, such as a user accessing a particular resource after being inactive for several months.

4. Real-Time Response and Mitigation

Once a compromised account is detected in real-time, AI systems can initiate various automated responses to mitigate damage and prevent further exploitation. Some potential actions include:

- **Locking the account**: Automatically disabling the account or requiring additional authentication to ensure the legitimacy of the user's activity.
- **Isolating the compromised system**: If the compromised account is part of a larger network, the system might isolate the affected machine to prevent lateral movement by the attacker.
- **Alerting security teams**: Sending alerts with detailed context on the compromised account and suspicious activity, allowing security teams to investigate further.
- **Triggering multi-factor authentication (MFA)**: Requiring the user to complete an additional authentication step, such as a fingerprint scan or a one-time password, to verify their identity.
- **Resetting credentials**: Prompting the user to reset their password, or locking the account while initiating a password recovery process.

Real-time response helps reduce the window of opportunity for attackers and minimizes the damage caused by compromised accounts.

5. Challenges and Considerations

While AI-driven systems for detecting compromised accounts are highly effective, there are several challenges to consider:

1. False Positives and Accuracy

Anomaly detection models may sometimes generate false positives, where legitimate actions are incorrectly flagged as suspicious. For instance, a user traveling abroad might log in from a new country, which could trigger an alert even though it's a legitimate activity. To reduce false positives, AI systems require continuous tuning, adjustment of thresholds, and context-aware algorithms that incorporate situational information.

2. Privacy Concerns

Monitoring user activities to detect compromised accounts raises privacy concerns, particularly when tracking personal login patterns or behavioral traits. Organizations must balance the need for security with privacy regulations, such as GDPR, and ensure that the monitoring process is transparent, ethical, and compliant with relevant laws.

3. Data Quality and Volume

AI systems rely on large volumes of data for training and analysis. Ensuring the quality and completeness of data is critical for accurate detection. Poor-quality data or missing context can lead to inaccurate results and missed threats.

Identifying compromised accounts in real time is critical for safeguarding sensitive information and preventing cyberattacks. AI and machine learning offer powerful tools to continuously monitor user activities, establish baselines of normal behavior, and detect anomalies that could signal a compromised account. With the ability to detect suspicious activity quickly and trigger automated responses, AI-driven systems help organizations minimize the damage from account compromises and reduce the time required to mitigate threats. However, challenges such as false positives, privacy concerns, and data quality must be addressed to ensure these systems operate effectively. As cyberattacks evolve, the use of AI for real-time account compromise detection will continue to play a central role in enhancing cybersecurity defenses.

6.4 Machine Learning Models for Role-Based Access Behavior

As organizations become increasingly digital, the complexity and volume of data they manage also grow. A critical part of maintaining strong cybersecurity involves managing access to this data, ensuring that only the right people can access sensitive systems and information. This is where Role-Based Access Control (RBAC) comes into play, offering a method to restrict system access based on a user's role within an organization. Machine learning (ML) can significantly enhance RBAC by analyzing role-based access behavior and detecting abnormal patterns that could indicate potential security risks.

In this section, we explore the concept of role-based access behavior in the context of cybersecurity, how machine learning models can be applied to improve access control, and the benefits and challenges associated with these techniques. We'll also look at how these models contribute to a proactive, dynamic security environment.

1. Understanding Role-Based Access Control (RBAC)

Role-Based Access Control is a system of managing access to computer systems based on the roles of individual users within an organization. Under this model, access rights are assigned to roles rather than individual users. Each user is then assigned to one or more roles, which in turn determine their access to specific resources.

For example:

- A system administrator may have unrestricted access to all servers, applications, and databases.
- A regular employee may only have access to specific files or software required for their daily tasks.
- A manager may have access to sensitive reports and data, but only within certain departments or projects.

This approach simplifies the management of user permissions by reducing the complexity of assigning access rights to individual users, ensuring that people can only access resources necessary for their job functions. However, as the scale and sophistication of attacks evolve, traditional RBAC might not be sufficient to detect unusual or unauthorized access behavior, especially when attackers compromise valid user credentials.

2. The Role of Machine Learning in Role-Based Access Behavior

Machine learning offers a significant advantage in role-based access management by continuously learning and analyzing access patterns associated with specific roles, identifying deviations from the normal behavior, and triggering alerts for potential security incidents. Here's how machine learning enhances traditional RBAC:

1. Continuous Monitoring of Access Behavior

Machine learning algorithms enable continuous monitoring of user access patterns, collecting data on who accesses what, when, and from where. These systems can learn from historical access logs and continuously refine their understanding of "normal" behavior for each role in the organization. The system can track various attributes such as:

- **Login times**: When a user typically accesses resources.
- **Access locations**: The geographic locations or IP addresses from which a user typically logs in.
- **Applications or data**: The specific tools, applications, or datasets a user frequently interacts with.
- **Volume of access**: How often the user requests or interacts with certain types of data.

By leveraging machine learning, these patterns are dynamically updated to accommodate any legitimate changes in user behavior, such as temporary role changes or shifts in workload. Machine learning models help avoid false positives by maintaining context about what constitutes typical behavior for each role.

2. Anomaly Detection for Abnormal Access

Once access behavior patterns are established, machine learning models can detect anomalies—any deviations from expected access behavior. For example:

- A sales manager who usually accesses customer records during business hours from the office might suddenly log in at midnight from a different country and access an entire company database.
- An HR personnel who normally handles employee records may suddenly attempt to access payroll data or project management tools—something outside their usual scope.

By using unsupervised learning techniques, such as clustering algorithms (e.g., k-means clustering), autoencoders, or Isolation Forests, machine learning models can detect such anomalies in real-time. These models do not require explicit labeling of abnormal behaviors and can uncover previously unknown threats or unauthorized access patterns.

3. Predictive Analytics for Access Behavior

Machine learning models are capable of using historical data to predict future access behaviors, which can help to identify abnormal behavior before it escalates into a security incident. By analyzing large datasets, ML algorithms can recognize patterns and forecast future activities that deviate from these trends. This helps proactively flag potential security risks, such as:

- **Account misuse**: An attacker may predictably access resources after a compromise, and the model can alert administrators in advance, allowing them to act before any significant damage occurs.
- **Privilege escalation**: If a user's access rights are gradually expanding, machine learning can detect unusual patterns that may indicate unauthorized privilege escalation and raise red flags.

Through predictive analytics, ML models allow organizations to preemptively respond to potential security breaches, improving the organization's overall defense posture.

3. Machine Learning Algorithms for Role-Based Access Behavior

Several machine learning techniques are particularly well-suited to the task of analyzing role-based access behavior. These algorithms can be categorized based on the type of analysis they perform:

1. Clustering Algorithms (Unsupervised Learning)

Clustering algorithms are used to group users with similar access patterns together. When analyzing access behavior, the algorithm can group users based on how they access data or interact with the system, identifying natural clusters of behaviors within each role. Any user whose access pattern differs significantly from their cluster can be flagged as suspicious.

- **K-means clustering**: Groups access behaviors into clusters based on similar patterns.
- **DBSCAN (Density-Based Spatial Clustering of Applications with Noise)**: Identifies anomalies based on spatial distance, which can highlight outlier behaviors in user access.

2. Classification Algorithms (Supervised Learning)

Supervised learning algorithms can be trained to differentiate between normal and anomalous access behaviors. These models require labeled data (normal vs. abnormal behavior) to train the system. Over time, the model becomes capable of predicting when access behavior is likely to be fraudulent or unauthorized, based on past labeled data.

- **Random Forests**: A tree-based algorithm that can classify access behavior into different categories.
- **Support Vector Machines (SVM):** Classifies users' access behaviors into normal or suspicious behavior based on a hyperplane.
- **Logistic Regression**: Can predict the likelihood of a user exhibiting abnormal access patterns based on prior features.

3. Neural Networks (Deep Learning)

For complex, high-dimensional datasets, deep learning algorithms like neural networks and recurrent neural networks (RNNs) can be applied. These models are particularly useful when access behavior involves sequential data (e.g., login times, resource access over time) or data with intricate patterns that are hard to detect using traditional methods.

- **Autoencoders**: Detect anomalies in access patterns by learning a compressed representation of normal behavior and flagging deviations from it.
- **LSTMs (Long Short-Term Memory networks):** An ideal choice for sequential data, allowing models to track the progression of user access over time, making it easier to detect abnormal patterns as they evolve.

4. Benefits of Using ML Models for Role-Based Access Behavior

Machine learning models provide a range of benefits when applied to role-based access behavior analysis:

- **Enhanced Accuracy**: By using dynamic learning techniques, ML models offer better accuracy in identifying true anomalies, reducing false positives and negatives.
- **Adaptability**: These models can adapt over time to changing user behaviors, accommodating shifts in job roles, workload, or access patterns without manual updates.
- **Scalability**: ML algorithms can process vast amounts of data across large organizations, enabling the detection of suspicious access behavior in real time, even in complex systems with many users.

- **Proactive Security**: Predictive capabilities allow organizations to respond to potential threats before they escalate, mitigating risks more effectively than traditional reactive approaches.

5. Challenges and Considerations

While ML models for role-based access behavior provide significant advantages, there are also challenges and considerations to be aware of:

- **Data Quality and Volume**: Machine learning models rely on high-quality data, and any inconsistencies or missing data can impact their effectiveness. Organizations must ensure that their access logs are complete and accurate.
- **False Positives**: Although ML algorithms are designed to reduce false positives, the complexity of human behavior and role-based variations can still result in occasional errors. Regular tuning and adjustment of the model are required.
- **Privacy Concerns**: Continuously monitoring user access behavior may raise privacy concerns, particularly in sensitive industries. Organizations must ensure compliance with data privacy regulations like GDPR.
- **Model Training**: Machine learning models require significant data and time for training to be effective. Inaccurate training data or overfitting to specific access patterns may reduce the model's generalizability to new situations.

Machine learning models for role-based access behavior represent a powerful tool in modern cybersecurity. By analyzing and learning from user behavior patterns, these models can detect anomalies and predict potential security risks associated with compromised accounts, insider threats, and privilege escalation. As cyber threats continue to evolve, integrating ML with RBAC enables organizations to continuously refine their access control policies, enhance detection capabilities, and proactively secure sensitive resources. While challenges like data quality, false positives, and privacy concerns remain, the benefits of using machine learning in managing role-based access behavior far outweigh these hurdles, making it a vital component of any modern cybersecurity strategy.

6.5 Adaptive Security Responses to User Anomalies

As the cybersecurity landscape grows increasingly complex, organizations must move beyond reactive security measures to adopt more dynamic, adaptive systems. Traditional security systems often rely on static rules or predefined thresholds to detect threats, but these systems can struggle to keep pace with sophisticated and rapidly evolving cyber threats. In this context, adaptive security responses represent a crucial advancement, allowing security systems to adjust in real-time to anomalous user behavior and dynamically respond to potential risks.

Adaptive security responses are particularly important in the context of user anomalies—deviations from the normal behavior of users within an organization. These anomalies can be indicative of various security threats, including insider threats, account compromise, or even data exfiltration attempts. By leveraging advanced machine learning (ML) and artificial intelligence (AI) techniques, adaptive security systems can automatically detect user behavior anomalies, assess their severity, and implement appropriate responses to neutralize threats.

In this section, we will explore the concept of adaptive security responses, the technologies that enable them, and how they can be used to protect organizations from a wide range of potential threats. We will also discuss the benefits, challenges, and best practices for implementing these systems in today's rapidly changing threat landscape.

1. Understanding Adaptive Security Responses

Adaptive security is an approach that uses real-time data and advanced technologies to continuously assess the security environment and adjust security measures accordingly. Unlike traditional reactive security measures, which typically only respond after an attack has been detected, adaptive security involves proactive, real-time analysis of user activity and behavior, enabling the system to respond automatically as potential threats arise.

In the context of user anomalies, an adaptive security system analyzes the behavior of users and creates baseline profiles of "normal" behavior. When it detects deviations from this baseline, the system can trigger an adaptive response. This might include limiting user access, requiring additional authentication, alerting security personnel, or even initiating automatic containment measures to prevent further damage.

2. Machine Learning and AI in Adaptive Security

The backbone of adaptive security responses is machine learning and artificial intelligence. These technologies allow the system to understand and model user behavior dynamically, learn from new data, and continuously improve its threat detection and response capabilities.

Behavioral Modeling

Machine learning models continuously analyze user behavior patterns to create baseline profiles. These profiles include details like:

- Login times and frequency
- Accessed resources and applications
- Geographical location of access
- Devices and IP addresses used
- Data access or modification behavior

As the system learns over time, it can more accurately distinguish between legitimate user actions and anomalies. The model's ability to adapt to changes in user behavior helps ensure that the system remains effective even as the organizational context evolves.

Anomaly Detection

Using a combination of supervised and unsupervised learning algorithms, adaptive security systems detect anomalies by identifying deviations from established patterns. For instance, an employee might typically access financial data only during office hours. If the system detects that the employee is accessing sensitive data at night from an unfamiliar location, this would be flagged as an anomaly.

Machine learning techniques such as clustering, decision trees, and neural networks can be used to model normal behavior and highlight outliers. These anomalies are then assessed in real time to determine whether they pose a threat, prompting a tailored response.

Predictive Analytics

Machine learning also plays a critical role in predicting potential security incidents before they occur. For example, a model trained on historical data might detect early signs of an impending account compromise by recognizing a gradual change in behavior that deviates from a user's usual pattern. Predictive analytics allows security teams to take proactive measures and prevent attacks from escalating into full-blown breaches.

3. Adaptive Responses to Anomalous User Behavior

Once a user anomaly is detected, adaptive security systems implement a tailored response to mitigate potential risks. The response can vary depending on the severity of the anomaly, the context of the user's behavior, and the specific security policies in place. Some common adaptive responses include:

1. Access Limitation or Isolation

When an anomaly is detected, the system can limit the user's access to sensitive data or applications. This might involve:

- Quarantining the user's account until further investigation is conducted.
- Limiting access to critical systems while allowing the user to continue their work in less sensitive areas.

For example, if an employee's account is flagged for accessing data outside of their normal scope, the system may automatically revoke access to certain resources until the issue is resolved.

2. Multi-Factor Authentication (MFA) Enforcement

For suspicious activity, an adaptive response could involve prompting the user for additional authentication factors. This could include:

- SMS-based authentication
- Biometric verification
- Behavioral biometrics (e.g., analyzing typing patterns or mouse movements)

For example, if a user attempts to log in from a new geographic location or device, the system might trigger MFA to ensure that the user is authorized.

3. Dynamic Risk-Based Responses

The system can apply risk-based policies to determine the severity of the anomaly and adjust its response accordingly. For example:

- **Low-risk anomaly**: If a minor deviation is detected, the system might simply log the event and send a warning to security personnel.
- **High-risk anomaly**: In more critical cases, the system might initiate an automatic lockdown of the affected account or prevent access to critical systems until further investigation can be conducted.

For example, if a user logs in from an unusual location, the system might verify the access as low-risk, but if the same user then attempts to download sensitive data, the response might escalate to account suspension.

4. Incident Alerting and Escalation

For anomalies that could indicate a high likelihood of an attack, the system will trigger alerts to security personnel, providing them with detailed information about the suspicious behavior. These alerts typically include:

- User identification
- Type of anomaly detected
- Contextual information (e.g., time of activity, access patterns)
- Suggested actions or recommended responses

In some cases, the system may also trigger an escalation, notifying higher-level administrators or initiating additional security protocols such as system-wide audits or forensic analysis.

5. Automatic Containment

In extreme cases, adaptive security systems can take the most aggressive action: automatic containment. This could involve locking or disabling the user account entirely, isolating the affected network segment, or even terminating active sessions that seem suspicious. This kind of response is typically reserved for high-confidence anomalies that suggest an ongoing security breach.

4. Benefits of Adaptive Security Responses

Adaptive security responses provide several significant benefits to organizations, particularly in the context of user anomaly detection:

1. Improved Real-Time Threat Detection

By continuously analyzing user behavior and implementing real-time responses, adaptive security systems can detect and mitigate threats much faster than traditional, static systems. This reduces the time between detection and response, minimizing the potential impact of a breach.

2. Proactive Defense Mechanisms

Adaptive systems can predict and prevent attacks before they escalate into major incidents, improving the organization's ability to respond proactively rather than reactively.

3. Reduced Risk of Insider Threats

Adaptive responses are particularly effective at identifying and mitigating insider threats, as these threats often involve subtle deviations from normal user behavior rather than external attacks. By recognizing these anomalies early, organizations can prevent damage before it occurs.

4. Enhanced User Experience

By allowing adaptive security systems to implement non-disruptive responses (e.g., MFA prompts or access limitation), the impact on users is minimized. This helps maintain user productivity while still ensuring that security measures are in place to protect against threats.

5. Challenges and Considerations

Despite the benefits, implementing adaptive security responses comes with challenges:

1. Data Privacy and Compliance

Constant monitoring and analysis of user behavior can raise concerns about privacy and compliance with data protection regulations (e.g., GDPR, HIPAA). Organizations must ensure that their systems are designed to comply with relevant regulations while still offering effective anomaly detection and response capabilities.

2. False Positives and Over-Response

One of the risks of adaptive security systems is that they might flag legitimate user activity as anomalous, leading to false positives. This could result in unnecessary interruptions, such as invalidating a user's credentials or locking down their access unnecessarily. Fine-tuning the system and calibrating its sensitivity are essential to avoid over-responses.

3. Integration Complexity

Integrating adaptive security systems with existing IT infrastructure can be complex, particularly in large organizations with diverse systems and applications. Ensuring seamless integration across systems, applications, and security layers is critical for the system to function effectively.

Adaptive security responses to user anomalies represent an essential shift in the way organizations defend against cyber threats. By leveraging AI and machine learning to continuously monitor user behavior and respond to anomalies in real time, organizations can significantly improve their ability to detect, mitigate, and prevent security incidents. While there are challenges in implementing these systems, the benefits of faster detection, proactive defense, and reduced impact of breaches make adaptive security responses a vital component of any modern cybersecurity strategy. As threats evolve, adaptive security will be a key enabler of resilient, flexible, and effective cyber defense systems.

7. The Double-Edged Sword: AI in Cyber Attacks

While AI and machine learning offer powerful tools for defending against cyber threats, they also present new opportunities for attackers. This chapter delves into how cybercriminals are leveraging AI to enhance their attack strategies, making them more sophisticated, evasive, and difficult to detect. From automating phishing campaigns to using machine learning to adapt malware and avoid traditional security measures, AI is a game-changer in the hands of cyber adversaries. Readers will explore case studies of AI-powered attacks and learn how cybersecurity professionals can adapt their defenses to address these evolving threats, creating a truly dynamic and resilient security posture.

7.1 How Cybercriminals Exploit AI for Their Benefit

The rise of artificial intelligence (AI) and machine learning (ML) has revolutionized the cybersecurity landscape, benefiting defenders in various ways, from threat detection to proactive protection. However, like any powerful tool, these technologies can also be harnessed by cybercriminals to improve the effectiveness of their attacks and evade detection. As AI continues to evolve, so too does its potential to be misused by malicious actors, making it essential for cybersecurity professionals to stay one step ahead.

In this section, we will explore how cybercriminals exploit AI for their benefit, delving into the ways in which attackers use AI-driven tools, techniques, and strategies to enhance the impact of their malicious activities. From sophisticated malware to social engineering tactics, AI is helping criminals improve their efficiency, automate attacks, and stay undetected. Understanding these threats is critical to countering them effectively.

1. Automating and Scaling Attacks

AI has significantly lowered the barrier to entry for cybercriminals, allowing them to automate and scale attacks that were previously complex, time-consuming, or resource-intensive. Here's how they use AI to enhance their operations:

1.1 Automated Phishing Attacks

Phishing, one of the most common forms of social engineering attacks, has been made more effective and scalable through AI. Traditionally, phishing attacks relied on attackers crafting convincing email templates, often relying on human input to create personalized content. With AI, cybercriminals can automate the creation of these emails, crafting messages tailored to individual targets by analyzing publicly available data such as social media profiles, email patterns, and behavior.

Machine learning models can also be trained to identify the most likely subjects, themes, and tones that would appeal to a particular user, thus improving the chances of the attack succeeding. These AI-powered phishing campaigns can target thousands, or even millions, of individuals, adapting to responses and continuously refining the attack based on the success rate of different tactics.

1.2 AI-Powered Social Engineering

Social engineering attacks often rely on understanding human psychology and exploiting individuals' emotions and behaviors. AI can enhance social engineering efforts by using natural language processing (NLP) and sentiment analysis to craft messages that manipulate emotions more effectively. Criminals can use AI-driven algorithms to parse large amounts of data from social media and other online platforms to identify potential victims, learning their interests, emotional triggers, and behavioral patterns.

For instance, by analyzing a victim's social media activity, an AI system could identify specific issues they are currently facing (e.g., a family member in the hospital, an important business deadline) and exploit those vulnerabilities by posing as a trusted individual offering help. These hyper-personalized attacks can make it significantly harder for victims to discern legitimate communication from malicious attempts.

2. Developing Advanced Malware

AI's ability to analyze data patterns and learn from its environment makes it an attractive tool for developing highly effective, adaptive malware. Cybercriminals can utilize AI to create malware that is more resilient, evasive, and difficult to detect. Some key ways AI is used in malware development include:

2.1 Self-Replicating and Evolving Malware

AI can be used to develop self-replicating malware that learns from its interactions with a network and adapts its behavior to avoid detection. For example, malware could analyze the network environment and choose the best strategy for evading antivirus software, intrusion detection systems (IDS), or even sandbox environments designed to catch malicious behavior. Over time, the malware learns how to optimize its methods, such as changing its code or behavior patterns, making it harder for defenders to identify and neutralize it.

2.2 Malware as a Service (MaaS)

AI is also making its way into the underground cybercrime marketplaces, where criminals sell ready-made tools and services. Malware-as-a-Service (MaaS) platforms use AI to make their malicious software more accessible and effective. Criminals can purchase AI-driven malware, which is often pre-configured to exploit specific vulnerabilities or systems. This means that individuals with minimal technical expertise can conduct sophisticated cyberattacks, making the threat landscape even more dangerous.

2.3 AI-Driven Ransomware

Ransomware attacks have evolved from simple demands for payment to complex systems that incorporate AI to maximize their effectiveness. AI-driven ransomware can autonomously identify critical systems, encrypt files, and adapt its methods based on the system's configuration. Additionally, AI can enhance the negotiation process by analyzing patterns in victim behavior to adjust ransom demands in real time, increasing the likelihood of payment.

3. Evasion and Obfuscation Techniques

Traditional security measures often rely on signature-based detection, looking for known patterns in code or behavior. AI-driven cyberattacks have moved beyond these limitations by introducing evasion techniques that make detection more difficult.

3.1 Polymorphic and Metamorphic Malware

AI can be used to develop polymorphic and metamorphic malware, which is designed to change its code every time it is executed, making it difficult for signature-based antivirus programs to recognize. In this context, machine learning algorithms are applied to obfuscate the malware code, ensuring that each version is unique, even though its malicious behavior remains the same.

Additionally, metamorphic malware can rewrite its own code to achieve complete transformation, evading even more advanced signature detection methods. This makes the malware resilient against both traditional antivirus software and newer AI-powered detection systems.

3.2 AI for Attack Obfuscation

AI-driven techniques can be used to mask or hide malicious activity within a network, evading network monitoring systems and other detection methods. Machine learning models can identify the normal traffic patterns on a network and adapt the attack traffic to blend in with legitimate operations. For example, malware can simulate normal user behavior by generating legitimate-looking requests or making small, inconspicuous modifications to system files over a long period of time, thus avoiding suspicion.

4. AI-Enhanced Distributed Denial of Service (DDoS) Attacks

DDoS attacks aim to overwhelm a target's resources, typically by flooding the target's servers with an overwhelming amount of traffic. Cybercriminals can exploit AI to create more sophisticated and scalable DDoS attacks that are harder to mitigate.

4.1 AI-Driven Botnets

AI allows cybercriminals to optimize the behavior of botnets used in DDoS attacks. Machine learning models can be used to direct large botnets of infected machines, enabling them to make decisions on the fly. These models can analyze the target's network defenses and adjust the botnet's tactics in real time to circumvent defenses, making the DDoS attack more effective.

4.2 Predictive DDoS Attacks

By analyzing historical data and identifying vulnerabilities in the target's infrastructure, AI can help cybercriminals predict the optimal time to launch a DDoS attack. AI systems can analyze past DDoS attack data to identify patterns in the target's response behavior, allowing attackers to time their efforts to create maximum disruption.

5. AI-Enhanced Cybercrime Networks and Ecosystems

AI is not only used to improve individual attacks but also to enhance the coordination and functioning of cybercriminal ecosystems. Cybercrime operates as a network of interconnected actors, from malware developers to money launderers, and AI enables them to coordinate and optimize their activities.

5.1 AI for Coordinating Multi-Stage Attacks

Cybercriminals can use AI to orchestrate complex, multi-stage attacks where the roles of different actors are coordinated and optimized for maximum impact. For example, an AI system can automate the process of compromising multiple targets and strategically deploying ransomware or exfiltrating data in stages, thus minimizing the chance of detection.

5.2 Leveraging AI for Financial Fraud

Financial fraud is another area where cybercriminals use AI. AI systems can analyze vast amounts of financial data to identify vulnerabilities in payment systems or detect weaknesses in fraud detection protocols. By automating the process of identifying loopholes and executing fraudulent transactions, cybercriminals can maximize their chances of success while avoiding detection.

As AI continues to evolve, so too will its role in the arsenal of cybercriminals. AI allows attackers to automate and scale attacks, evade detection, and develop more sophisticated malware and attack strategies. The potential misuse of AI by cybercriminals highlights the need for defenders to adopt similarly advanced AI-driven technologies to protect against these evolving threats. The cat-and-mouse game between attackers and defenders will continue to intensify, and understanding how cybercriminals exploit AI is crucial in staying ahead of the curve in cybersecurity.

7.2 Examples of AI-Powered Phishing and Malware Campaigns

As artificial intelligence (AI) becomes more accessible, cybercriminals are increasingly using it to enhance the sophistication and effectiveness of their cyberattacks. One of the most concerning ways in which AI is exploited is in phishing and malware campaigns, where cybercriminals can automate and refine attacks, making them harder to detect and more likely to succeed. This section explores some prominent examples of AI-powered phishing and malware campaigns, illustrating how these technologies are leveraged by malicious actors.

1. AI-Driven Phishing Campaigns

Phishing attacks, in which cybercriminals impersonate legitimate entities to steal sensitive information, have been a major concern in cybersecurity for years. However, AI has made phishing attacks even more convincing and scalable. Below are a few examples where AI has been integrated into phishing campaigns.

1.1 Deepfake Phishing Emails

Deepfakes, a form of AI-generated media that manipulates or generates fake videos, audio, or images, have made their way into phishing schemes. Cybercriminals can use deep learning models to create audio or video content that mimics the voice or appearance of trusted individuals, such as company executives or key partners. This can be used in voice phishing (vishing) or video phishing.

Example: A cybercriminal could use a deepfake audio model to replicate the voice of a CEO or manager. The attacker could then use this voice to impersonate the CEO in a phone call, instructing an employee to transfer funds or release sensitive data. Alternatively, they could create a convincing video of the CEO requesting an urgent meeting or document upload.

With deepfake technology, the social engineering aspect of phishing becomes much more effective because targets are more likely to trust a communication that feels personal and legitimate. This is especially effective in corporate environments where senior leaders are typically trusted by employees.

1.2 AI-Powered Email Personalization

AI and machine learning can be used to make phishing emails more personalized and convincing, significantly increasing the likelihood of success. Traditional phishing emails often had generic content that was easy to spot due to poor grammar or irrelevant information. AI-powered phishing attacks, however, leverage natural language processing (NLP) algorithms to analyze and replicate email structures, tone, and even language specific to a target.

Example: AI tools can scrape publicly available information from social media profiles, company websites, and even data breaches to gather information about the target, such as their name, position, interests, and recent activities. The AI then crafts a phishing email that is highly tailored to the recipient, using familiar terminology and referencing recent work projects or personal interests. This increases the likelihood of the recipient interacting with the phishing email or clicking on a malicious link.

An AI-driven phishing attack can also mimic specific communication styles used within an organization, increasing its chances of bypassing spam filters and fooling employees or clients into believing the message is legitimate.

1.3 Chatbot-Driven Phishing Scams

AI-powered chatbots can also be used in phishing attacks to engage victims in conversation, extract information, and guide them through fraudulent processes. Chatbots can be integrated into phishing websites, such as fake customer service portals or spoofed websites, to communicate with users in real time.

Example: Cybercriminals set up a fake website impersonating a well-known service, like an online banking portal. An AI-driven chatbot then interacts with the user, asking them for account credentials, personal information, or payment details. The chatbot is programmed to give realistic, empathetic responses to keep the victim engaged, encouraging them to complete the interaction.

The use of AI chatbots in phishing scams increases the level of interactivity and realism, making it harder for victims to recognize the fraudulent nature of the attack. Furthermore, chatbots can learn from interactions and adjust their tactics based on user responses, making them increasingly efficient over time.

2. AI-Driven Malware Campaigns

AI's potential to enhance the sophistication of malware campaigns is another significant concern for cybersecurity professionals. By using machine learning and other AI techniques, attackers can create more evasive, self-replicating, and adaptive malware that can bypass traditional security measures and adapt to the environment.

2.1 Polymorphic Malware

Polymorphic malware is designed to change its appearance every time it infects a new system, evading detection by traditional antivirus software that relies on signature-based detection. With the help of AI, malware can now self-modify its code using machine learning algorithms to create endless variations of itself.

Example: A polymorphic AI-driven Trojan could change its code each time it is downloaded or executed, ensuring that traditional signature-based antivirus tools cannot identify it. The AI in the malware can even analyze the target system's defenses and adapt its behavior to avoid detection. It might modify its own code in response to an antivirus program or security scan, effectively "learning" how to bypass the system and maintain persistence in the infected network.

This form of AI-driven polymorphism enhances the ability of malware to persist undetected for long periods, making it difficult for security teams to identify and eliminate the threat.

2.2 AI-Powered Ransomware

Ransomware, which encrypts victims' data and demands payment for its release, is another area where AI is improving the capabilities of cybercriminals. Traditional ransomware simply locks files and demands payment, but AI-enhanced ransomware can engage in advanced evasion tactics and dynamic encryption strategies.

Example: AI-powered ransomware could leverage machine learning algorithms to identify which files are most valuable to the victim—such as sensitive documents or proprietary data—and prioritize encrypting those first. It can also learn the victim's behavior patterns and decide the most opportune moment to strike for maximum impact. AI allows ransomware to automate the negotiation process with victims, adjusting ransom amounts based on previous interactions or the victim's ability to pay.

Some AI-driven ransomware even includes anti-debugging techniques, making it more difficult for researchers or security professionals to reverse-engineer the ransomware and identify its origin.

2.3 Fileless Malware Powered by AI

Fileless malware is an advanced form of malware that operates in the memory (RAM) of the victim's system rather than leaving traditional files behind. This makes it harder for antivirus programs to detect. AI is used to optimize the behavior of fileless malware, allowing it to operate stealthily and adapt to various environments.

Example: An AI-powered fileless malware attack could leverage machine learning to identify vulnerabilities in a target system in real time and use this information to inject malicious code directly into the system's memory. Once active, the malware can establish a backdoor for continuous access and can modify its behavior based on the environment or changes to the system, making it highly evasive.

AI's role in fileless malware campaigns is significant because it enables the malware to adapt to new environments quickly and evade detection, even in the most secure systems. This type of malware can also use AI to detect and disable security programs running on the system, further increasing its chances of success.

2.4 Autonomous Malware Distribution

AI can also enhance the autonomous distribution of malware by optimizing the way it spreads across networks. Traditionally, malware spreads through social engineering or vulnerabilities in software, but AI can help automate this process to make it more efficient.

Example: An AI-driven botnet could autonomously scan for vulnerabilities across a network of devices, identifying the most effective attack vectors and distributing malware through the fastest and most undetectable methods. Machine learning algorithms can be used to optimize the botnet's behavior, adjusting its tactics based on the layout of the target network and even predicting where vulnerabilities are most likely to exist.

AI-powered malware can also improve self-propagation by adapting to changes in the network environment. For example, if a botnet detects that one method of spreading is being blocked, it can quickly shift to an alternative, making it more difficult for defenders to shut down the attack.

AI-powered phishing and malware campaigns are becoming increasingly prevalent and sophisticated, allowing cybercriminals to execute attacks more efficiently, at scale, and with greater success rates. By leveraging AI-driven tools such as deepfake technology, AI chatbots, polymorphic malware, and AI-enhanced ransomware, cybercriminals can craft attacks that are highly targeted, evasive, and adaptive. As AI technologies continue to advance, the cybersecurity landscape will need to evolve rapidly to defend against these threats. For organizations, it's crucial to stay vigilant and invest in next-generation defenses powered by AI to counter the increasing sophistication of cybercriminal activities.

7.3 Detecting AI-Driven Social Engineering Attacks

Social engineering attacks, where cybercriminals manipulate individuals into divulging confidential information or performing actions that compromise security, have long been one of the most effective ways for attackers to gain access to sensitive data. With the increasing integration of artificial intelligence (AI) and machine learning (ML) technologies, the complexity and success rates of these attacks have grown significantly. AI-driven social engineering is particularly concerning because it can be used to automate and personalize attacks at an unprecedented scale, making it more difficult for traditional defense systems to detect and prevent them.

In this section, we will explore the challenges posed by AI-driven social engineering attacks and outline strategies and tools for detecting these sophisticated threats. AI can be used to craft highly convincing phishing emails, automate interactions, and predict human behavior, all of which make AI-driven social engineering attacks particularly effective. However, there are emerging techniques for identifying these attacks, which leverage behavioral analytics, anomaly detection, and natural language processing (NLP) to detect patterns associated with malicious activity.

1. Understanding AI-Driven Social Engineering

Before diving into detection strategies, it is crucial to understand the mechanics of AI-driven social engineering attacks. These attacks rely on AI's ability to analyze and process vast amounts of data, which can then be used to tailor messages, predict responses, and automate interactions with the target.

1.1 AI-Powered Phishing and Spear Phishing

Phishing attacks involve cybercriminals impersonating legitimate individuals or organizations to trick victims into revealing sensitive information, such as login credentials or financial details. Spear phishing is a more targeted form of phishing that uses personalized content based on information gathered from social media profiles, company websites, or previous interactions.

With AI, attackers can now automatically gather data from publicly available sources and craft highly personalized messages that are tailored to the individual's behavior, interests, or recent activities. AI-driven phishing campaigns can adjust the tone, content, and urgency of the message in real-time based on the target's social profile and response.

1.2 Automated Chatbots and Voice Phishing (Vishing)

AI-powered chatbots and voice phishing (vishing) are other forms of social engineering that use machine learning to simulate human-like conversations. Chatbots can interact with targets on websites or messaging platforms, while AI-generated voice calls can mimic real human voices to convince victims that they are communicating with a trusted entity.

In these attacks, the AI system learns from each interaction to refine its responses, making the attack more persuasive and tailored to each individual's communication style. This adaptive learning makes it harder for traditional security systems to detect these attacks, as they appear more legitimate and are highly personalized.

1.3 Deepfake Technology for Social Engineering

Deepfake technology uses AI to create convincing fake audio or video content that mimics real people. Cybercriminals can exploit deepfakes in social engineering attacks by creating videos or audio clips of individuals (such as company executives, government officials, or family members) asking for sensitive information or urging certain actions, such as transferring funds or downloading a file.

Deepfakes take social engineering to a new level because they exploit the victim's trust in visual and auditory cues. The AI-driven ability to manipulate faces, voices, and even the tone of speech makes these attacks significantly harder to detect and defend against.

2. Challenges in Detecting AI-Driven Social Engineering Attacks

The introduction of AI into social engineering attacks presents several challenges for cybersecurity professionals tasked with identifying and mitigating these threats.

2.1 Increased Scale and Speed

AI-driven social engineering attacks can be launched at a much larger scale than traditional methods. Machine learning algorithms can automate the generation of personalized messages, making it easy to target thousands or even millions of individuals simultaneously. Furthermore, the speed at which these attacks can be executed has increased dramatically, with AI enabling attackers to craft and deploy phishing emails or initiate phone calls in real-time.

The scale and speed of AI-driven attacks pose a significant challenge for traditional defense mechanisms, which may struggle to keep up with the volume of interactions or detect malicious activity within the short timeframes associated with these fast-moving campaigns.

2.2 Greater Personalization and Precision

AI's ability to analyze large amounts of data and extract meaningful insights makes social engineering attacks more precise. Traditional phishing attacks often have telltale signs of generic content, suspicious sender addresses, and poor grammar. AI, however, can create highly personalized messages that are tailored to the victim's interests, behaviors, and interactions.

For example, AI can scrape social media to gather details about a target's life, such as their job, location, hobbies, and recent interactions, and use this information to craft a convincing email or message. This level of personalization makes AI-driven social engineering attacks much more difficult for the victim to recognize as fraudulent.

2.3 Evasion of Detection Systems

Traditional signature-based detection systems look for known indicators of phishing or fraudulent activity, such as specific keywords, URLs, or email addresses. However, AI-driven social engineering attacks can constantly adapt to bypass these systems. Machine learning models can learn from past interactions and continuously modify the language, structure, and timing of the attack to evade detection.

Moreover, deepfake technology and AI-powered chatbots make it harder for users to discern between legitimate and malicious communications, as they often mimic real-world interactions very convincingly.

3. Strategies for Detecting AI-Driven Social Engineering Attacks

While AI-driven social engineering attacks present significant challenges, there are several strategies and tools that cybersecurity professionals can use to detect these threats.

3.1 Behavioral Analytics and Anomaly Detection

Behavioral analytics is a powerful tool for detecting AI-driven social engineering attacks. This technique involves establishing a baseline of normal user behavior and then monitoring for deviations from that baseline. For example, if an employee typically does not transfer large sums of money, but suddenly receives an urgent email from what appears to be the CEO, requesting a fund transfer, the system can flag this as an anomaly.

AI and machine learning can also be applied to detect patterns of behavior that may indicate social engineering tactics, such as unexpected requests for sensitive information, frequent interactions with unrecognized contacts, or sudden changes in communication tone. Anomaly detection systems can automatically raise alerts when suspicious activities are detected, allowing security teams to investigate further.

3.2 Natural Language Processing (NLP) for Content Analysis

Natural language processing (NLP) is a branch of AI that can analyze and understand human language. By applying NLP to email content, messages, or phone conversations, cybersecurity systems can identify certain patterns or cues that suggest an attack is underway. For example, NLP algorithms can be trained to detect phrases or sentence structures commonly used in phishing emails or vishing calls, such as phrases like "urgent action required" or "confirm your account details."

NLP can also be used to analyze the context of messages and detect subtle inconsistencies or signs of impersonation. By evaluating the communication style, tone, and content, NLP algorithms can flag suspicious interactions that might otherwise appear legitimate.

3.3 Multi-Factor Authentication (MFA) and Verification Protocols

While AI-driven social engineering is highly sophisticated, it is often still reliant on manipulating human behavior. One of the most effective ways to defend against these attacks is to implement multi-factor authentication (MFA) and verification protocols. Even if a social engineering attack succeeds in obtaining login credentials or initiating a fraudulent request, MFA can serve as an additional layer of defense, requiring the attacker to provide additional verification (e.g., a one-time code or biometric scan).

MFA reduces the likelihood that stolen credentials can be used to execute fraudulent actions, providing a safety net in case an AI-driven social engineering attack successfully compromises user credentials.

3.4 AI-Enhanced Threat Intelligence Platforms

Advanced AI-powered threat intelligence platforms can be used to gather data from a wide range of sources, including dark web forums, social media, and known phishing campaigns, to identify emerging patterns of AI-driven social engineering attacks. These platforms can use machine learning to detect indicators of compromise (IOCs) associated with specific types of attacks, such as phishing kits or chatbots used for vishing.

By staying informed about the latest tactics, techniques, and procedures (TTPs) used by cybercriminals, threat intelligence platforms can help organizations proactively defend against evolving AI-driven social engineering attacks.

AI-driven social engineering attacks represent a growing and evolving threat to individuals and organizations alike. The ability of attackers to craft highly personalized, automated, and convincing attacks using AI technologies such as deepfake audio and video, chatbots, and machine learning makes these threats particularly challenging to detect and prevent. However, by leveraging modern cybersecurity techniques such as behavioral analytics, natural language processing, and multi-factor authentication, organizations can better defend against these attacks. It is essential for cybersecurity professionals to stay vigilant and continually adapt their defense strategies to keep up with the sophisticated tools and tactics employed by cybercriminals in the age of AI.

7.4 Strategies to Counter AI-Augmented Attacks

As artificial intelligence (AI) continues to advance, so too do the capabilities of cybercriminals to exploit AI in crafting more sophisticated and devastating cyberattacks. AI-augmented attacks leverage machine learning, deep learning, natural language processing, and other AI techniques to automate and scale malicious activities, making them more effective, evasive, and harder to detect. These types of attacks, such as AI-powered phishing, malware, and social engineering, represent a significant challenge for traditional cybersecurity defenses. As a result, cybersecurity professionals must adopt new strategies, tools, and approaches to counter AI-augmented attacks effectively.

In this section, we will explore various strategies that organizations can use to counter AI-driven cyber threats. These strategies encompass a combination of advanced detection techniques, proactive defense mechanisms, and adaptation of AI technologies to turn the tide against malicious use of AI.

1. Enhancing Threat Detection with AI and Machine Learning

AI is not just a tool for attackers; it can also be a powerful ally for defenders. The first step in countering AI-augmented attacks is to integrate AI-powered threat detection systems that can identify emerging threats in real-time. Machine learning (ML) and deep learning algorithms can be used to improve the detection of unknown malware, advanced persistent threats (APTs), and AI-driven social engineering attacks.

1.1 Leveraging Behavioral Analytics

AI can be used to monitor user and entity behavior across the network. By establishing a baseline of normal activities, AI-powered behavioral analytics can detect deviations from the norm that indicate potential malicious actions, such as unauthorized data access, unusual file transfers, or atypical login patterns.

For example, if an employee typically logs in at 9 a.m. from an office IP address, but suddenly logs in from an overseas location at 3 a.m., the system would flag this as anomalous behavior and alert security personnel. Behavioral analytics powered by machine learning can detect patterns of AI-driven deception, such as impersonation attempts or abnormal email activity associated with phishing or social engineering campaigns.

1.2 AI-Based Threat Hunting

AI-based threat hunting platforms use machine learning to analyze large volumes of data across the network and identify subtle signals of cyber threats that traditional methods may miss. By automating the data analysis and correlating it with historical attack patterns, these platforms can assist security teams in discovering hidden threats faster, particularly those that are AI-powered and adaptive in nature.

Machine learning models can be trained to recognize AI-driven tactics like polymorphic malware that alters its code to avoid detection or malware that mimics legitimate traffic patterns. These systems provide real-time threat intelligence, enabling security teams to rapidly respond to AI-powered attacks before they can cause damage.

1.3 Predictive Analytics for Attack Forecasting

Predictive analytics uses AI to forecast potential threats based on historical data and threat intelligence. By leveraging machine learning models that analyze attack vectors, attack patterns, and system vulnerabilities, organizations can predict future attack attempts, including those leveraging AI.

Predictive AI can help spot weaknesses in the organization's defenses before the attacker does. For instance, if AI-based models detect an emerging trend of AI-enhanced ransomware targeting similar organizations, proactive measures like enhanced email filtering, patching known vulnerabilities, and increasing network segmentation can be implemented to mitigate the potential risk.

2. Strengthening Human Defenses Through Education and Training

While AI is becoming more sophisticated, human error remains one of the weakest links in cybersecurity. To counter AI-augmented attacks, organizations must ensure that employees are properly trained to recognize and respond to evolving AI-driven threats, such as phishing emails, deepfake impersonation, and AI-powered social engineering.

2.1 Simulated Attack Training

AI-driven cyber attacks often rely on social engineering tactics that exploit human psychology. By training employees through simulated AI-driven phishing campaigns, organizations can help their workforce become more adept at spotting suspicious activity and avoiding malicious links or attachments. AI-based training platforms can simulate realistic phishing attacks that mirror the tactics of actual AI-powered threats, allowing employees to practice and improve their response.

Simulated attacks can also be tailored based on the individual's role within the organization. For example, executives can be trained to identify targeted spear-phishing emails, while finance teams can focus on recognizing fraudulent wire transfer requests.

2.2 Regular Security Awareness Programs

Incorporating security awareness into everyday work routines is crucial in combating AI-driven social engineering attacks. Security awareness programs should educate employees on the types of AI-augmented attacks, such as deepfake impersonation, where attackers use AI-generated media to impersonate executives or colleagues.

Employees should also be trained on best practices for recognizing AI-driven voice phishing (vishing) attacks, where a malicious actor uses AI to mimic a trusted voice or a corporate chatbot to extract sensitive information. Multi-factor authentication (MFA), when combined with employee education, can significantly reduce the success rate of AI-driven social engineering attacks.

3. Employing Advanced Security Technologies

Traditional cybersecurity solutions, such as firewalls and antivirus software, are insufficient to protect against AI-powered threats that evolve rapidly and autonomously. To effectively counter AI-augmented attacks, organizations need to integrate advanced security technologies designed to detect, respond to, and mitigate AI-based attacks in real-time.

3.1 Next-Gen Endpoint Detection and Response (EDR)

AI-enhanced Endpoint Detection and Response (EDR) solutions utilize machine learning algorithms to analyze endpoint activities and detect suspicious behaviors such as AI-driven malware execution, abnormal file access, or the execution of malicious scripts. These solutions can automatically block suspicious activity, provide real-time alerts, and support rapid containment of AI-based threats before they can propagate across the network.

EDR tools are increasingly adopting AI algorithms to recognize novel attack techniques, including those designed by attackers using AI tools to bypass traditional security measures.

3.2 AI-Powered SIEM (Security Information and Event Management) Systems

Security Information and Event Management (SIEM) systems provide centralized monitoring, detection, and response to security events within an organization. AI-powered SIEM systems enhance traditional SIEM by integrating machine learning to analyze large amounts of security data and correlate events in real-time.

These systems can detect AI-driven attacks more effectively by identifying unusual patterns of behavior that are difficult for traditional rule-based systems to detect. For example, an AI-driven SIEM could detect an AI-powered malware campaign that constantly changes its signatures to avoid detection by traditional signature-based detection systems.

3.3 Automation and Orchestration in Incident Response

Automated incident response systems can help mitigate the damage caused by AI-augmented attacks. Using AI, these systems can respond to attacks in real-time, isolate compromised endpoints, block malicious IP addresses, and perform other essential actions automatically, based on preconfigured playbooks.

For example, an AI-driven incident response system could automatically recognize signs of an AI-driven DDoS attack (distributed denial-of-service) by analyzing traffic patterns, and instantly implement countermeasures such as rate limiting or blocking suspicious traffic. This speed and precision help prevent the attack from spreading or causing significant damage.

4. Continuous Improvement and Adaptation

Given that AI-powered cyberattacks are evolving constantly, it is crucial for organizations to continuously improve their security measures to stay one step ahead of cybercriminals. Adaptation and ongoing learning are key to countering AI-augmented threats.

4.1 Adversarial Machine Learning Defense

AI-based attack models, such as adversarial machine learning (AML), are designed to manipulate machine learning models to evade detection. Organizations should adopt countermeasures that incorporate adversarial training into their security systems. This involves training AI models to recognize and defend against adversarial manipulation by simulating adversarial AI techniques and incorporating defenses into detection algorithms.

4.2 Red-Teaming with AI

Red-teaming exercises, where simulated attacks are launched against a network to test its defenses, should also evolve to include AI-driven attack simulations. This allows organizations to better understand how AI-powered attacks will behave in real-world scenarios and refine their defense strategies.

By leveraging AI in these exercises, red teams can simulate the use of AI-driven malware or deepfake impersonations, allowing the organization to assess how effective their defenses are in detecting and countering these evolving threats.

AI-augmented attacks represent a significant challenge for organizations, but they also provide an opportunity for cybersecurity professionals to harness AI for defense. By adopting advanced detection systems powered by machine learning, enhancing employee training, and employing cutting-edge security technologies, organizations can build resilient defenses against these sophisticated threats. As AI continues to shape both the offense and defense sides of cybersecurity, it is crucial for organizations to adapt, innovate, and remain vigilant in order to stay ahead of cybercriminals using AI for malicious purposes.

7.5 The Future of AI Arms Races in Cybersecurity

The integration of Artificial Intelligence (AI) into both cyberattack strategies and defense mechanisms has sparked a new form of digital arms race in the cybersecurity world. As both attackers and defenders increasingly rely on AI technologies, the battlefield is evolving at a rapid pace, forcing organizations to continually adapt to increasingly sophisticated tactics, techniques, and procedures. In this section, we will explore the potential future of the AI arms race in cybersecurity, considering the impact of emerging technologies, evolving attack strategies, and the ongoing arms race between threat actors and cybersecurity defenders.

The AI arms race refers to the escalating competition between attackers and defenders, where both sides leverage cutting-edge AI to gain an advantage. As attackers use AI to craft more targeted, evasive, and adaptive attacks, defenders are equally motivated to adopt AI-driven tools and solutions to enhance threat detection, mitigate damage, and respond more quickly to potential breaches. The outcome of this arms race will have a profound impact on the cybersecurity landscape, shaping the way organizations approach digital security in the future.

1. The Evolving Threat Landscape: AI-Powered Attacks at Scale

As cybercriminals and state-sponsored actors continue to advance their use of AI, the sophistication, scale, and speed of cyberattacks will increase significantly. In the future, we are likely to see the development of AI-powered malware that can automatically evolve to evade detection, tailor itself to specific targets, and even optimize its strategies to maximize damage.

For example, AI-driven ransomware could develop the ability to use machine learning to identify the most critical files on a network, dynamically encrypt high-value data, and demand targeted ransom based on the value of that data to the victim. In the case of Advanced Persistent Threats (APTs), AI will allow attackers to infiltrate systems with greater stealth, using deep learning to mimic normal user behavior and blend in with legitimate network activity.

Another potential scenario is the rise of AI-assisted social engineering attacks that utilize natural language processing (NLP) and deep learning to craft personalized, hyper-realistic phishing emails or phone calls. These attacks could be designed to exploit specific vulnerabilities or emotions within individuals, resulting in highly successful social engineering campaigns.

The rapid evolution of AI-powered attack techniques could lead to the automation of these threats, allowing attackers to deploy and control large-scale cyberattacks with minimal effort, further outpacing traditional defense strategies.

2. The Rise of Autonomous Defense Systems

To counter increasingly sophisticated AI-driven attacks, cybersecurity professionals will have to adopt autonomous defense systems that can continuously learn, adapt, and respond to threats in real time. As the arms race escalates, the need for highly adaptive and self-learning defense systems will become more urgent.

AI-powered security platforms will evolve to provide more dynamic responses to AI-powered threats. These systems will use machine learning algorithms that not only detect and respond to known attack patterns but also analyze and adapt to new, previously unseen threats. By doing so, these platforms will be able to protect networks, devices, and data in a way that is both scalable and efficient.

In particular, AI-driven incident response systems could automate many of the time-consuming processes involved in threat detection, analysis, and mitigation. These systems will be able to identify suspicious activities, quarantine infected systems, and trigger security protocols faster than human teams, all while learning from each attack to improve responses in the future.

Furthermore, autonomous systems will likely collaborate across industries, sharing threat intelligence and responding collectively to large-scale, AI-driven cyberattacks. This network of interconnected, AI-powered defense systems could provide a form of global cybersecurity collaboration, where AI systems communicate and exchange data to protect against emerging threats in real-time.

3. AI in Threat Attribution and Attribution Wars

As AI continues to be a tool of choice for both attackers and defenders, the question of attribution—identifying the origin and motive behind an attack—becomes increasingly complex. AI-driven attacks can easily obscure their origins by using techniques such as proxy networks, deepfake personas, and AI-powered social manipulation. The ability to accurately attribute attacks to specific threat actors, especially state-sponsored groups, will become a crucial aspect of the arms race.

AI will play a pivotal role in helping defenders identify and trace the origins of cyberattacks by using advanced attribution models. Machine learning algorithms can analyze attack patterns, network traffic, and digital forensics to link attacks to specific actors or groups. However, attackers are likely to use AI to obfuscate their activities, creating new layers of complexity in the attribution process.

This dynamic could lead to a new form of attribution warfare, where both sides of the arms race use AI to influence perceptions of responsibility. Attackers may use AI to create disinformation or confusion, while defenders will seek to use AI to bolster their claims of attribution. This "war" over cyber credibility could have geopolitical implications, especially if cyberattacks are linked to national security interests.

4. Ethical and Legal Considerations in the AI Arms Race

As both attackers and defenders rely on AI in the cybersecurity domain, questions surrounding the ethics and legal implications of these technologies will become more pressing. In particular, the deployment of autonomous defense systems raises concerns about the potential for unintended consequences, such as collateral damage or overreaction in defense mechanisms.

For example, an AI-driven defense system might automatically shut down critical infrastructure in response to a suspected attack, potentially disrupting business operations or public services. Additionally, AI-powered surveillance technologies could inadvertently infringe on privacy rights, leading to concerns about mass surveillance or violations of civil liberties.

On the offensive side, the use of AI in cyberattacks could lead to escalating cyber conflicts, as attackers gain the ability to conduct attacks with increasing sophistication, precision, and speed. These types of attacks could have devastating consequences, particularly in the context of critical infrastructure or financial systems.

As AI technologies continue to play a larger role in cybersecurity, international organizations, governments, and corporations will need to develop robust legal frameworks to regulate their use and ensure accountability. Ethical standards will need to be established to guide the responsible use of AI in both defense and offense, while minimizing the risks associated with misuse or abuse.

5. The Arms Race Between Cybersecurity Vendors

The AI arms race is not just limited to attackers and defenders. Cybersecurity vendors will also find themselves in a constant battle to develop and deploy the most effective AI-driven solutions. As the demand for AI-powered security tools grows, vendors will compete to create cutting-edge technologies that offer faster detection, better accuracy, and more comprehensive protection.

The market will see continued innovation in AI security tools, with new solutions aimed at addressing emerging threats such as AI-powered phishing, machine learning malware, and automated vulnerability exploitation. Some vendors will likely develop AI-driven threat intelligence platforms that provide real-time insights into global threat landscapes, while others may focus on next-gen firewalls and intrusion detection systems (IDS) that incorporate advanced machine learning to identify anomalies in network traffic.

As organizations increasingly rely on AI-powered defense mechanisms, the vendor arms race will drive both competition and collaboration across the cybersecurity industry. Companies will need to strike a balance between adopting the latest innovations and ensuring that these AI-powered tools are effective, ethical, and scalable.

6. Conclusion: Navigating the Future of AI in Cybersecurity

The AI arms race in cybersecurity is set to become one of the defining features of the digital age. As AI-powered attacks and defenses continue to evolve, the strategies, tools, and tactics used by both attackers and defenders will become increasingly sophisticated. The challenge for cybersecurity professionals will be to stay ahead of this rapidly changing landscape by continually adapting their defenses, leveraging AI for proactive protection, and mitigating the risks associated with AI-driven threats.

The future of cybersecurity will require a dynamic, multi-layered approach that includes collaboration between AI-driven defense systems, international cooperation, and ethical standards for the use of AI in both defense and attack. As AI continues to shape the cybersecurity domain, the ultimate goal will be to achieve a balance between utilizing its power for protection while minimizing the potential for its misuse.

8. Simulating Attacks with AI

One of the most effective ways to strengthen cybersecurity defenses is by anticipating and simulating potential attacks. This chapter explores how AI is revolutionizing penetration testing and red team exercises by automating attack simulations. Using machine learning algorithms and reinforcement learning, AI can simulate adversarial tactics, identify vulnerabilities, and predict attack paths with greater precision and speed than traditional methods. Readers will learn how AI-driven attack simulations help security teams assess their defenses, uncover hidden weaknesses, and improve response strategies in real-time, offering a proactive approach to cybersecurity that anticipates threats before they strike.

8.1 AI-Powered Penetration Testing Tools

Penetration testing (often referred to as pen testing) is a crucial component of a comprehensive cybersecurity strategy, designed to identify vulnerabilities in systems, networks, and applications before malicious hackers can exploit them. Traditional pen testing involves human experts manually simulating attacks on an organization's infrastructure to find weaknesses. However, as cyber threats become more complex and sophisticated, the integration of Artificial Intelligence (AI) into penetration testing has begun to revolutionize the process. AI-powered penetration testing tools use machine learning algorithms, automated processes, and advanced analytics to enhance the speed, accuracy, and efficiency of security assessments.

In this section, we will explore the various ways in which AI is transforming penetration testing, the types of AI-powered tools available, and how these tools are enabling organizations to conduct more effective and proactive security assessments.

1. The Role of AI in Penetration Testing

AI-powered tools have the potential to dramatically improve the way penetration tests are conducted by automating many of the repetitive and time-consuming tasks traditionally handled by human testers. These tools are capable of scanning vast amounts of data, identifying vulnerabilities, and even simulating complex attack scenarios in a fraction of the time it would take for a human expert to do so.

Key benefits of AI integration in penetration testing include:

- **Speed**: AI can process large datasets and perform tests much faster than manual testing, allowing for more frequent and comprehensive assessments.
- **Accuracy**: By leveraging machine learning algorithms, AI can reduce the risk of human error, ensuring that vulnerabilities are identified with greater precision.
- **Scalability**: AI can easily scale to assess large, complex networks or systems that would be impractical for a human tester to evaluate manually.
- **Advanced Simulation**: AI can simulate attack patterns and scenarios based on real-world tactics, techniques, and procedures (TTPs) used by cybercriminals, helping to test defenses against increasingly sophisticated threats.

In addition to the traditional process of vulnerability scanning, AI-powered penetration testing tools can simulate realistic attack chains, analyze system behavior in response to attacks, and continuously adapt to discover new weaknesses, providing more comprehensive results.

2. Types of AI-Powered Penetration Testing Tools

AI-powered penetration testing tools can be broadly categorized based on the specific aspects of the pen testing process they enhance. Some of the key tools and technologies that leverage AI in penetration testing include:

2.1 Automated Vulnerability Scanners

AI-driven vulnerability scanners can identify security weaknesses in a system's infrastructure, such as outdated software versions, missing patches, or weak configurations, much more efficiently than traditional scanners. By leveraging machine learning algorithms, these tools can prioritize vulnerabilities based on their potential risk and the likelihood of exploitation.

AI-powered scanners can also learn from previously discovered vulnerabilities, improving their detection capabilities over time. For instance, if a vulnerability in a specific type of software or network configuration is frequently targeted in cyberattacks, an AI-based scanner can be trained to prioritize testing for that vulnerability in future scans.

2.2 AI-Enhanced Web Application Testing Tools

Web applications are frequent targets for cybercriminals due to their online presence and complex structures. AI-powered web application penetration testing tools can scan websites and applications for vulnerabilities such as SQL injection, Cross-Site Scripting (XSS), and broken authentication. These tools use AI to simulate sophisticated attacks on the application, identifying vulnerabilities in the code or logic that would otherwise be difficult to spot.

Machine learning models can analyze historical attack patterns and web traffic to simulate targeted attacks, providing insights into potential vulnerabilities that could be exploited by attackers. These AI-based tools can even identify logical flaws and issues with application design that are often missed by traditional scanners.

2.3 AI for Network Penetration Testing

Network penetration testing tools powered by AI can assess the security posture of an organization's network infrastructure by simulating attacks against the network perimeter, internal systems, and devices. AI algorithms are used to automate tasks such as network mapping, vulnerability scanning, and identifying weak spots in the network defenses.

These tools can simulate Distributed Denial of Service (DDoS) attacks, Man-in-the-Middle (MitM) attacks, and other network-based threats. AI-based network testers can also learn from ongoing test results and dynamically adjust their attack techniques, mimicking the adaptive strategies used by real-world attackers.

2.4 AI for Exploit Development and Payload Simulation

Some AI-powered penetration testing tools go beyond identifying vulnerabilities by automating the process of developing exploits and simulating real-world attacks. These tools leverage deep learning algorithms to analyze known exploits, malware samples, and attack code in order to create custom payloads tailored to specific vulnerabilities.

By using AI to generate exploit payloads, penetration testers can automate the process of testing vulnerabilities with real-world attack scenarios, reducing the need for manual intervention. AI can also analyze how the system responds to payloads and adjust the attack strategy based on the system's defenses.

2.5 Continuous Testing and AI-Assisted Red-Teaming

Unlike traditional pen testing, which typically occurs at set intervals, AI-assisted red-teaming enables continuous testing of an organization's defenses. By using machine learning, these tools can simulate persistent, evolving attacks over extended periods, mimicking long-term threat actor behavior. Red-teaming exercises powered by AI can generate new attack vectors over time, adapting to the changes in the organization's security posture and mimicking real-world threat actors' strategies.

AI can also optimize the red-teaming process by prioritizing areas of attack based on historical data, vulnerability assessments, and exploitability analyses. This enables security teams to stay ahead of potential threats and prepare for a range of possible attack scenarios.

3. Advantages of AI-Powered Penetration Testing

The integration of AI into penetration testing brings numerous advantages that can improve the overall security of an organization. These include:

3.1 Speed and Efficiency

AI-powered tools can automate many repetitive tasks in the penetration testing process, such as vulnerability scanning, exploit testing, and system mapping, which would take human testers significantly longer to perform manually. This allows security teams to conduct more frequent and comprehensive assessments across large, complex environments.

3.2 Enhanced Accuracy and Precision

Traditional pen testing can be prone to human error, and even the most experienced security experts may miss vulnerabilities. AI-driven tools, on the other hand, leverage vast amounts of data and patterns from past attacks, reducing the likelihood of overlooking critical weaknesses. Furthermore, AI-powered systems can continuously improve their accuracy as they learn from each test.

3.3 Adaptability and Evolution

AI systems can dynamically adapt to new threats as they arise. For example, machine learning algorithms can learn from zero-day vulnerabilities, adjusting their testing methods to detect previously unknown attack techniques. This adaptability enables AI-powered tools to remain effective even as cyber threats evolve.

3.4 Cost-Effectiveness

While the initial cost of AI-powered penetration testing tools may be higher than traditional methods, their ability to automate and speed up many aspects of the testing process can significantly reduce overall testing costs in the long term. Additionally, AI tools can identify vulnerabilities more effectively, minimizing the costs associated with security breaches and damage control.

4. Limitations and Considerations

Despite their many advantages, AI-powered penetration testing tools also come with limitations and considerations:

4.1 Lack of Human Insight

While AI can automate and optimize many aspects of penetration testing, it still lacks the nuanced understanding that human experts bring to the table. For example, AI may struggle to simulate certain social engineering attacks or to understand the broader business context in which an attack might occur. Human expertise is still crucial in interpreting the results of AI-driven tests and providing actionable insights.

4.2 False Positives and Model Tuning

AI-powered tools are not immune to false positives, where legitimate system behavior is flagged as a vulnerability. Continuous model tuning and training are required to refine the AI's accuracy and minimize false positives. Additionally, these tools rely on historical data and patterns, which means they may not always recognize novel or highly creative attack techniques that deviate from established patterns.

4.3 Ethical and Privacy Concerns

Automated penetration testing tools, particularly those that simulate real-world attacks, could raise ethical concerns regarding privacy and the potential for unintended consequences, such as disrupting live systems or exposing sensitive data during testing. Organizations should ensure that AI-driven penetration tests are carefully planned and controlled to avoid causing any harm.

5. Conclusion: The Future of AI in Penetration Testing

AI-powered penetration testing tools are reshaping the landscape of cybersecurity by automating, accelerating, and improving the effectiveness of vulnerability assessments and security testing. These tools bring significant benefits, including faster testing, more accurate vulnerability identification, and enhanced adaptability to new threats. However, while AI can handle many aspects of penetration testing, human expertise remains essential in interpreting results, addressing complex attack scenarios, and refining AI models. As AI technology continues to evolve, we can expect even more advanced, adaptive, and efficient penetration testing tools to emerge, ultimately improving the overall security of organizations and helping them stay one step ahead of cybercriminals.

8.2 Using ML to Predict Adversarial Behavior

In the ever-evolving world of cybersecurity, anticipating and mitigating adversarial behavior is a critical challenge for security teams. As attackers become more sophisticated, traditional defense mechanisms often struggle to keep pace. Machine Learning (ML) has emerged as a powerful tool to help predict, identify, and respond to adversarial behavior before it can cause significant damage. By analyzing patterns in data and adapting to new behaviors, machine learning models can provide a proactive defense strategy, turning the tables on attackers who typically rely on exploiting vulnerabilities.

In this section, we will explore how Machine Learning (ML) can be used to predict adversarial behavior, the types of adversarial actions that ML models can anticipate, and how organizations can deploy these models as part of their security arsenal.

1. The Role of Machine Learning in Predicting Adversarial Behavior

Machine learning is fundamentally about building algorithms that learn from data to make predictions, identify patterns, or make decisions without explicit programming. In the context of cybersecurity, ML algorithms can analyze vast amounts of data to detect abnormal behavior, uncover hidden patterns, and predict potential malicious activities before they materialize.

Unlike traditional security systems that rely on predefined rules and signatures, ML-based models can continuously improve their accuracy and efficiency by learning from both historical and real-time data. This allows them to predict adversarial behavior by identifying deviations from normal patterns, flagging potential threats even in the face of new and sophisticated attack strategies. Over time, these models become more adept at recognizing subtle changes in behavior that might indicate an emerging cyberattack, making them far more effective at predicting adversarial tactics than legacy security systems.

By leveraging machine learning to predict adversarial behavior, organizations can implement more proactive defense mechanisms, reducing the time between detecting a threat and responding to it. This shift from a reactive to a predictive security model is critical in an era where cyberattacks are becoming increasingly sophisticated, dynamic, and fast-moving.

2. Types of Adversarial Behavior That Machine Learning Can Predict

Adversarial behavior in cybersecurity often refers to malicious actions that attackers undertake to infiltrate systems, steal data, or disrupt services. Machine learning can be used to predict a variety of adversarial behaviors, including:

2.1 Evolving Attack Techniques

Cybercriminals are constantly evolving their tactics to evade detection and maximize their impact. ML models can predict the likelihood of new attack strategies based on trends in the data, identifying early signs of emerging threats. For example, malware authors may modify their code to avoid signature-based detection systems, or attackers may employ zero-day exploits targeting previously unknown vulnerabilities. Machine learning models can help predict such changes by analyzing historical attack patterns and adapting their detection algorithms accordingly.

2.2 Insider Threats and Anomalous User Behavior

Insider threats are one of the most difficult adversarial behaviors to predict because they involve legitimate users abusing their access for malicious purposes. Behavioral analytics powered by ML can monitor and analyze user activities in real time, detecting deviations from typical behavior that could indicate an insider threat. For example, if an employee accesses sensitive files they have never interacted with before or begins downloading large amounts of data at odd hours, an ML model could flag these behaviors as suspicious, prompting further investigation.

2.3 Phishing and Social Engineering Attacks

Phishing and social engineering attacks rely on manipulating individuals into revealing sensitive information or performing actions that compromise security. Machine learning algorithms, particularly those utilizing natural language processing (NLP), can predict phishing attempts by analyzing patterns in communication (e.g., emails, messages, or websites) for signs of deception. ML models can analyze the tone, syntax, and structure of emails to predict whether a message is a phishing attempt. They can also monitor changes in communication patterns, such as increased urgency or unexpected requests, which are typical characteristics of social engineering tactics.

2.4 Automated Reconnaissance and Scanning for Vulnerabilities

Attackers often begin their campaigns by scanning networks for vulnerabilities, looking for exposed systems or open ports that they can exploit. ML models can predict this type of adversarial behavior by identifying scanning activity patterns in network traffic. For example, by analyzing the frequency, timing, and location of incoming requests, ML systems can recognize when an attacker is performing network reconnaissance and can trigger automated defenses to block these attempts. These systems can also adapt their analysis to spot novel scanning techniques that attackers may use to evade detection.

2.5 Advanced Persistent Threats (APTs)

Advanced Persistent Threats (APTs) are long-term, highly targeted attacks aimed at infiltrating and remaining undetected within an organization's network. ML can predict APT behaviors by identifying small, seemingly innocuous activities that collectively signal a more significant threat. By analyzing data across multiple attack vectors (such as network traffic, endpoint behavior, and application logs), ML models can detect the early signs of APTs, such as lateral movement, privilege escalation, or the exfiltration of data. This predictive capability is crucial for detecting APTs before they cause significant damage.

3. Machine Learning Techniques for Predicting Adversarial Behavior

To predict and prevent adversarial behavior, cybersecurity professionals rely on a range of machine learning techniques, each suited to different aspects of threat detection and prediction:

3.1 Supervised Learning for Threat Classification

Supervised learning models are trained on labeled datasets, where the correct outcomes (e.g., malicious or benign behavior) are provided. In cybersecurity, this can be used to classify incoming network traffic, system logs, or user activities as either legitimate or suspicious. The model is trained to recognize the patterns associated with both normal and adversarial behaviors, improving its ability to classify future activities. These models are particularly effective at identifying known attack patterns or malware signatures.

3.2 Unsupervised Learning for Anomaly Detection

Unsupervised learning algorithms are ideal for detecting unknown threats, as they do not require labeled training data. Instead, they analyze large volumes of data to identify patterns and deviations from the norm. In cybersecurity, this technique is particularly effective for identifying anomalous behaviors that may indicate a new attack or compromised system. For example, unsupervised learning can flag unusual network traffic, sudden spikes in system resource usage, or unexplained access to sensitive files—all of which may point to adversarial activities.

3.3 Reinforcement Learning for Adaptive Defense

Reinforcement learning (RL) algorithms are designed to continuously learn and adapt based on feedback from their environment. In the context of cybersecurity, reinforcement learning can be used to predict adversarial moves and develop adaptive defense strategies. RL models interact with simulated attack environments and adjust their responses to minimize the impact of potential threats. Over time, the system learns the best strategies for counteracting specific adversarial behaviors, making it a useful tool for real-time defense.

3.4 Deep Learning for Complex Pattern Recognition

Deep learning, a subset of machine learning, uses artificial neural networks with multiple layers to learn complex patterns in large datasets. In cybersecurity, deep learning models can predict adversarial behavior by analyzing raw data from various sources, such as network traffic, endpoint logs, and user interactions. These models are highly effective in recognizing subtle patterns and interactions that indicate a sophisticated attack. For example, deep learning can be used to detect advanced malware that evades traditional signature-based detection systems by analyzing the way the malware interacts with the operating system.

4. Real-World Applications of Machine Learning for Predicting Adversarial Behavior

Several organizations have already begun to integrate machine learning into their cybersecurity strategies to predict adversarial behavior. Examples of real-world applications include:

4.1 Predicting Phishing Attacks

By using natural language processing (NLP) and machine learning, several email filtering systems can predict and block phishing attempts before they reach the inbox. For example, Google's Gmail uses machine learning to detect phishing emails by analyzing the sender's behavior, language patterns, and overall email structure. Over time, the system learns to recognize new forms of phishing and adapt its detection capabilities to defend against emerging threats.

4.2 Predicting Insider Threats

Many organizations have implemented machine learning-driven insider threat detection systems to monitor employee behavior and predict potential insider threats. By analyzing user activity, including login patterns, file access, and email communications, these systems can identify deviations that might indicate an insider is engaging in malicious behavior, such as stealing data or accessing unauthorized areas of the network.

4.3 Identifying APTs in Network Traffic

ML-based intrusion detection systems (IDS) can predict and detect Advanced Persistent Threats (APTs) by analyzing patterns in network traffic. For example, Darktrace, a cybersecurity company, uses machine learning to identify emerging APTs in real-time by monitoring traffic and flagging abnormal communication patterns between devices. The system adapts and evolves as new attack vectors emerge, providing continuous protection against advanced threats.

5. Conclusion: The Future of Predicting Adversarial Behavior with Machine Learning

Machine learning has already proven to be an invaluable tool for predicting and preventing adversarial behavior in cybersecurity. By harnessing the power of ML, organizations can better anticipate and mitigate threats before they cause significant damage. As cybercriminals become more sophisticated and employ increasingly complex attack techniques, the ability to predict adversarial behavior using ML will become even more critical. As machine learning models continue to improve and evolve, they will provide a more proactive and adaptive defense against the growing wave of cyber threats.

8.3 Creating Attack Scenarios with Reinforcement Learning

In the rapidly evolving cybersecurity landscape, understanding and anticipating the tactics and techniques employed by cyber adversaries is crucial. One of the most promising approaches to achieving this understanding is Reinforcement Learning (RL), a subset of machine learning that focuses on how agents can learn optimal behaviors through trial and error. Reinforcement learning enables systems to simulate attack scenarios and adapt to various threat tactics, creating realistic attack simulations that can help organizations improve their defense mechanisms.

In this section, we will explore how Reinforcement Learning (RL) can be used to create attack scenarios, simulate adversarial behavior, and enhance cybersecurity defenses. By using RL to simulate attacks, security teams can better prepare for and counter real-world cyberattacks, enhancing their preparedness against both known and unknown threats.

1. Introduction to Reinforcement Learning and Its Role in Attack Simulations

Reinforcement learning is a type of machine learning where an agent (or system) interacts with an environment and learns to achieve specific goals by performing actions and receiving feedback. Unlike supervised learning, where models are trained on labeled data, RL relies on an agent receiving positive or negative feedback based on its actions and adjusting its strategy over time.

In the context of cybersecurity, RL allows an agent to simulate the behavior of an attacker within a controlled environment. The agent can explore various attack strategies, learn from the outcomes of its actions, and adapt its approach to maximize the chances of success. By using reinforcement learning to create realistic attack scenarios, security teams can test and refine their defenses before a real attack occurs.

In essence, reinforcement learning allows cybersecurity professionals to create dynamic and adaptable attack simulations that mimic real-world adversarial tactics. These simulations can help organizations assess their vulnerabilities, improve their defensive measures, and ultimately strengthen their security posture.

2. Creating Realistic Attack Scenarios with RL

Reinforcement learning can be used to generate complex and realistic attack scenarios by mimicking the decision-making processes of cyber adversaries. In a typical RL setup, the "agent" represents the attacker, and the "environment" represents the network, system, or infrastructure that is being targeted. Through interactions with the environment, the agent learns optimal attack strategies by receiving feedback based on the effectiveness of its actions.

2.1 Simulating Advanced Persistent Threats (APTs)

One of the most significant applications of RL in attack simulations is the creation of Advanced Persistent Threats (APTs), which are sophisticated, long-term cyberattacks typically carried out by state-sponsored or highly organized criminal groups. APTs often involve multiple stages, including reconnaissance, lateral movement, privilege escalation, and data exfiltration.

Reinforcement learning models can simulate these multi-stage attacks by allowing the agent to experiment with various tactics, techniques, and procedures (TTPs) associated with APTs. As the agent interacts with the system, it learns how to move through the network, compromise different systems, evade detection, and maintain persistence—all while adjusting its approach based on the outcomes of previous actions.

This creates a more realistic attack simulation that mirrors the complexity and adaptability of real-world APTs. Organizations can use these simulations to test their defenses against these types of persistent and evolving threats.

2.2 Evasion Techniques and Exploit Development

Another key area where RL can be used to simulate attacks is in the development of evasion techniques and the exploitation of vulnerabilities. Attackers often use sophisticated methods to bypass traditional security defenses, such as firewalls, intrusion detection systems, and antivirus software. By simulating attack scenarios using reinforcement learning, security teams can better understand the effectiveness of these evasion techniques.

For instance, an RL agent can simulate an attacker's efforts to evade detection while exploiting a zero-day vulnerability. Through repeated interactions with the system, the agent can refine its methods for avoiding detection and leveraging system weaknesses to gain unauthorized access. By continuously adjusting its tactics, the agent can simulate a range of evasion techniques, such as polymorphic malware, which changes its code to avoid signature-based detection, or living off the land tactics, where attackers use legitimate system tools to carry out their malicious activities.

By using RL to simulate such attacks, organizations can gain insights into potential weaknesses in their defenses and develop more robust security systems capable of detecting even the most sophisticated evasion methods.

2.3 Testing Phishing and Social Engineering Tactics

Phishing and social engineering attacks rely on manipulating individuals to gain access to sensitive information or systems. Reinforcement learning can be used to simulate the tactics used by attackers to craft effective phishing campaigns and other social engineering schemes. The RL agent can experiment with different phishing strategies, such as crafting convincing email messages, exploiting trust relationships, or impersonating legitimate entities.

Through repeated interactions with the environment, the RL agent can refine its phishing tactics, learning how to improve the chances of success for each campaign. For example, it may adjust the timing of the attack, modify the language used in the phishing email, or test different delivery channels (e.g., email, text messages, social media) to find the most effective method of tricking the target.

By using RL to simulate phishing and social engineering tactics, organizations can better understand how attackers exploit human behavior and vulnerabilities, helping them create better awareness training and more effective defenses against these types of attacks.

3. Advantages of Using Reinforcement Learning for Attack Simulations

There are several advantages to using reinforcement learning for creating attack scenarios and simulations in cybersecurity:

3.1 Realistic and Adaptive Attack Models

Reinforcement learning enables the creation of adaptive, dynamic attack models that continuously evolve based on the feedback received. Unlike traditional attack simulations, which are often static and predefined, RL-based simulations allow adversaries to adjust their tactics in real time based on the effectiveness of their previous actions. This leads to more realistic and unpredictable attack scenarios that closely mirror real-world adversarial behavior.

3.2 Customizable Attack Strategies

One of the key benefits of RL-based attack simulations is the ability to create highly customizable attack strategies. Security teams can modify the environment (e.g., the network topology or defense mechanisms) and instruct the RL agent to focus on specific attack vectors, such as exploiting vulnerabilities, social engineering, or using malware. This flexibility allows security professionals to tailor attack simulations to their specific threat landscape, ensuring that the tests are relevant and comprehensive.

3.3 Identifying Weaknesses in Security Posture

By using reinforcement learning to simulate attacks, organizations can identify vulnerabilities and weaknesses in their cybersecurity defenses that might not be apparent through traditional testing methods. For example, RL simulations can help uncover blind spots in detection systems, areas where security policies are too permissive, or flaws in incident response plans. This proactive testing approach helps organizations stay one step ahead of attackers and strengthens their overall security posture.

3.4 Continuous Learning and Improvement

Reinforcement learning models are capable of continuous improvement, adapting to new scenarios and learning from past interactions. As the RL agent simulates attacks, it refines its approach, improving its effectiveness over time. This ongoing learning process ensures that the attack simulations remain relevant as adversaries evolve their tactics, making it an essential tool for staying ahead of emerging threats.

4. Implementing Reinforcement Learning for Attack Simulations

To implement reinforcement learning for creating attack scenarios, cybersecurity teams must first set up a simulation environment that accurately represents their network and systems. This environment needs to include:

- **Data Inputs**: Realistic system logs, network traffic, and user behaviors that the RL agent can interact with.
- **Reward Structure**: A feedback mechanism that rewards the agent for successful actions (e.g., exploiting vulnerabilities, evading detection) and penalizes it for unsuccessful actions (e.g., being detected, failing to exploit a vulnerability).
- **Security Countermeasures**: Simulated defenses such as intrusion detection systems, firewalls, endpoint protection, and monitoring tools that the RL agent will attempt to bypass or exploit.

Once the environment is set up, the RL agent can begin its learning process, continually refining its strategies and adapting its behavior based on feedback from the system. Security teams can then analyze the results to identify areas of weakness, improve detection capabilities, and develop stronger defensive measures.

5. Conclusion: The Future of Attack Simulations with Reinforcement Learning

As cyber threats become increasingly sophisticated, traditional defense strategies must evolve to keep pace. Reinforcement learning represents a powerful tool for simulating adversarial behavior and testing cybersecurity defenses in dynamic and realistic scenarios. By using RL to create attack simulations, organizations can anticipate and prepare for emerging threats, enhance their incident response capabilities, and continuously improve their security posture.

In the future, as reinforcement learning models become more advanced and widely adopted, they will play an essential role in building adaptive, resilient cybersecurity systems that can outmaneuver even the most sophisticated cyber adversaries.

8.4 Benefits of AI-Driven Red Team Simulations

AI-driven red team simulations are rapidly becoming a cornerstone of modern cybersecurity strategies. A Red Team refers to a group of ethical hackers who simulate real-world cyberattacks to test an organization's defenses, processes, and response mechanisms. Traditionally, red team operations were conducted by human experts who manually crafted attack scenarios based on their understanding of adversarial tactics. However, the introduction of AI and machine learning into this domain has significantly enhanced the capabilities and effectiveness of red team simulations. This section explores the key benefits of using AI-driven red team simulations in modern cybersecurity.

1. Improved Realism and Complexity in Attack Simulations

One of the most significant advantages of AI-driven red team simulations is the enhanced realism they bring to cyberattack scenarios. Traditional red team exercises rely on predefined attack methods and static attack vectors. While these are useful, they often fail to account for the evolving tactics and adaptive strategies used by real-world cyber adversaries. AI, especially when combined with machine learning, can dynamically adapt its attack techniques in response to the defensive mechanisms in place, making the simulation more representative of actual adversarial behaviors.

For example, an AI-driven red team can continuously learn from the organization's defense responses and adjust its tactics accordingly. This creates a highly adaptive and realistic attack model that simulates how a determined, sophisticated adversary might evolve their attack strategy over time. The AI agent might begin by attempting common attack vectors, such as phishing or exploiting known vulnerabilities, then adapt its behavior based on how the target system defends itself. This adaptability allows for a more complex, evolving attack pattern that is closer to the tactics used by advanced persistent threats (APTs).

2. Increased Efficiency and Scalability

In traditional red teaming, human red team members can only conduct a limited number of attack simulations due to the time and resources required to plan and execute each attack. The involvement of AI, on the other hand, allows for greater scalability and efficiency. AI-driven simulations can run autonomously, testing multiple attack vectors across various environments at a fraction of the time it would take human red teamers to do so manually.

AI agents can simultaneously conduct hundreds or even thousands of attack scenarios, testing defenses across various attack surfaces in parallel. This significantly speeds up the process of identifying vulnerabilities and weaknesses in a network or system, making it more feasible for organizations to conduct continuous, real-time red teaming exercises. Moreover, AI-driven red teams can operate 24/7, ensuring that the organization's defenses are constantly being tested without requiring the deployment of a large team of human testers at all times.

This scalability is particularly useful for large, complex organizations or enterprises with extensive networks and systems that need frequent, exhaustive testing. AI can rapidly identify security gaps in systems that may otherwise be overlooked during periodic human-conducted red team operations.

3. Enhanced Threat Intelligence Integration

AI-driven red team simulations have the added benefit of being able to integrate real-time threat intelligence into their attack strategies. Threat intelligence refers to data and insights regarding current and emerging cyber threats, including attack tactics, techniques, and procedures (TTPs) used by cybercriminals and state-sponsored actors. AI can use this intelligence to craft highly targeted attack simulations based on the most up-to-date threat landscape.

By incorporating threat intelligence into red team exercises, AI agents can simulate cutting-edge attack methods and focus on the specific risks and vulnerabilities most likely to affect the organization. This makes the red team exercises far more relevant, helping organizations to identify vulnerabilities that may not be part of traditional attack patterns but are instead part of more advanced, real-world threats.

For example, AI can incorporate information about newly discovered vulnerabilities (such as zero-day exploits), recent phishing campaigns, or evolving ransomware tactics into its simulations. This ensures that the red team exercises reflect the current threat landscape, allowing organizations to stay ahead of attackers and reduce the risk of being caught off guard by emerging threats.

4. Continuous Improvement and Learning

One of the standout features of AI-driven simulations is their ability to continuously learn from interactions with the environment, often referred to as reinforcement learning. With each attack simulation, the AI agent refines its strategies based on feedback from the results of the previous interactions. In other words, the AI learns from its own successes and failures, enabling it to improve over time.

In a red team context, this continuous improvement means that AI agents can progressively enhance the sophistication and complexity of their attack strategies. As the AI learns, it begins to simulate more advanced attack methods, making it a dynamic and evolving adversary. This ongoing evolution in attack tactics ensures that the simulations remain realistic and are always pushing the boundaries of what an organization's defenses are prepared to handle.

For instance, if a particular defense mechanism blocks an attack strategy, the AI can immediately attempt different tactics or attempt to bypass the defense in new ways. This learning loop ensures that red team simulations grow more challenging over time, helping organizations develop increasingly effective and adaptive defense strategies.

5. Cost Efficiency and Resource Optimization

Human red team operations can be costly and resource-intensive, especially when large-scale or frequent exercises are required. Traditional red team testing often requires a team of ethical hackers, each with specialized expertise in various attack vectors and techniques. This setup involves costs related to personnel, training, and the time spent on planning and executing the simulation. Additionally, the engagement of external consultants or security firms can add significant financial burden.

In contrast, AI-driven red team simulations reduce these costs by automating many aspects of the attack simulation process. AI models can autonomously conduct the simulations, test a variety of attack scenarios, and generate comprehensive reports on the effectiveness of the defense mechanisms. This reduces the need for large teams of human experts, enabling organizations to conduct more frequent tests at a fraction of the cost.

Moreover, AI-driven red team exercises allow organizations to optimize their resources. Rather than allocating large sums to extensive one-off red team engagements, AI-driven simulations allow for continuous, low-cost testing. This cost-effective and sustainable approach to red teaming ensures that organizations can maintain strong security postures without the financial strain of frequent manual testing.

6. Objective and Data-Driven Results

Human red teamers may sometimes introduce biases into their assessments or favor specific attack vectors based on their experience or preferences. In contrast, AI-driven simulations are inherently data-driven and objective, providing organizations with clear, quantitative insights into the effectiveness of their defenses.

AI agents evaluate a wide range of attack vectors and analyze vast amounts of system data to identify weaknesses, generating comprehensive, actionable reports. These reports often include metrics such as attack success rates, time-to-compromise, lateral movement speed, and methods used to evade detection. This objective data can help organizations understand their vulnerabilities in more concrete terms, guiding decisions on where to invest resources in defense improvements.

7. Better Incident Response Testing

AI-driven red team simulations also play a crucial role in incident response testing. By simulating complex, multifaceted cyberattacks, these simulations test not only the organization's defensive mechanisms but also its ability to respond effectively to security breaches. AI-driven simulations can trigger alerts, test incident response workflows, and assess the speed and effectiveness of defensive actions in real-time.

For example, an AI-driven red team might simulate a ransomware attack, testing how quickly the organization can detect the threat, isolate affected systems, and initiate recovery procedures. The simulation can identify weak points in the incident response plan, ensuring that the organization is better prepared to respond to actual cyberattacks.

AI-driven red team simulations offer a transformative approach to proactive cybersecurity testing. By improving the realism and complexity of attack simulations, increasing efficiency and scalability, integrating real-time threat intelligence, providing continuous learning, optimizing resources, offering objective results, and testing incident response protocols, AI is enhancing the effectiveness of red team operations. As organizations face increasingly sophisticated and persistent cyber threats, AI-driven red teaming offers a critical tool for improving defenses, identifying vulnerabilities, and ultimately building a more resilient cybersecurity posture.

8.5 Integrating Simulation Results into Defense Strategies

As the frequency and sophistication of cyberattacks continue to rise, cybersecurity teams are under constant pressure to not only identify vulnerabilities but to also enhance their ability to defend against evolving threats. Simulation results from tools like AI-driven red team exercises, penetration tests, and attack simulations provide valuable insights into the weaknesses in an organization's defenses. However, these results must be effectively integrated into defense strategies to be actionable and beneficial.

This section explores how organizations can leverage the results from attack simulations to improve their cybersecurity posture, refine their defenses, and establish a proactive, continuous cycle of improvement. By ensuring that simulation insights are not merely collected and analyzed but actively fed back into security processes, companies can create a more resilient and adaptive defense system.

1. Analyzing Simulation Results to Identify Vulnerabilities

The first step in integrating simulation results into defense strategies is analyzing the findings from red team exercises, penetration tests, or other simulated attacks. These results typically highlight areas where defenses failed or were bypassed during the simulation, such as misconfigured systems, gaps in monitoring, or human errors that facilitated the attack.

1.1 Prioritize Vulnerabilities

To make the results actionable, organizations should prioritize the identified vulnerabilities based on their potential impact. Critical vulnerabilities that could lead to severe data breaches, business disruptions, or long-term damage to the organization should be addressed first. These include zero-day exploits, privilege escalation issues, and misconfigured access controls.

Simulations often reveal defensive gaps that may not be immediately obvious through routine vulnerability scanning. For example, if a red team successfully bypasses a firewall or compromises a user account through phishing, it signals a need for a deeper analysis of how defenses could be strengthened in these areas. By prioritizing these vulnerabilities, organizations can implement the most effective countermeasures.

1.2 Review and Reproduce Attack Scenarios

Another critical aspect of integrating simulation results is the ability to reproduce the attack scenarios in real-world conditions. This allows security teams to verify how effectively they can replicate the circumstances in which the vulnerabilities were exploited. This includes reviewing attack paths, methods of compromise, and tactics used by attackers during the simulation. By testing these scenarios in a controlled environment, teams can refine their defensive measures based on concrete evidence of what went wrong.

2. Enhancing Detection and Response Mechanisms

AI-driven simulations often uncover detection failures that may have allowed an attack to progress undetected, whether through lack of visibility, inadequate threat detection systems, or ineffective incident response procedures. Integration of these findings into defense strategies is crucial for improving an organization's ability to identify and stop threats before they cause significant damage.

2.1 Fine-tuning Detection Systems

Simulations can reveal gaps in intrusion detection systems (IDS) and intrusion prevention systems (IPS), such as the failure to detect lateral movement, privilege escalation, or exfiltration of sensitive data. By analyzing the specific tactics used by the attacker during simulations, cybersecurity teams can fine-tune their detection systems to catch similar behavior in real-time.

For example, AI-driven simulations often highlight that certain attack patterns were missed by traditional signature-based detection systems. In response, security teams might adopt anomaly-based detection systems powered by machine learning, which can flag irregular behavior even when there are no known signatures for the attack. This enhances early detection and minimizes the time between compromise and response.

2.2 Strengthening Incident Response Playbooks

Simulation results also shed light on the efficiency of the incident response process. Organizations can assess whether their playbooks are effective in mitigating an attack after detection. Did the response time meet predefined goals? Were security teams able to contain the attack quickly and efficiently? Were critical actions, such as isolating compromised systems or notifying stakeholders, performed according to the plan?

By analyzing how well the response played out during simulated attacks, organizations can update and enhance their incident response plans, integrating lessons learned. For instance, if a simulated ransomware attack revealed slow containment due to poor communication or lack of coordination, the incident response playbook can be updated to address these issues, streamlining the process and minimizing the attack's impact in future events.

3. Improving Security Awareness and Training Programs

Another essential area where simulation results can make an impact is in security awareness and training programs. Simulated attacks, particularly those that focus on social engineering tactics like phishing or vishing, provide critical insights into how employees respond to these attacks and how susceptible they are to manipulation.

3.1 Addressing Human Vulnerabilities

Human error is often the weakest link in cybersecurity defenses. Attack simulations frequently reveal that employees fail to recognize phishing emails or social engineering attempts, allowing attackers to gain unauthorized access. Simulation results can identify common mistakes that need to be addressed through training, such as failing to spot suspicious email attachments, clicking on harmful links, or disclosing sensitive information under pressure.

Using these insights, organizations can tailor phishing simulations and other training exercises to focus on the specific vulnerabilities revealed in the simulations. This includes offering employees more targeted training on recognizing phishing attempts, implementing regular security awareness campaigns, and encouraging a culture of cyber vigilance. Regular simulations that mimic common attack tactics can also help employees stay alert and improve their response to potential threats.

3.2 Simulated Tabletop Exercises

In addition to automated training modules, simulations can be used to run tabletop exercises that engage employees in real-time response scenarios. These simulated tabletop exercises encourage security staff, incident responders, and leadership to work together and practice handling attacks in a controlled environment. They can be based on specific attack types revealed through red teaming and tailored to the unique risks the organization faces.

For example, a red team simulation might reveal that the organization is particularly vulnerable to a business email compromise (BEC) attack. To address this, a tabletop exercise could be organized where employees and security teams practice responding to such an attack, discussing strategies, and refining their response processes in real-time.

4. Closing Gaps in Security Architecture and Configuration

Attack simulations often expose weaknesses in an organization's security architecture and system configuration that could leave systems exposed to exploitation. These gaps can include misconfigured firewalls, weak access controls, or unpatched systems. By integrating the results of simulations into the organization's defense strategy, security teams can prioritize architectural changes and system hardening efforts.

4.1 System Patching and Hardening

Simulated attacks may reveal instances where attackers were able to exploit unpatched vulnerabilities in software or hardware. By incorporating these findings into the defense strategy, IT teams can prioritize patch management and ensure that critical updates are applied as soon as they are released. Additionally, simulations can reveal areas where systems may not be sufficiently hardened (e.g., weak default settings or excessive system privileges). These areas can then be prioritized for hardening to minimize attack surfaces.

4.2 Reviewing Access Control Policies

Simulations may also expose excessive or poorly implemented access controls, where attackers were able to escalate privileges or gain access to sensitive systems without appropriate authorization. Security teams can use these insights to review and tighten access control policies, ensuring that users only have the minimal permissions necessary to perform their duties.

5. Continuously Updating Security Posture

The process of integrating simulation results into defense strategies is not a one-time exercise but rather a continuous process. As new threats emerge, attack simulations must be regularly conducted, and security strategies must be updated to address the latest findings. This continuous feedback loop allows organizations to keep pace with evolving threats and ensures that their defenses remain strong.

By making simulation-driven security improvements an integral part of the organization's cybersecurity strategy, organizations can ensure that they are always adapting to new risks. Regular testing, review, and refinement will help organizations maintain a robust defense posture, capable of thwarting both current and future attacks.

Integrating simulation results into defense strategies is an essential practice for modern cybersecurity. By leveraging the insights gained from red team exercises, penetration tests, and AI-driven simulations, organizations can identify vulnerabilities, improve detection and response mechanisms, enhance employee training, and strengthen their overall security architecture. This integration transforms insights into actionable steps, ensuring that cybersecurity defenses evolve in step with the ever-changing threat landscape. Ultimately, by continuously improving and adapting based on simulation results, organizations can build a more resilient, proactive cybersecurity posture capable of defending against even the most sophisticated adversaries.

9. Natural Language Processing (NLP) in Phishing Detection

Phishing remains one of the most common and effective cyberattack techniques, exploiting human behavior and trust. This chapter explores how Natural Language Processing (NLP), a subset of AI, is enhancing phishing detection by analyzing and understanding the content of emails, messages, and other communication forms. Using NLP, AI can assess the linguistic features, tone, and structure of messages to identify potential phishing attempts, even those that evade traditional security filters. Readers will learn how NLP models can detect malicious links, suspicious language patterns, and impersonation tactics, providing organizations with a powerful tool to combat phishing in real time and reduce the risk of credential theft and fraud.

9.1 How NLP Works: Basics for Cybersecurity Professionals

Natural Language Processing (NLP) is a subfield of artificial intelligence (AI) that focuses on enabling computers to understand, interpret, and respond to human language in a way that is both meaningful and useful. In the context of cybersecurity, NLP can be a powerful tool for analyzing and detecting various forms of cyber threats that involve communication, such as phishing emails, social engineering attacks, and malicious communications. Understanding the fundamentals of NLP is crucial for cybersecurity professionals, as it allows them to leverage this technology to enhance threat detection, automate analysis, and improve response efforts.

This section provides an introduction to the basics of NLP, its key concepts, and its relevance to cybersecurity professionals. By understanding how NLP works, cybersecurity teams can better integrate this technology into their defense strategies and tools, such as email filtering systems, threat intelligence platforms, and automated incident response systems.

1. What is Natural Language Processing?

At its core, Natural Language Processing (NLP) is a set of computational techniques that allow machines to process and analyze human language, whether written or spoken. The goal of NLP is to bridge the gap between human communication and computer understanding. In cybersecurity, this is particularly useful for analyzing large volumes of unstructured data, such as emails, messages, logs, and social media content, to identify potential threats or malicious activities.

NLP combines various techniques from linguistics, computer science, and statistical modeling to enable machines to perform tasks like:

- Understanding syntax (structure of sentences)
- Recognizing semantics (meaning of words or phrases)
- Contextual analysis (interpreting meaning based on surrounding text)
- Text classification (sorting information into categories, such as spam detection)

Cybersecurity professionals leverage NLP to process large-scale textual data from emails, documents, and chat logs to detect and respond to suspicious activities, including phishing attempts, fraud, and other types of social engineering attacks.

2. Key Components of NLP

NLP involves several key components and techniques that enable machines to process and understand natural language. Below are some of the most important concepts that cybersecurity professionals should know when working with NLP:

2.1 Tokenization

Tokenization is the process of breaking down a stream of text into smaller units, called tokens, which are usually words, phrases, or symbols. For example, in the sentence "The quick brown fox jumps over the lazy dog," the tokens could be the individual words: "The," "quick," "brown," etc.

Tokenization is one of the first steps in any NLP process because it helps the system structure the raw text data into manageable chunks, making it easier for algorithms to process and analyze.

2.2 Part-of-Speech Tagging

Part-of-speech (POS) tagging is the process of identifying the grammatical categories of words in a sentence (e.g., noun, verb, adjective). This helps machines understand the role each word plays in a sentence, which is essential for accurately interpreting the meaning.

For example, in the phrase "Urgent action required," NLP systems would tag "Urgent" as an adjective and "action" as a noun. In the context of phishing detection, this can help to flag messages with specific language that exhibits urgency, a common tactic used in malicious emails.

2.3 Named Entity Recognition (NER)

Named Entity Recognition (NER) is a technique used to identify and classify entities in text, such as names of people, organizations, locations, dates, and other key information. For instance, in a phishing email, the names of banks, brands, or corporate titles might be identified as entities, helping to detect socially engineered attacks.

NER helps NLP systems focus on extracting relevant entities from documents, emails, and messages, which can be used to categorize threats or identify suspicious patterns in communications.

2.4 Sentiment Analysis

Sentiment analysis involves determining the sentiment or emotional tone behind a piece of text, whether positive, negative, or neutral. In cybersecurity, this can be used to detect fraudulent or threatening communications by analyzing the tone of the message. For example, a threatening email might convey urgency or hostility, which could be flagged by an NLP system as suspicious.

For example, a message that uses threatening language such as "If you don't respond immediately, we'll take legal action" may be flagged as potentially malicious due to its aggressive tone.

2.5 Contextual Understanding

Contextual understanding refers to the ability of NLP systems to interpret text based on its surrounding content, rather than treating words in isolation. This is essential for accurately interpreting ambiguous language and detecting phishing attempts or social engineering tactics. For instance, a seemingly benign phrase like "Please send your account details" may not appear harmful by itself, but when viewed in the context of an urgent request, it could indicate a phishing attempt.

Contextual NLP models, such as those based on deep learning (e.g., transformers), can capture the nuance and intent of the text in ways that traditional methods could not.

3. How NLP Enhances Cybersecurity

NLP plays an increasingly vital role in enhancing cybersecurity measures by automating and improving threat detection, analysis, and response. Here are several ways in which NLP contributes to cybersecurity:

3.1 Phishing Detection

Phishing attacks are one of the most common and successful forms of social engineering. NLP is particularly effective in identifying phishing attempts by analyzing the content of emails, messages, and web pages for suspicious patterns, such as:

- **Urgency**: Phrases like "Immediate action required," "Account suspended," or "You've won a prize" can trigger warnings.
- **Mimicking trusted sources**: NLP can detect attempts to impersonate brands or trusted entities by recognizing patterns in language or domain names.
- **Suspicious links**: NLP models can flag unusual URLs or domains embedded in email texts.

By using text classification techniques, NLP systems can automatically filter out phishing emails and prevent them from reaching end-users, thereby reducing the risk of successful social engineering attacks.

3.2 Malware Analysis

NLP can be used to analyze malware or threat intelligence reports, extracting key information from security logs, reports, and command-and-control communications. NLP helps cybersecurity teams automate the process of extracting valuable threat data from unstructured text, such as identifying IP addresses, file hashes, or malicious behavior patterns described in reports. This allows analysts to quickly assess and respond to emerging threats.

Additionally, NLP can be used in reverse engineering malware samples to automatically decode suspicious messages, commands, or signatures hidden within the text.

3.3 Threat Intelligence Processing

Threat intelligence data often comes in the form of raw, unstructured text—such as blog posts, social media updates, and email communications—that needs to be analyzed and processed. NLP can automate the extraction of relevant threat intelligence, identify trends or new vulnerabilities, and classify the data based on severity. This helps cybersecurity teams stay ahead of evolving cyber threats and respond more rapidly to emerging attacks.

For example, by analyzing text from multiple sources, NLP can help identify new malware strains, attack techniques, or vulnerabilities that may be exploited by attackers.

3.4 Automated Incident Response

NLP is increasingly being used in incident response processes to help automate the analysis and categorization of security events. When an incident occurs, NLP tools can sift through emails, logs, and other textual data to identify key events or indicators of compromise (IOCs). By parsing through large volumes of unstructured text, NLP systems help incident responders triage alerts more efficiently, quickly distinguishing between high-priority incidents and false alarms.

NLP can also be used in automated response systems, where predefined actions are triggered based on the content of an incident report. For example, if a potential ransomware attack is detected through NLP analysis of a communication, the system could automatically isolate affected systems or block suspicious IP addresses.

Understanding the basics of Natural Language Processing (NLP) is becoming increasingly important for cybersecurity professionals, as the technology plays a crucial role in identifying and mitigating cyber threats. From phishing detection and malware analysis to threat intelligence processing and automated incident response, NLP offers powerful tools to enhance cybersecurity defense mechanisms.

By mastering NLP techniques, cybersecurity professionals can better leverage this technology to identify patterns, automate threat analysis, and reduce response times, ultimately strengthening their overall security posture. As cyber threats continue to evolve, understanding how NLP works will enable cybersecurity teams to stay ahead of attackers who are using increasingly sophisticated methods to evade traditional defense mechanisms.

9.2 Using NLP to Analyze Email and Text Patterns

In the rapidly evolving cybersecurity landscape, Natural Language Processing (NLP) is emerging as a powerful tool to enhance the detection and prevention of cyber threats, especially in the context of email and text-based communications. Phishing attacks, spam, and other forms of social engineering rely heavily on text patterns to deceive users into taking malicious actions. NLP offers cybersecurity professionals an automated way to identify suspicious patterns, categorize content, and respond to these threats more effectively.

This section explores how NLP can be applied to analyze email and text patterns in order to detect phishing, spam, and other malicious activities that exploit human language for cyberattacks. Through the use of various NLP techniques such as text classification, pattern recognition, and semantic analysis, organizations can enhance their security measures and significantly reduce the risk of successful attacks.

1. Detecting Phishing with NLP

Phishing is one of the most common and successful cyberattacks that targets individuals and organizations alike. Attackers use emails, messages, and other forms of communication to deceive recipients into revealing sensitive information, such as login credentials or financial details. Traditional email filtering methods, such as keyword-based rules, often fail to detect sophisticated phishing attempts because they rely on rigid patterns that attackers can easily circumvent.

NLP helps overcome this limitation by allowing systems to analyze not just specific keywords but the entire context of an email or message. By leveraging machine learning algorithms and deep learning techniques, NLP systems can detect patterns in phishing emails that are harder for rule-based filters to recognize. Some of the ways NLP can help detect phishing emails include:

1.1 Identifying Suspicious Language and Urgency

Phishing emails often rely on urgency and emotional manipulation to prompt recipients into action, such as "Immediate action required" or "Your account has been compromised." NLP systems can be trained to identify these emotional cues by analyzing the sentiment and tone of the email. This can help flag emails that contain a sense of urgency or emotional appeal, which are common indicators of phishing.

1.2 Recognizing Impersonation Techniques

Phishers often try to impersonate trusted entities like banks, government agencies, or popular brands. NLP tools can analyze the writing style, language, and structure of the email to detect mimicry of official communication. By comparing the content of the email to a database of legitimate emails from trusted sources, NLP systems can flag emails that are trying to impersonate known entities, even if they contain no obvious signs of a scam.

1.3 Analyzing URL Patterns

Phishing emails often contain suspicious links that lead to fake websites designed to steal sensitive information. NLP can be used to analyze the text surrounding URLs in an email and flag hyperlinks that appear suspicious, based on their structure, domain names, or contextual clues. While URL analysis is not purely an NLP task, combining it with linguistic features can help improve the accuracy of phishing detection.

2. Spam Detection in Emails and Messages

Another common threat in the digital world is spam, which consists of unsolicited or unwanted messages, often for the purpose of advertising or spreading malware. Traditional spam filters may rely on simple keyword matching or blacklists, but these methods can be circumvented by attackers who change the wording or structure of the message.

NLP approaches are more effective because they analyze the entire text of the email or message, enabling the detection of patterns that indicate spam. Here's how NLP helps in detecting spam:

2.1 Text Classification and Feature Extraction

One of the primary techniques for spam detection in NLP is text classification. In this approach, a machine learning algorithm is trained on a labeled dataset of known spam and non-spam emails to classify new messages. NLP tools extract features such as keywords, word frequency, sentence structure, and tone, allowing the system to distinguish between legitimate emails and spam.

Over time, as the system is exposed to more data, it can become more adept at identifying subtle patterns that human users may overlook.

2.2 Detecting Repeated or Malicious Patterns

Spam emails often exhibit repetitive language or patterns aimed at delivering the same message to a large audience. NLP techniques like n-gram analysis and entity recognition can identify repeated phrases, common sales tactics, or suspicious URLs that are characteristic of spam campaigns. Additionally, some spam messages may be designed to trick users into clicking on malicious links or downloading harmful attachments. By detecting these patterns early, NLP systems can quarantine or filter these messages before they reach the user's inbox.

3. Detecting Social Engineering Attacks

Social engineering attacks involve manipulating individuals into divulging confidential information by exploiting human psychology. Attackers often use emails or text messages to impersonate trusted entities and trick users into clicking malicious links, downloading malware, or providing sensitive data. NLP can play a key role in analyzing text patterns to detect these attacks and prevent them from succeeding.

3.1 Analyzing Language for Deceptive Tactics

NLP can be used to identify deceptive language in emails or messages. For instance, attackers often use words that suggest urgency, authority, or alarm to pressure recipients into taking immediate action. Analyzing the text for psychological cues such as fear, pressure, or guilt can help identify emails that may be part of a larger social engineering attack.

NLP-based sentiment analysis can also help detect messages that attempt to create a sense of urgency or fear by flagging phrases like "Immediate action required," "Account locked," or "Time-sensitive." These types of psychological triggers are often used in Business Email Compromise (BEC) attacks, where an attacker impersonates a trusted executive or vendor to trick employees into wiring money or sharing sensitive information.

3.2 Identifying Impersonation in Text

In social engineering attacks, attackers often impersonate individuals the target knows, such as colleagues, friends, or company executives. NLP can be used to analyze emails and identify patterns of impersonation based on known writing styles or the use of specific names, titles, or companies. By comparing the email's tone, phrasing, and language to previous messages from the same sender, NLP systems can flag suspicious or anomalous communications that deviate from the norm.

4. Language Models and Phishing Site Detection

One of the most sophisticated applications of NLP in cybersecurity is the use of language models to detect phishing attempts through analysis of the content of phishing websites and their URLs. Attackers often create fake websites that mimic legitimate ones, using deceptive text to trick users into entering sensitive information.

NLP can help detect phishing sites by analyzing their content for signs of fraudulent behavior, such as:

- Fake product names or brand logos
- Unusual wording or sentence structure
- Mismatch between the site's language and its claimed origin

By analyzing the textual content of the website, NLP can identify inconsistencies in the language or discrepancies between the domain name and the content, flagging these websites as potential phishing attempts.

5. Building an NLP-Based Phishing and Spam Detection System

To implement an effective NLP-based phishing and spam detection system, security teams need to:

5.1 Collect and Prepare Datasets

The first step is to gather a large and diverse dataset of phishing and legitimate emails, messages, and texts. This dataset is used to train the NLP model to recognize common patterns, phrases, and structures indicative of phishing or spam.

5.2 Train and Fine-Tune NLP Models

Once the dataset is prepared, the next step is to train a machine learning model using algorithms such as logistic regression, decision trees, or neural networks. Fine-tuning the model involves adjusting parameters and continually updating it with new data to improve its accuracy over time.

5.3 Integrate with Existing Security Infrastructure

NLP-based detection systems need to be integrated with other security measures, such as email filtering, endpoint protection, and network monitoring tools. This integration ensures that suspicious messages are flagged in real-time and that response actions, such as quarantining the message or alerting security teams, can be automated.

Using Natural Language Processing (NLP) to analyze email and text patterns is an essential tool for detecting and preventing phishing, spam, and other text-based cyber threats. By analyzing the context, language, sentiment, and structure of communications, NLP systems can identify suspicious patterns that traditional security tools may overlook.

As cyberattacks become increasingly sophisticated, incorporating NLP into cybersecurity strategies can provide an additional layer of defense, helping organizations stay one step ahead of cybercriminals.

9.3 Detecting Phishing and Malicious Links with AI

Phishing attacks, often regarded as one of the most prevalent forms of cybercrime, involve the use of fraudulent communications—typically in the form of emails, SMS, or even social media messages—designed to trick individuals into divulging sensitive information such as login credentials, financial data, or personal identification. These attacks are often accompanied by malicious links that lead to fake websites mimicking legitimate ones, where unsuspecting users are prompted to enter their private information. In the digital age, where phishing techniques have evolved in sophistication, detecting and mitigating these threats has become increasingly challenging. This is where Artificial Intelligence (AI) comes into play, offering advanced tools and methodologies to combat phishing and malicious links more effectively.

In this section, we will explore how AI, through a combination of machine learning (ML), natural language processing (NLP), and other algorithms, helps to detect phishing attempts and identify malicious links with greater precision and efficiency than traditional methods.

1. Understanding the Role of AI in Phishing Detection

Phishing detection traditionally relied on keyword-based filters or blacklists that identified known malicious domains or email addresses. While these systems provide some level of protection, they are easily bypassed by sophisticated attackers who constantly alter their tactics—such as changing their messaging or using new domains and URLs. AI, on the other hand, has the capability to adapt and learn over time, improving its ability to detect new forms of phishing and malicious links as they evolve.

AI-based systems for phishing detection employ machine learning models to identify subtle patterns within the data. These models are trained on large datasets of legitimate and phishing emails, websites, and links, enabling them to generalize and identify previously unseen phishing attempts. AI uses a variety of methods to improve detection, including:

Supervised Learning: In supervised learning, a model is trained on labeled data that includes examples of both phishing and non-phishing emails or websites. Once trained, the model can predict whether new, unseen content is malicious based on the patterns it has learned.

Unsupervised Learning: In cases where labeled data is scarce, unsupervised learning techniques can be used to detect anomalies or outliers in the data, which might indicate phishing attempts. These methods can identify suspicious patterns even without explicit training on phishing content.

Deep Learning: With deep learning models, AI can analyze complex patterns and hierarchies within the data, making it particularly effective in detecting sophisticated phishing attacks, such as spear-phishing or attacks that use personalized content to deceive the target.

2. AI Techniques for Detecting Malicious Links

Phishing attacks often use malicious URLs to trick users into visiting counterfeit websites that look similar to legitimate ones, such as a fake bank login page designed to steal user credentials. AI is crucial in analyzing the structure and content of these links to determine whether they are safe or malicious. Here's how AI can help detect malicious links:

2.1 URL Analysis and Domain Classification

AI models can perform domain classification to evaluate whether a URL is linked to a known malicious domain. However, rather than relying solely on a pre-existing list of blacklisted domains, AI systems analyze various features of the URL itself, such as the domain name, path structure, query parameters, and even the length of the URL. Attackers often use slight variations of legitimate domain names or create URLs that are longer and more complex to evade detection, making it difficult for traditional methods to catch them.

AI models can analyze these features and compare them with a database of known safe and malicious domains, classifying a URL as suspicious or legitimate based on the URL's characteristics.

2.2 Machine Learning and Link Reputation

AI-powered systems can evaluate the reputation of a URL based on various signals. For instance, AI can leverage datasets of known safe or malicious URLs and use pattern recognition to identify characteristics commonly associated with malicious links. Links from newly registered domains, domains with strange character strings, or URLs with unusual patterns (such as excessive use of special characters) are often red flags.

AI systems can also evaluate historical data to assess whether the link has been previously involved in a cyberattack or if it points to a domain or IP address that has been flagged for malicious activity.

2.3 URL Content Analysis Using NLP

When users click on a link, the destination website may load various content, such as text, images, forms, and more. AI can utilize Natural Language Processing (NLP) to analyze the text content of the linked web page to determine whether it is likely to be malicious. Phishing websites often use language that mimics legitimate sites, but subtle linguistic patterns or unusual grammar can indicate a fraudulent site.

NLP algorithms can analyze the language style, tone, and semantic meaning of the content on the linked page to identify anomalies. For example, a financial institution's website should use formal, professional language, and any signs of poor grammar, improper formatting, or discrepancies in the messaging could suggest phishing activity.

3. Detecting Phishing Emails and Links in Real-Time

AI can be used to not only detect phishing emails or malicious links in advance but also to perform real-time scanning to catch phishing attempts as they happen. When an email is received or a user clicks on a link, AI-based tools can scan the message or the URL instantly, flagging suspicious elements before the user interacts with them. This can be done using real-time machine learning models that continuously evaluate incoming data and automatically respond when a threat is detected. Several key approaches include:

3.1 Real-Time URL Scanning with AI

Once an email with a link is received, AI-powered systems can scan the URL against databases of known malicious domains and use pattern recognition to detect if the link is attempting to impersonate a legitimate site. This can be done in real time, with instant alerts to users if a malicious link is detected.

3.2 Content Filtering for Phishing Emails

AI models can also analyze the content of emails to identify common phishing tactics such as spoofing, misleading sender names, or manipulative language. This real-time filtering allows email clients to block or quarantine suspicious emails before they reach the inbox, minimizing the risk of phishing attacks.

4. Leveraging AI for Phishing Prevention and User Awareness

AI doesn't just help detect phishing and malicious links—it can also be used to prevent these attacks from succeeding by providing enhanced user awareness and training. AI systems can offer real-time warnings when a user is about to click a suspicious link or visit a potentially dangerous website, helping to reinforce security best practices and reduce human error.

Additionally, AI-powered training programs can simulate phishing scenarios, educating users on how to recognize suspicious links and avoid falling victim to social engineering attacks. By analyzing a user's behavior and email history, AI can personalize training and recommend actions for improving awareness based on their specific risks.

5. Building a Comprehensive Phishing Detection System with AI

To effectively combat phishing attacks, organizations can integrate AI-driven phishing detection and malicious link identification into a comprehensive security system. This system should include the following components:

5.1 Continuous Learning and Model Updates

AI models should be continuously trained with new phishing data, as attackers evolve their tactics regularly. By implementing a feedback loop, AI systems can be updated with new phishing patterns and incorporate user feedback to improve accuracy over time.

5.2 Integration with Existing Security Infrastructure

AI-powered phishing detection can be integrated with existing cybersecurity infrastructure, such as email filters, web gateways, and endpoint protection solutions, to provide a layered defense against phishing attacks.

5.3 Real-Time Threat Intelligence Sharing

AI systems can be connected to global threat intelligence feeds, enabling real-time sharing of malicious URLs, phishing tactics, and attack patterns across organizations and industries. This ensures that AI models are constantly exposed to new threat intelligence, enhancing their ability to detect emerging phishing techniques.

Phishing and malicious links remain a significant threat in the digital landscape, but AI is a powerful tool in the fight against these attacks. Through the use of machine learning, natural language processing, and real-time scanning, AI can help detect phishing attempts and malicious links with higher accuracy and efficiency than traditional methods. By continuously evolving and adapting to new phishing tactics, AI systems not only protect users from the most common threats but also provide a more proactive and automated defense against phishing and malicious links in today's increasingly sophisticated cyberattack environment.

9.4 Preventing Voice Phishing (Vishing) with AI Solutions

Voice phishing, or vishing, is a rapidly growing threat in the cybersecurity landscape, where attackers attempt to deceive individuals into revealing sensitive personal information, such as credit card numbers, passwords, or Social Security numbers, over the phone. These attacks often involve spoofed phone numbers or AI-generated voices that impersonate legitimate entities such as banks, government agencies, or even family members. With the rise of sophisticated AI tools, vishing has become a more challenging threat to detect and prevent, as attackers can now mimic human speech patterns and voices with alarming accuracy. In this section, we will explore how AI solutions can be used to prevent and detect vishing attacks, enhancing both individual and organizational security.

1. Understanding Voice Phishing and Its Techniques

Vishing attacks typically involve phone calls or voicemails that aim to manipulate or coerce victims into sharing confidential information. Cybercriminals may impersonate a variety of trusted sources, such as bank representatives, tech support agents, or law enforcement officers, often employing fear-based tactics to persuade individuals to take immediate actions, like transferring funds or disclosing passwords.

Vishing is particularly dangerous because it preys on human psychology, leveraging trust in the voice as a communication medium. While traditional phishing relies on emails or texts, vishing targets the voice, making it harder to identify malicious activity until it's too late. Recent advancements in voice synthesis technologies and the use of AI tools like deepfake voices make it even more difficult for victims to differentiate between legitimate and fraudulent calls.

2. AI-Powered Voice Recognition for Detection and Prevention

AI solutions offer powerful tools to combat vishing by identifying and analyzing suspicious voice patterns and detecting anomalies in the tone, cadence, and content of the call. Several AI-driven techniques are being used to detect and prevent voice phishing in real-time:

2.1 Voice Biometrics and Authentication

One of the most effective AI-driven techniques for preventing vishing attacks is voice biometrics. By analyzing an individual's unique voice features—such as pitch, tone, cadence, and speech patterns—voice biometrics can verify whether the person on the phone is truly who they claim to be. This technology is already being implemented by financial institutions, healthcare providers, and customer service departments to authenticate users during phone-based transactions or interactions.

Voice biometric systems can capture a person's vocal characteristics and create a voiceprint, a unique digital representation of their voice. This voiceprint is then used as a form of authentication, ensuring that the caller is legitimate. During a potential vishing attack, AI can immediately flag or block calls from unauthorized voices, preventing attackers from successfully impersonating trusted figures.

2.2 Anomaly Detection in Speech Patterns

AI can also be used to detect anomalies in speech patterns and identify potential threats based on specific characteristics of the call. In typical vishing scams, attackers may exhibit unnatural speech behaviors, such as using overly scripted dialogue, a sense of urgency, or hesitation. AI algorithms can analyze these speech patterns and flag them as suspicious.

For example, AI-powered systems can analyze:

- **Speech cadence**: Natural speech patterns have a rhythm and flow that AI can recognize. Suspicious or forced speech, such as unnatural pauses or robotic intonations, can trigger alerts.

- **Voice inconsistencies**: With AI, systems can identify voice modulation, such as changes in tone or voice inconsistencies, that may suggest the voice is being altered or synthesized by deepfake technologies.
- **Contextual and linguistic analysis**: AI tools can also analyze the context and language used in conversations. For instance, if the caller is making unusually vague requests or urging the victim to act in a hurry, the system can flag the call as suspicious.

3. Real-Time AI-Driven Call Monitoring and Filtering

In addition to post-call analysis, AI solutions can provide real-time monitoring and filtering of voice-based interactions to prevent vishing attacks from occurring in the first place. By leveraging advanced natural language processing (NLP) and speech-to-text technologies, AI systems can transcribe phone calls in real-time, making it easier to analyze and identify potentially fraudulent behavior.

These systems can automatically scan incoming calls and identify suspicious phrases or patterns in the conversation. For example, if the caller is asking for sensitive information like bank account details or passwords, the AI system can recognize these patterns and alert the recipient of the potential threat. Additionally, AI can block or redirect suspicious calls before the attacker can complete their objectives.

3.1 Intelligent Call Screening and Blocking

AI-powered call screening systems can flag and block suspicious phone numbers before they reach the target. These systems can work in conjunction with Caller ID spoofing detection technology to prevent attackers from masking their true identity. If a call is flagged as a potential vishing attempt, the system can automatically reject it or direct it to a secure platform for further verification.

3.2 Integration with Voice-Based Authentication Systems

AI-powered voice authentication systems can also be integrated into existing phone networks or customer service platforms to authenticate callers before they can interact with the system. For example, a user calling into a bank might be asked to provide a spoken passphrase or authentication code that the system can verify. If the call is determined to be fraudulent, it can be blocked before any personal information is revealed.

4. AI-Enhanced Detection of Deepfake Voices

One of the major challenges in combating vishing attacks is the rise of deepfake voices, generated through AI technologies. These voices can convincingly mimic a real person's voice, making it nearly impossible for humans to detect deception without advanced analysis tools. However, AI is also capable of identifying these synthetic voices.

4.1 Deepfake Voice Detection Algorithms

AI systems can use advanced algorithms to analyze and detect signs of voice synthesis in real-time. These algorithms focus on inconsistencies that may be imperceptible to human ears but are noticeable to machines, such as unnatural speech pauses, unnatural tonal variations, or overly consistent modulation. By analyzing these anomalies, AI can flag the call as suspicious and prevent it from succeeding.

4.2 Forensic Audio Analysis

Forensic audio analysis is another AI-driven technique used to detect deepfake voices in vishing calls. By examining the underlying audio features of the voice—such as waveforms, frequency spectrums, and compression patterns—AI can identify synthetic voices that do not have the same natural qualities as real human speech. This technology can provide strong evidence to distinguish a deepfake voice from a legitimate one, significantly improving the accuracy of vishing detection.

5. Enhancing Consumer Awareness and Preventive Measures

In addition to technical defenses, AI solutions can be leveraged to educate consumers about vishing risks and encourage proactive self-protection. AI-driven systems can deliver:

- Personalized security alerts to warn individuals about common vishing tactics, helping users recognize suspicious calls.
- Interactive AI chatbots to assist individuals in reporting and verifying potential vishing calls in real-time, enhancing their awareness.
- AI-powered mobile apps that provide consumers with a platform to block suspected vishing calls, share threat intelligence, and receive real-time fraud alerts.

By using AI in combination with educational initiatives, individuals can better identify vishing attacks and respond to them appropriately.

Vishing is a significant and growing threat that takes advantage of human trust and the inherent nature of voice communication. AI solutions, however, offer an array of tools to effectively prevent and detect vishing attacks. Through voice biometrics, speech anomaly detection, real-time call monitoring, and deepfake voice detection, AI can significantly reduce the risks associated with vishing and protect individuals and organizations from falling victim to these deceptive attacks. As vishing evolves and attackers adopt increasingly sophisticated tactics, AI will play a central role in defending against these threats, providing an advanced, automated, and proactive approach to securing voice-based communications.

9.5 Case Studies: Real-World NLP Applications in Cybersecurity

Natural Language Processing (NLP), a subfield of artificial intelligence (AI), has seen transformative applications across various industries, and cybersecurity is no exception. With the increasing complexity of cyber threats, leveraging NLP in the fight against cybercrime has provided organizations with powerful tools for automating threat detection, analyzing vast amounts of unstructured data, and enhancing security measures. NLP helps in understanding, interpreting, and generating human language, making it especially useful in identifying threats hidden in emails, documents, chat messages, and other forms of communication.

In this section, we will explore several real-world case studies that illustrate the application of NLP in cybersecurity. These case studies highlight how organizations have successfully employed NLP technologies to detect phishing attempts, automate threat intelligence, identify malicious content, and safeguard their digital environments.

1. Case Study: Phishing Detection in Email Systems

Overview: Phishing remains one of the most significant cyber threats today, with attackers using emails to deceive users into disclosing sensitive information like login credentials, personal details, or financial data. The growing sophistication of phishing attempts, especially spear-phishing (targeted attacks), means that traditional rule-based filters often fail to detect the subtle cues of fraudulent messages.

NLP Application: A large financial institution implemented an NLP-based phishing detection system to combat phishing emails. The system analyzes email content, looking for anomalous language patterns that are indicative of phishing attempts, such as:

- **Urgency cues**: Phrases like "Immediate action required," "Account suspended," or "Click here to verify" are common in phishing emails, aiming to rush recipients into taking action without critical thinking.
- **Deceptive language**: Phishing emails often contain subtle inconsistencies in tone, grammar, or phrasing that can be flagged by NLP systems.
- Suspicious hyperlinks: NLP algorithms analyze embedded URLs and identify suspicious patterns that may link to phishing sites.

The NLP system was trained on a dataset of known phishing emails, learning from previous attack patterns. It leverages classification models to categorize incoming emails as legitimate or suspicious. Emails identified as phishing are automatically flagged and routed for further review or blocked before reaching users' inboxes.

Results:

- The financial institution reported a 30% reduction in successful phishing attempts.
- The system's ability to learn from emerging threats helped the organization stay ahead of new phishing tactics.
- The use of NLP helped reduce the burden on human analysts by automating the detection of potentially harmful emails.

2. Case Study: Detecting Malicious Content in Social Media

Overview: Social media platforms are a popular target for cybercriminals, who use them to spread malicious content, launch phishing attacks, and recruit users for scams. The challenge for security teams is the massive volume of unstructured data generated daily, making it difficult to manually monitor every post, message, or comment for malicious activity.

NLP Application: A global social media platform deployed an NLP-based content moderation system to detect and filter harmful or malicious content in real-time. The system analyzes posts, comments, and private messages for various indicators of cyber threats, including:

- **Phishing links**: The NLP system scans messages for suspicious URLs, such as shortened or obfuscated links, which could redirect users to fraudulent websites.
- **Toxic or threatening language**: NLP algorithms detect phrases commonly associated with social engineering attacks, bullying, harassment, or fraud.

- **Suspicious patterns in user behavior**: NLP models can detect patterns of anomalous behavior such as a user sending out a high volume of identical messages (a tactic used in phishing scams).

The system uses a combination of text classification and sentiment analysis to differentiate between benign and potentially malicious content. Additionally, NLP is used to track patterns in language that evolve with the changing tactics of cybercriminals.

Results:

- The system successfully identified malicious accounts, such as fake profiles spreading phishing links or recruitment messages for scams.
- A significant reduction in cyberbullying incidents and financial scams was reported.
- The ability to detect malicious content in real-time prevented attacks before they could spread to a wider audience.

3. Case Study: Automating Threat Intelligence with NLP

Overview: Threat intelligence involves collecting, analyzing, and disseminating information about potential or existing threats to a network or system. The vast amount of unstructured data generated from blogs, news articles, social media, and dark web forums makes it challenging for security teams to manually sift through and extract valuable intelligence.

NLP Application: A cybersecurity firm developed an NLP-powered threat intelligence platform that automates the process of gathering and analyzing data from a variety of sources, including dark web forums, social media platforms, and threat reports. The platform uses several NLP techniques, such as:

- **Named Entity Recognition (NER):** This technique identifies and extracts entities (e.g., names, IP addresses, malware names) from unstructured text, allowing the system to gather specific pieces of information related to emerging threats.
- **Topic modeling**: The platform uses NLP algorithms to cluster related topics, such as newly discovered vulnerabilities or attack campaigns, allowing analysts to quickly identify and prioritize emerging threats.
- **Sentiment analysis**: The system can detect the tone and intent behind threat actor communications, such as the sentiment of discussions around a new zero-day vulnerability or a potential targeted attack.

By automating the analysis of threat data using NLP, the platform provides real-time intelligence that helps organizations quickly adapt their security posture to emerging threats.

Results:

- The firm's threat intelligence platform was able to automatically process and analyze millions of documents per day, saving analysts significant time.
- The automated system helped identify zero-day vulnerabilities and attack indicators much faster, allowing organizations to take proactive measures.
- Security teams reported a 40% improvement in the speed at which they identified and responded to cyber threats.

4. Case Study: Detecting Insider Threats with NLP in Enterprise Environments

Overview: Insider threats, where employees or contractors intentionally or unintentionally cause harm to an organization's digital assets, are a significant concern. Detecting insider threats is often difficult due to the lack of outwardly malicious behavior. Anomalous communication patterns and subtle shifts in language can serve as indicators of potential insider threats, but identifying these changes requires advanced analysis of internal communications.

NLP Application: A global technology firm implemented an NLP-based system to analyze employee communications (emails, chat logs, and internal reports) for signs of potential insider threats. NLP is used to:

- **Detect anomalous language patterns**: Employees exhibiting signs of frustration, resentment, or dissatisfaction may express these emotions in emails or messages, potentially indicating a higher risk of committing an insider attack.
- **Monitor for signs of malicious intent**: NLP models are trained to detect suspicious conversations that might indicate planning an attack or sharing sensitive information inappropriately.
- **Behavioral analysis:** NLP helps in identifying employees who are sending unusually high volumes of sensitive data or engaging in risky activities.

By using NLP to monitor employee communication, the organization could identify warning signs of potential insider threats before they escalated into major incidents.

Results:

- The system detected potential insider threats based on changes in language and communication patterns, such as an employee requesting access to unauthorized data or exhibiting signs of frustration toward the company.
- Early detection allowed the firm to intervene before any major damage occurred, leading to a 60% reduction in the number of insider threats.
- The system also improved overall employee behavior awareness by flagging risky actions before they could lead to breaches.

5. Case Study: Automated Malware Analysis with NLP

Overview: Cybersecurity teams often face challenges in manually analyzing the increasing volume of malware samples, each with its own signature or behavior. Automating the identification and classification of malware can be a complex task, especially when malware authors use obfuscation techniques to hide their code's true nature.

NLP Application: A leading cybersecurity firm employed an NLP-driven malware analysis system to analyze malware samples in real-time. The system leverages NLP techniques such as:

- **Text mining and feature extraction**: The system uses NLP to extract relevant keywords from malware-related communications (e.g., forum posts, hacking manuals, and malware descriptions) to understand the tactics, techniques, and procedures (TTPs) of attackers.
- **Clustering and classification**: NLP tools are used to classify malware samples based on their language features (e.g., suspicious code structures, function calls) and group similar samples together for faster analysis.
- **Behavioral analysis**: By analyzing the commands and scripts within malware, NLP systems can predict the malware's intent and classify it accordingly.

By integrating NLP with malware analysis workflows, the cybersecurity firm significantly enhanced its ability to respond to new threats faster.

Results:

- The system reduced manual malware analysis time by 50% and identified new variants of malware that had evaded traditional detection methods.
- The automated system flagged malicious code based on contextual language, improving detection rates of evasive malware techniques.

- The firm was able to stay ahead of rapidly evolving malware trends, providing faster response times and more effective threat mitigation.

These case studies illustrate how Natural Language Processing (NLP) is becoming an indispensable tool in modern cybersecurity. From detecting phishing attempts and malicious content to automating threat intelligence and insider threat detection, NLP enables organizations to manage and mitigate the growing complexity of cyber threats in real time. As cybercriminals continue to evolve their tactics, the integration of NLP into cybersecurity strategies will play a crucial role in maintaining effective digital defense systems.

10. AI in Malware Detection and Reverse Engineering

As cyber threats become more sophisticated, traditional malware detection methods often struggle to identify novel or polymorphic malware. This chapter explores how AI and machine learning are revolutionizing malware detection and reverse engineering by enabling systems to recognize previously unknown threats based on their behavior rather than relying solely on signature-based detection. Using deep learning and anomaly detection techniques, AI can analyze vast amounts of code and identify malicious patterns, even in zero-day vulnerabilities. Additionally, AI aids in the reverse engineering process, automating the dissection of malware to understand its functionality and origins. Readers will discover how these AI-driven methods improve the speed, accuracy, and effectiveness of malware defense, making them essential tools in the fight against modern cyber threats.

10.1 Identifying Malware Using AI-Based Signatures

Malware has evolved significantly over the years, becoming more sophisticated and capable of evading traditional detection methods. Traditional methods of malware detection typically rely on signature-based techniques, which compare the characteristics of files to known malware signatures. While effective against known threats, signature-based detection struggles with identifying new or polymorphic malware, which changes its appearance to evade detection. To address these challenges, Artificial Intelligence (AI) is being used to improve malware detection, particularly through the development of AI-based signatures.

AI-based malware detection represents a significant leap forward by allowing security systems to not only detect known threats but also identify new, previously unseen malware. These AI-based signatures are not based on exact file matches but rather on the underlying patterns of behavior, structure, and characteristics found within malware. AI systems can analyze large datasets of files, classify their features, and learn from these characteristics to create dynamic signatures that evolve over time, increasing detection accuracy.

How AI-Based Signatures Work

AI-based signatures are built through the application of machine learning (ML) and other AI techniques. These systems process large volumes of data, extracting relevant features from both benign and malicious files to develop models that can identify malware based on patterns or behaviors instead of exact matches. Here's how AI-based signatures typically work:

Data Collection and Feature Extraction: AI-based malware detection starts by collecting a large set of data containing both malware and clean files. This data could include executable files, system logs, or even metadata. AI systems extract features that may not be immediately visible to traditional signature-based methods, such as API calls, file structures, file sizes, code sequences, and behavioral patterns. For example, malware might exhibit unusual file manipulation, network traffic patterns, or other abnormal behaviors that AI can detect.

Model Training: Once the features are extracted, machine learning models are trained to recognize patterns within the data. A supervised learning model might be trained on labeled data, where files are tagged as "malicious" or "benign." The AI system uses this training data to understand the differences between malware and non-malicious files. It learns to generalize based on these patterns, creating an AI signature or model that can detect malware without relying on exact matches.

Anomaly Detection: In addition to recognizing known malware signatures, AI systems are often used in anomaly detection. Instead of simply matching a file's characteristics to an existing malware signature, the AI system identifies deviations from expected behavior or normal patterns within a file or system. For example, if a file attempts to encrypt large portions of the system unexpectedly or attempts to access sensitive system resources, it could be flagged as anomalous. This approach is particularly effective in identifying new, unknown malware.

Continuous Learning: One of the key benefits of AI-based malware detection is its ability to learn and adapt. As new malware is discovered, AI systems can be retrained with updated data to recognize emerging threats. This continuous learning process helps ensure that AI-based malware detection systems remain effective even as malware authors use advanced obfuscation and evasion techniques to avoid detection. AI systems can even flag malware variants that may share common behaviors or characteristics, helping to build a more robust database of AI signatures.

Dynamic Signatures: Unlike traditional signature-based systems, AI-based signatures are dynamic, meaning they can evolve over time based on the data the AI models are exposed to. As malware changes its form or modifies its behavior, AI models can adapt to these changes without requiring new signatures to be manually created. This dynamic adaptability is one of the main advantages over static signature-based methods, as it allows AI systems to respond faster to new and emerging threats.

Advantages of AI-Based Malware Detection

The use of AI-based signatures in malware detection offers several significant advantages over traditional methods:

Detection of Unknown Malware: One of the most important benefits of AI-based malware detection is its ability to identify previously unseen malware. Traditional signature-based methods rely on known patterns and definitions, so they cannot detect new, zero-day threats until they are added to the signature database. In contrast, AI-based systems can analyze the behaviors or characteristics of files and classify them as malicious based on learned patterns, even if they have never been encountered before.

Higher Accuracy and Lower False Positives: AI-based malware detection systems often achieve higher accuracy compared to traditional methods because they rely on advanced pattern recognition rather than exact matches. By analyzing the behavior and features of files, AI can distinguish between legitimate applications and malware more effectively. This results in fewer false positives, which are common with traditional signature-based detection systems. By reducing false alarms, AI systems allow security teams to focus their efforts on genuine threats.

Evasion Resistance: Malware developers often use techniques such as polymorphism (changing the file's appearance) or metamorphism (completely rewriting code to avoid detection). Traditional signature-based methods often struggle with these tactics because the malware can look different with each attack. However, AI-based systems analyze behavioral traits and structural patterns, making them more resistant to evasion tactics. Even if malware modifies its code, the AI model can still detect the underlying malicious behavior.

Speed and Scalability: AI-based systems can process and analyze vast amounts of data far more quickly than humans or traditional methods. This enables real-time malware detection across multiple endpoints, networks, and devices. AI systems can also scale more efficiently, allowing them to handle the growing volume and complexity of malware samples. This scalability ensures that even as attack surfaces increase with the proliferation of IoT devices, cloud computing, and mobile technologies, AI-powered detection systems can keep up.

Continuous Improvement and Adaptability: AI-based malware detection systems have the ability to evolve over time. As they encounter new data, they can retrain themselves to improve detection capabilities, ensuring they stay ahead of evolving malware tactics. This continuous learning process helps AI systems remain effective as new malware strains emerge, without requiring manual updates to the system's signature database.

Challenges of AI-Based Malware Detection

Despite its advantages, there are some challenges that come with implementing AI-based malware detection:

Data Quality and Quantity: For AI models to be accurate, they require high-quality and large datasets for training. Inadequate or unbalanced datasets could lead to poor performance, especially in detecting new or rare malware variants. Additionally, collecting and labeling large amounts of data for training can be resource-intensive and time-consuming.

Complexity and Interpretability: AI models, especially deep learning models, can be highly complex, making them difficult to interpret. This lack of transparency, often referred to as the "black-box" problem, can be a concern for organizations looking to understand why certain files were flagged as malicious. In a security context, understanding the reasoning behind a detection is important for both trust and compliance.

Adversarial Attacks: Like all machine learning models, AI-based malware detection systems are vulnerable to adversarial attacks. Malware developers could use techniques that deliberately manipulate AI systems by introducing slight changes in the data to trick the model into misclassifying it. Developing more robust models that can resist such attacks is an ongoing challenge in the AI field.

Resource Requirements: AI models, particularly deep learning models, can be resource-intensive to train and deploy. They require significant computational power and memory, which can be a challenge for organizations with limited infrastructure. However, cloud-based AI solutions are increasingly mitigating this issue by providing scalable resources on demand.

AI-based signatures represent a significant step forward in the detection of malware, offering several advantages over traditional signature-based methods. By leveraging machine learning and advanced pattern recognition, AI systems are able to detect both known and unknown malware with higher accuracy and efficiency. While there are challenges associated with implementing AI-based detection systems, such as data quality and adversarial attacks, the potential benefits make them an invaluable tool for modern cybersecurity defense strategies. As malware continues to evolve, AI-driven solutions will play an increasingly important role in safeguarding digital environments.

10.2 Behavioral Detection with Deep Learning Models

As cyber threats become more sophisticated, the limitations of traditional signature-based detection methods have become increasingly apparent. These conventional approaches rely on matching malware or attack signatures with known threats, which can be ineffective against new, unknown, or polymorphic malware that changes its appearance to evade detection. To counter this, behavioral detection powered by deep learning models is emerging as an advanced and powerful method for identifying malicious activities in real-time.

Behavioral detection focuses on identifying abnormal or suspicious activities by analyzing the behavior of files, applications, users, or systems, rather than relying on the characteristics of specific files or known attack signatures. This approach has become particularly effective in detecting previously unseen malware, zero-day vulnerabilities, and insider threats, which can exploit vulnerabilities before security teams have a chance to create specific signatures. Deep learning, a subset of machine learning, plays a pivotal role in advancing behavioral detection by enabling systems to autonomously learn complex patterns and behaviors without explicit human intervention.

How Deep Learning Models Enable Behavioral Detection

Deep learning models are a class of artificial intelligence algorithms that excel at identifying intricate patterns in large datasets. These models are based on artificial neural networks, particularly deep neural networks (DNNs), which consist of multiple layers that allow the model to process and analyze data at various levels of abstraction. For behavioral detection, deep learning models are trained to recognize normal and abnormal behaviors by analyzing large volumes of system or network data, such as process activities, system calls, file operations, network traffic, or user actions.

Here's how deep learning models work for behavioral detection:

Data Collection and Feature Extraction: Behavioral detection relies on continuous monitoring of user activity, system behavior, and network traffic. This data can include a wide variety of inputs, such as system logs, file access patterns, CPU usage, network traffic logs, or user login behaviors. Once data is collected, deep learning models can automatically extract meaningful features from this raw information. For example, they may identify specific patterns like unusual API calls, abnormal sequences of file accesses, or spikes in CPU usage that could signal a potential security incident.

Training the Model: Deep learning models are trained using a large dataset that includes both normal (benign) behavior and known malicious behavior. The system learns to differentiate between these behaviors through supervised or unsupervised learning techniques. During the training process, the deep learning model builds a complex understanding of what constitutes "normal" behavior based on the data it is provided, allowing it to detect deviations from this baseline that might indicate malicious activity.

Detection of Abnormal Behavior: Once trained, the deep learning model can be used in real-time environments to monitor system activities and flag behaviors that significantly deviate from the baseline. For instance, if a system typically experiences moderate file access during working hours but suddenly experiences a large number of read/write operations at odd times, the model might classify this as suspicious activity. Similarly, an unusually high volume of network traffic or abnormal system calls could trigger alerts for further investigation.

Anomaly Detection: A key aspect of behavioral detection is anomaly detection, where deep learning models identify actions that are statistically unusual or different from the established pattern. The model might not necessarily know whether a particular action is explicitly malicious, but it can flag it as an anomaly that warrants closer inspection. The ability to detect zero-day attacks, where no signature or prior knowledge exists, is one of the strengths of deep learning-based behavioral detection.

Continuous Learning and Adaptation: One of the most powerful aspects of deep learning for behavioral detection is its ability to learn continuously. As new data becomes available and threats evolve, deep learning models can adapt to these changes by retraining themselves, adjusting to new patterns of behavior. This dynamic learning ability allows deep learning systems to maintain high detection accuracy as attackers modify their tactics to evade detection.

Advantages of Behavioral Detection with Deep Learning

Deep learning-powered behavioral detection systems offer several significant advantages over traditional security approaches, particularly in terms of detecting sophisticated, novel, or evasion-based attacks.

Detection of Unknown Threats: Traditional signature-based systems rely on previously known malware signatures to detect attacks. However, they are ineffective against zero-day threats (previously unknown vulnerabilities) or polymorphic malware that constantly changes its code. Deep learning models, on the other hand, focus on the behavior of the malware rather than its signature. By detecting deviations from the norm, deep learning models can identify previously unseen threats, making them invaluable for identifying new attack techniques and tactics.

Reduction of False Positives: Deep learning models are designed to learn and adapt to the unique baseline behavior of each system or user. This helps to reduce the occurrence of false positives (benign activities incorrectly flagged as malicious). By distinguishing between legitimate deviations and genuine attacks, deep learning models can make more accurate assessments and provide a more reliable indication of malicious behavior.

Real-Time Detection: Deep learning models can analyze data in real-time, providing near-instantaneous detection of suspicious or malicious activities. This real-time analysis enables immediate response to potential threats, reducing the window of opportunity for attackers. Whether it's detecting unusual file access, abnormal network traffic, or suspicious login patterns, deep learning models can quickly identify potential attacks and notify security teams to take appropriate action.

Adaptation to Evolving Threats: Cybercriminals are constantly evolving their techniques to evade traditional detection methods. Deep learning models are capable of adapting to new behaviors and attack methods. As attackers deploy new tactics, deep learning models can recognize and learn from these changes, ensuring that the detection system remains relevant and capable of identifying emerging threats.

Improved Response Times: Because deep learning models can continuously analyze data and adapt in real-time, they can significantly improve response times to cyber threats. Instead of relying on manual rule updates or signature additions, which can take time, deep learning-based behavioral detection systems provide automated responses to potential threats, enabling quicker mitigation and containment of attacks.

Applications of Behavioral Detection with Deep Learning

The applications of behavioral detection using deep learning models extend across various domains of cybersecurity, including:

Endpoint Security: On individual devices, deep learning models can monitor user and application behavior to detect anomalous activities indicative of malware, ransomware, or unauthorized access attempts. By continuously analyzing file activity, system resource usage, and user actions, the model can identify malicious behaviors that might indicate a breach, even if no specific malware signature exists.

Network Traffic Analysis: Behavioral detection can be applied to network traffic to monitor for unusual patterns, such as data exfiltration, lateral movement, or command-and-control (C&C) communications. Deep learning models can flag abnormal network activity, such as unexpected connections to external servers, or large data transfers, as potential indicators of a cyberattack.

Insider Threat Detection: One of the most challenging threats to detect is insider threats, where employees or contractors intentionally or unintentionally cause harm to the organization. Behavioral detection powered by deep learning can help identify abnormal behavior, such as unauthorized access to sensitive data, unusual file transfers, or an employee's actions deviating from their normal routine. By detecting anomalies in their work patterns, deep learning models can highlight potential insider threats early in the attack cycle.

Fraud Detection: In industries like finance or e-commerce, deep learning-based behavioral detection is useful for identifying fraudulent activities. By analyzing transactional data, spending patterns, and user behavior, deep learning models can flag unusual or suspicious activities that deviate from a user's normal behavior, helping to prevent financial fraud and identity theft.

Challenges of Behavioral Detection with Deep Learning

Despite its many advantages, there are some challenges associated with implementing deep learning-based behavioral detection systems:

High Computational Requirements: Deep learning models require significant computational power, especially when processing large volumes of data in real-time. This can be resource-intensive and may require specialized hardware such as GPUs to process and analyze data efficiently.

Data Privacy Concerns: Behavioral detection often requires continuous monitoring of users' activities, which can raise privacy concerns. Balancing security with privacy regulations such as GDPR and CCPA is essential, and organizations must implement measures to ensure data is handled appropriately while maintaining effective behavioral detection.

Model Interpretability: One challenge with deep learning models is their "black-box" nature, meaning that the decision-making process of the model can be difficult to understand. For security teams to trust and act on the model's findings, it is important that they can interpret why the model flagged certain activities as anomalous or malicious.

Behavioral detection powered by deep learning represents a significant advancement in the cybersecurity landscape, offering real-time detection, reduced false positives, and the ability to identify unknown and evolving threats. By focusing on the behavior of systems, applications, and users, deep learning models provide a robust defense against sophisticated attacks, including zero-day threats and insider threats. While there are challenges to overcome, such as computational requirements and model interpretability, the potential benefits make deep learning an essential tool in modern cybersecurity strategies. As cyber threats continue to evolve, deep learning will play a central role in securing digital systems and data against increasingly complex adversaries.

10.3 Automating Malware Analysis Workflows

Malware analysis is a critical aspect of cybersecurity that involves examining suspicious files or software to understand their behavior, origins, and potential impact on systems. Traditionally, malware analysis has been a manual and time-consuming process, requiring skilled security experts to inspect and reverse-engineer malware samples. However, with the rapid increase in the volume and sophistication of malware, it has become clear that traditional, manual methods are no longer sufficient to detect and mitigate emerging threats in real time. To address this challenge, automating malware analysis workflows using artificial intelligence (AI) and machine learning (ML) has become a vital strategy for cybersecurity professionals.

Automated malware analysis leverages advanced AI techniques to streamline and accelerate the process of detecting, analyzing, and responding to malware threats. By utilizing AI-powered systems, cybersecurity teams can reduce the time required to identify and mitigate malware, minimize human error, and gain deeper insights into new and unknown threats. In this section, we will explore how automated workflows are transforming the field of malware analysis and the various technologies and techniques involved.

Key Components of an Automated Malware Analysis Workflow

An automated malware analysis workflow typically involves several key stages that allow for the efficient detection, analysis, and classification of malware. These stages often work together to quickly identify new threats, understand their behavior, and enable prompt mitigation.

Collection and Preparation of Malware Samples: The first step in the automated analysis workflow is the collection of malware samples. This can be done through various channels, such as security vendors, honeypots, threat intelligence feeds, or samples submitted by users or security researchers. Once collected, these malware samples need to be prepared for analysis, which involves extracting relevant metadata and ensuring that they are appropriately categorized for further analysis.

Automation's Role: Automation tools can streamline the sample collection process, ensuring that malware samples are continuously collected, classified, and prepared without manual intervention. This enables the system to process a high volume of malware samples in a short period of time.

Dynamic Analysis in a Sandbox Environment: Dynamic analysis refers to executing the malware sample in a controlled environment (a sandbox) to observe its behavior during runtime. This is a critical stage of the analysis as it allows security experts to monitor how the malware interacts with the system—what files it modifies, what network connections it attempts to make, and what processes it starts.

Automation's Role: AI-powered sandbox environments can automatically execute the malware, track its activities in real time, and generate detailed reports on its behavior. These reports can highlight key indicators of compromise (IoCs), such as changes in the file system, registry modifications, network traffic, or attempts to exploit vulnerabilities. Automated systems can even simulate a range of operating systems and applications, enabling the analysis of malware across different environments without manual intervention.

Static Analysis: Static analysis involves examining the malware's code without executing it. This can be done through reverse engineering, looking at the binary, inspecting the metadata, and searching for known patterns or signatures. Static analysis helps identify the structure of the malware, the coding language used, and potential indicators such as hardcoded IP addresses, URLs, or encryption keys.

Automation's Role: Automated tools can analyze malware code at scale, using predefined algorithms to identify suspicious patterns, compare it to existing malware signatures, and match it to known malware families. Machine learning algorithms can also be trained to recognize unusual coding patterns or identify novel threats based on historical data. By automating static analysis, security teams can rapidly identify potential threats without needing to manually reverse engineer each sample.

Malware Classification and Threat Intelligence Integration: After the malware's behavior and code are analyzed, the next step is to classify the sample and determine its threat level. This often involves comparing the malware to a library of known threats or malware families and using advanced AI techniques to detect similarities between known and unknown malware. This helps to assign risk levels to each malware sample and prioritize it for further investigation or mitigation.

Automation's Role: AI-based malware classification systems can use unsupervised machine learning to identify new types of malware that do not match known signatures but exhibit similar behavior to known threats. By clustering malware samples based on their behavior or features, automated systems can detect previously unknown malware, assign it to a threat family, and integrate the findings into threat intelligence platforms for rapid response.

Reporting and Alerting: Once the malware analysis is complete, automated systems generate detailed reports that summarize the findings and provide actionable insights. These reports typically include information about the malware's origin, the vulnerabilities it exploits, the techniques it uses to persist or spread, and any IoCs that can be used for detection or prevention. Automated systems can also trigger alerts or responses based on predefined rules, such as isolating an infected machine or blocking a malicious URL.

Automation's Role: Automation speeds up the reporting process, ensuring that security teams receive real-time alerts and reports. These reports can be integrated into security information and event management (SIEM) systems, enabling security analysts to correlate malware activity with other security events and respond faster.

Benefits of Automating Malware Analysis Workflows

The automation of malware analysis offers several key benefits, enabling organizations to enhance their threat detection and response capabilities.

Faster Detection and Response: Automated malware analysis drastically reduces the time it takes to analyze and respond to threats. With automated workflows, malware samples are analyzed in real time, allowing security teams to quickly detect new and emerging threats and respond proactively. This is especially critical in the case of zero-day threats, where timely detection and containment can prevent widespread damage.

Increased Scalability: The volume of new malware strains is growing exponentially, and manually analyzing each sample would be impractical. Automation enables organizations to scale their malware analysis efforts to handle a larger volume of samples without overwhelming their security teams. AI-powered systems can process thousands of samples simultaneously, ensuring that new threats are identified and analyzed quickly.

Reduced Human Error: Manual malware analysis is prone to human error, especially when dealing with large volumes of data or complex malware samples. By automating the process, organizations can eliminate the risk of oversight or misclassification. AI systems are highly consistent and can analyze malware based on predefined parameters, ensuring that no critical indicators are missed.

Improved Accuracy and Efficiency: AI and machine learning models can continuously improve their performance by learning from new malware samples. This leads to more accurate analysis and more efficient workflows over time. Automated systems can also reduce the number of false positives, as they learn to distinguish between benign behavior and genuine threats.

Enhanced Threat Intelligence: Automated malware analysis workflows contribute to building and enhancing threat intelligence databases by continuously updating them with new malware samples and IoCs. This provides organizations with up-to-date information about emerging threats and improves the overall detection and prevention capabilities of their cybersecurity infrastructure.

Technologies Enabling Automated Malware Analysis

Several technologies play a key role in enabling the automation of malware analysis:

Machine Learning (ML): Machine learning models, especially supervised and unsupervised learning, are used to identify patterns in malware behavior and classify new samples based on their similarity to known threats. These models can be trained on vast datasets of malware samples, enabling them to predict new malware families or detect zero-day threats.

Deep Learning: Deep learning algorithms, particularly convolutional neural networks (CNNs) and recurrent neural networks (RNNs), are used for analyzing complex data such as malware code, network traffic, and system behavior. These models can automatically extract features and learn deep representations of malware, enabling more accurate detection and classification.

Sandbox Environments: Virtualized environments or sandboxes are used to execute malware samples safely and analyze their runtime behavior. Automation can ensure that these sandboxes are set up and torn down quickly, allowing malware to be analyzed in isolated environments without human intervention.

Threat Intelligence Platforms: Automated malware analysis systems often integrate with threat intelligence platforms to share new insights, signatures, and IoCs with other security tools in real-time. This ensures that security defenses across the organization are continuously updated with the latest threat information.

Challenges and Considerations

While automating malware analysis brings numerous benefits, it also presents challenges, including:

Evasion Tactics: Malware authors are increasingly aware of automated analysis tools and may use evasion tactics, such as delays in execution or anti-sandbox techniques, to avoid detection. Automated systems must be equipped to handle such tactics and adapt accordingly.

Resource Intensiveness: Running automated malware analysis workflows, especially for large datasets, requires substantial computational resources. Organizations must ensure they have sufficient infrastructure to support these workflows.

Accuracy of Machine Learning Models: Automated systems rely on machine learning models that need to be continuously updated and trained with new data. Ensuring that these models are accurate and able to detect emerging threats is essential for the success of automated malware analysis.

Automating malware analysis workflows is a game-changer in the fight against cyber threats. By leveraging AI and machine learning, organizations can process large volumes of malware samples quickly, reduce human error, and improve the accuracy of threat detection and response. As cyber threats become more complex and dynamic, automation will play an increasingly important role in keeping systems secure. Through automated malware analysis, organizations can enhance their overall cybersecurity posture and stay ahead of the rapidly evolving threat landscape.

10.4 AI-Powered Reverse Engineering Tools

Reverse engineering is a crucial discipline in cybersecurity that involves deconstructing software or malware to understand its structure, functionality, and behavior. This technique is often used to uncover vulnerabilities, identify malicious code, and discover attack vectors within systems. However, traditional reverse engineering methods require skilled professionals to manually analyze complex code and software, which can be time-consuming, error-prone, and resource-intensive. In the context of increasingly sophisticated cyber threats, such as malware and advanced persistent threats (APTs), this manual process is no longer sufficient to keep pace with the scale and speed of attacks.

AI-powered reverse engineering tools are transforming the way cybersecurity professionals approach this critical task. By integrating artificial intelligence (AI) and machine learning (ML) into the reverse engineering process, these tools automate and accelerate the analysis of malicious software, improving the efficiency, accuracy, and scalability of reverse engineering workflows. This section explores how AI-powered reverse engineering tools work, the benefits they offer, and how they can help cybersecurity professionals tackle the challenges of analyzing and mitigating advanced threats.

How AI-Powered Reverse Engineering Tools Work

AI-powered reverse engineering tools leverage machine learning algorithms, data analysis techniques, and pattern recognition to automate the process of disassembling and analyzing software. These tools can perform a wide range of functions, including code analysis, decompilation, dynamic behavior analysis, and anomaly detection. Below, we'll delve into how AI enhances various aspects of reverse engineering:

Automated Code Analysis: Traditional reverse engineering often involves manually reviewing assembly code, decompiled source code, and binary files to identify code structures, functions, and vulnerabilities. AI-powered tools can analyze these code elements automatically, detecting patterns, instructions, and function calls that indicate malicious intent or unusual behavior. Machine learning algorithms can be trained to recognize specific malware behaviors or exploit patterns, reducing the need for human intervention.

AI's Role: Using supervised and unsupervised learning models, AI tools can classify code segments, identify suspicious code patterns, and flag known malware signatures. These systems continuously improve their detection capabilities as they analyze new malware samples, learning to identify novel threats even if they have not been encountered before.

Decompilation and Decompiled Code Understanding: Decompilation is the process of converting machine-readable code (such as binary or executable files) into a human-readable source code format. AI-powered reverse engineering tools can enhance decompilation by improving the accuracy of converting complex binaries into high-level programming languages, making it easier for security experts to understand the functionality of malware.

AI's Role: Deep learning models, particularly neural networks, can help automate decompilation by predicting and converting lower-level machine instructions into higher-level language constructs, making the process faster and more accurate. This allows security analysts to understand how malware behaves and what actions it performs once executed.

Dynamic Analysis in Sandboxes: Dynamic analysis involves running malware in a controlled environment (sandbox) to observe its behavior during execution. AI tools can enhance dynamic analysis by automatically detecting and analyzing behavioral patterns such as file modifications, registry changes, network activity, or system calls. This is particularly useful for analyzing polymorphic or obfuscated malware that may change its structure during execution to avoid detection.

AI's Role: AI systems can monitor and analyze real-time behavior, generating detailed reports on malware actions and identifying previously unseen indicators of compromise (IoCs). Machine learning algorithms can also recognize when malware uses anti-debugging, anti-virtualization, or evasion techniques and adapt their analysis strategies to bypass these defenses.

Anomaly Detection in Reverse Engineering: In traditional reverse engineering, analysts look for known signatures or specific patterns of malicious behavior. However, this approach can miss new or highly obfuscated threats that do not match any known signatures. AI can address this by focusing on anomaly detection—identifying deviations from normal system behavior or code structures.

AI's Role: By leveraging unsupervised learning and outlier detection algorithms, AI-powered reverse engineering tools can spot anomalous code or behavior that may not be immediately recognizable as malicious but could still pose a threat. AI can detect new attack techniques, even when they don't follow typical patterns seen in known malware families.

Automated Vulnerability Discovery: One of the primary goals of reverse engineering is to discover vulnerabilities within a piece of software or system. AI-powered tools can assist in this process by automatically identifying potential vulnerabilities in code, such as buffer overflows, race conditions, or logic flaws. These vulnerabilities can be exploited by cybercriminals to gain unauthorized access to systems or execute malicious payloads.

AI's Role: Using machine learning models, AI tools can recognize vulnerable code snippets that are prone to exploitation, even if they are not explicitly listed in known vulnerability databases. AI can also prioritize vulnerabilities based on their potential impact, allowing security teams to focus on the most critical issues first.

Benefits of AI-Powered Reverse Engineering Tools

AI-powered reverse engineering tools offer several key advantages over traditional reverse engineering methods, making them indispensable in modern cybersecurity.

Increased Speed and Efficiency: Manual reverse engineering is a time-consuming process, often requiring hours or even days to analyze a single malware sample. AI tools can automate many aspects of this process, reducing the time needed for analysis and enabling cybersecurity teams to analyze thousands of malware samples quickly. This is especially important in environments where rapid detection and response are crucial to preventing large-scale breaches.

Scalability: The sheer volume of malware and potential threats that organizations face requires a scalable approach to reverse engineering. AI-powered tools can handle large datasets and analyze many samples in parallel, providing security teams with scalable solutions to detect and respond to threats across an entire organization or network.

Enhanced Detection of Unknown and Novel Threats: AI algorithms are adept at identifying patterns that may not be immediately obvious to human analysts, especially when it comes to previously unknown or polymorphic malware. Through continuous learning, AI-powered tools can detect new malware families or previously unseen attack methods, enhancing the overall detection capabilities of reverse engineering.

Improved Accuracy: While traditional reverse engineering relies heavily on the expertise and experience of human analysts, AI tools offer a high degree of consistency and accuracy in their analyses. Machine learning models are less prone to human error, and AI systems can analyze malware in a repeatable, objective manner, reducing the risk of missed threats or misidentification.

Reduction of Human Resource Burden: Reverse engineering is a highly specialized task that requires skilled cybersecurity experts. AI-powered tools can automate many aspects of reverse engineering, freeing up human analysts to focus on higher-level tasks, such as interpreting results, responding to incidents, or developing proactive security measures. This allows cybersecurity teams to allocate their resources more effectively and improves the overall efficiency of threat detection efforts.

Challenges and Considerations

Despite the many advantages, there are challenges and considerations when using AI-powered reverse engineering tools:

Evasion Techniques: Malware authors are aware of AI-powered detection methods and often employ evasive tactics, such as obfuscation, polymorphism, or anti-sandbox techniques, to avoid detection. AI tools need to be constantly updated and trained to recognize these techniques, making continuous learning and adaptation a key requirement for success.

Data Privacy and Security Concerns: Automated reverse engineering tools may require access to sensitive data or files, raising concerns about data privacy and the risk of leaks or inadvertent exposure. Organizations need to ensure that reverse engineering processes are carried out in secure environments with strict access controls.

Model Accuracy and False Positives: While AI tools can improve the efficiency and accuracy of reverse engineering, they are not infallible. Machine learning models may still generate false positives or misclassify certain malware, especially when dealing with highly obfuscated or sophisticated attacks. Human oversight is still necessary to validate the results of AI-driven analyses.

AI-powered reverse engineering tools represent a significant advancement in the field of cybersecurity. By automating and enhancing key aspects of reverse engineering, these tools enable faster, more accurate detection and analysis of malware, improving the overall effectiveness of cybersecurity defenses. As cyber threats become increasingly complex, AI-powered tools will continue to play a crucial role in identifying and mitigating risks before they can cause significant damage. While challenges remain, the potential for AI to revolutionize reverse engineering processes offers an exciting path forward in the battle against malicious software and cybercriminals.

10.5 Case Studies of AI in Zero-Day Exploit Prevention

Zero-day exploits represent one of the most critical threats in the cybersecurity landscape. These are vulnerabilities in software that are unknown to the vendor or security community, meaning there are no patches or defenses available when they are first discovered. Once discovered by attackers, zero-day exploits can be used to infiltrate systems, steal sensitive data, or disrupt operations. The ability to prevent or mitigate zero-day attacks is a major challenge for cybersecurity professionals. However, AI-powered solutions are proving to be invaluable in identifying and stopping these threats before they can cause significant damage.

In this section, we will explore several case studies that illustrate how artificial intelligence has been effectively used to detect and prevent zero-day exploits, highlighting the significant role that AI plays in modern cybersecurity.

Case Study 1: AI-Based Vulnerability Detection in Web Applications

In this case study, a large financial institution was facing persistent threats from zero-day vulnerabilities in their web applications. The organization was using traditional security tools, such as intrusion detection systems (IDS) and firewalls, to protect its infrastructure. However, despite these measures, sophisticated attackers were able to exploit unpatched vulnerabilities in their web applications.

To address this, the organization adopted an AI-driven approach using behavioral analysis and anomaly detection to identify potential zero-day exploits in real time. A machine learning model was trained to detect anomalous patterns in web traffic that deviated from the typical behavior of legitimate users.

How AI Prevented Zero-Day Exploits: The AI system used a combination of supervised and unsupervised learning algorithms to analyze normal user behavior and establish baselines for the web application's traffic. By continuously monitoring the network and user interactions, the AI system was able to flag abnormal activities, such as unauthorized access attempts, unusual data requests, and attempts to exploit known vulnerabilities.

When the AI detected unusual traffic patterns indicative of a zero-day exploit, it triggered an immediate alert and automatically blocked the potentially harmful traffic. This enabled the organization to prevent an attack that could have led to a significant data breach, despite the vulnerability being previously unknown.

Outcome: The implementation of AI-based vulnerability detection significantly improved the organization's ability to prevent zero-day exploits in real-time. By leveraging machine learning algorithms to analyze large amounts of traffic and recognize patterns indicative of potential exploits, the financial institution could respond faster and more accurately than with traditional methods.

Case Study 2: AI-Powered Endpoint Protection for Zero-Day Malware

A leading software company that developed enterprise resource planning (ERP) software faced repeated threats from zero-day malware that targeted vulnerabilities in their application suite. The company had tried traditional antivirus solutions and endpoint detection systems but struggled to prevent sophisticated attacks that exploited unpatched vulnerabilities in their software.

To combat this, the company decided to implement an AI-powered endpoint protection solution. The new system leveraged machine learning and deep learning to analyze and detect potential zero-day malware behaviors, even in cases where signatures or known patterns of the malware were not available.

How AI Prevented Zero-Day Exploits: The AI endpoint protection system worked by analyzing the behavior of every process running on the endpoints in real-time. Using behavioral analysis, the system could identify suspicious activities that were out of the ordinary for the environment, such as unusual file access patterns or attempts to exploit unpatched vulnerabilities.

When a new form of malware attempted to exploit an unpatched vulnerability on the endpoint, the AI system detected its malicious behavior before it could execute a damaging payload. Instead of relying on known malware signatures, the system was able to identify malware based on its behavior, which allowed it to detect novel zero-day exploits.

Outcome: The AI-powered endpoint protection solution successfully blocked several zero-day malware attacks, providing a significant improvement over traditional endpoint protection tools. The ability to detect malicious behavior without relying on known signatures ensured that the software company was protected against new and evolving threats.

Case Study 3: AI in Network Traffic Analysis for Zero-Day Exploit Detection

A major healthcare provider was experiencing an increasing number of zero-day exploit attempts against its network infrastructure. These exploits targeted vulnerabilities in the company's web servers and cloud applications, but since the vulnerabilities were unknown, the security systems couldn't provide protection.

The healthcare provider implemented an AI-driven network traffic analysis system that used unsupervised machine learning models to detect anomalies in the network. The system analyzed millions of data points related to network traffic, including packet size, source/destination IP addresses, protocols used, and the volume of traffic, to detect abnormal behavior that could indicate a zero-day exploit.

How AI Prevented Zero-Day Exploits: The AI system used deep learning algorithms to learn the normal traffic patterns across the network. Over time, the system became adept at recognizing subtle deviations from this baseline, such as unusual port scanning activity or requests for resources that were out of character for the users' typical activities.

When a zero-day exploit was attempted, the attackers used encrypted traffic and sophisticated evasion techniques to bypass traditional signature-based systems. However, the AI system detected the abnormal traffic pattern associated with the exploit and blocked the attack before it could infiltrate the healthcare provider's systems.

Outcome: By incorporating AI into their network traffic monitoring system, the healthcare provider successfully identified and prevented multiple zero-day exploit attempts, including several that had bypassed traditional security defenses. The AI system's ability to detect anomalous behaviors in real-time was key to preventing these attacks.

Case Study 4: AI and Zero-Day Detection in Cloud Environments

A global e-commerce company operating a large cloud infrastructure was concerned about the increasing threat of zero-day vulnerabilities in the cloud services they used. Attackers were actively searching for vulnerabilities in the cloud applications and infrastructure, and the organization needed a proactive solution to prevent potential zero-day attacks.

The company deployed an AI-based cloud security solution that combined machine learning with real-time vulnerability scanning and dynamic behavior analysis. The AI system was designed to identify unusual behavior across the cloud infrastructure, such as irregular resource usage, unauthorized access attempts, and deviations in cloud service interactions.

How AI Prevented Zero-Day Exploits: AI models continuously monitored the interactions between cloud applications, services, and users. When the AI system detected irregularities in cloud traffic or behavior that might be linked to an unpatched vulnerability, it immediately flagged the activity as a potential zero-day exploit. The system would then cross-reference known attack patterns with its behavior models to determine if the activity was indicative of a zero-day threat.

In one instance, the AI system detected an abnormal spike in requests to a specific API endpoint. The behavior was consistent with an attack attempting to exploit a vulnerability in a widely-used cloud service. The AI system was able to block the exploit in real-time, preventing the attackers from gaining access to sensitive data.

Outcome: By using AI to monitor and analyze cloud interactions, the e-commerce company successfully mitigated the risk of zero-day exploits. The AI-powered solution was able to identify zero-day threats in a rapidly changing cloud environment, significantly enhancing the organization's overall cybersecurity posture.

These case studies highlight the effectiveness of AI-powered systems in detecting and preventing zero-day exploits across various environments. By leveraging machine learning, deep learning, and behavioral analysis, AI systems can identify unknown vulnerabilities and malicious behavior, providing an essential layer of defense against sophisticated cyberattacks. As zero-day exploits continue to evolve, the use of AI in cybersecurity is proving to be a critical component in securing systems, networks, and data from emerging threats. With continuous improvements in AI technologies, we can expect even more powerful and adaptive defense mechanisms against the growing threat of zero-day attacks.

11. Securing IoT with Machine Learning

The Internet of Things (IoT) has introduced unprecedented connectivity, but it has also significantly expanded the attack surface, making IoT devices a prime target for cybercriminals. This chapter explores how machine learning (ML) is playing a crucial role in securing IoT ecosystems by monitoring, detecting, and responding to threats in real-time. Machine learning algorithms can analyze data from millions of IoT devices, identifying unusual behavior, network anomalies, or unauthorized access attempts that might otherwise go undetected. Readers will learn how ML models can help safeguard these devices by continuously learning from new data, improving their ability to predict and prevent attacks as the IoT environment evolves. With IoT security challenges growing rapidly, this chapter provides practical insights into how ML can be leveraged to build resilient and adaptive security systems for the interconnected world.

11.1 The Unique Challenges of IoT Security

The Internet of Things (IoT) has revolutionized the way we interact with the world, enabling devices ranging from everyday household objects like refrigerators and thermostats to critical infrastructure components such as industrial machinery and healthcare equipment to connect to the internet and each other. This growing network of interconnected devices offers immense convenience, efficiency, and innovation, but it also introduces a host of unique security challenges. As IoT devices proliferate in both consumer and industrial sectors, securing these devices and their communications becomes increasingly difficult and critical to ensuring safety, privacy, and operational continuity.

In this section, we explore the distinctive security challenges associated with the IoT ecosystem, explaining why traditional cybersecurity measures often fall short and outlining the impact these challenges can have on organizations and individuals.

1. The Vast and Diverse Attack Surface

One of the most significant challenges in securing IoT environments is the vast and diverse attack surface. IoT devices come in all shapes, sizes, and functionalities, from simple sensors that monitor temperature or humidity to complex systems like autonomous vehicles and connected healthcare devices. The sheer number and variety of these devices create a challenge for security professionals, as they must secure a wide range of hardware, operating systems, and communication protocols that were often designed without robust security in mind.

Challenges:

- **Variety of Devices**: IoT encompasses everything from small embedded sensors to large, complex devices with varying capabilities and operating systems. This diversity makes it difficult to implement standardized security protocols across the entire ecosystem.
- **Limited Device Resources**: Many IoT devices have limited processing power, memory, and storage, which restricts the ability to implement advanced security measures like encryption, anomaly detection, or regular updates.
- **Impact**: As IoT expands across different sectors, this heterogeneous environment creates opportunities for attackers to exploit weak points. Even a small device with minimal computing resources can act as an entry point to larger systems, potentially compromising the entire network.

2. Lack of Standardization and Security Protocols

Unlike traditional IT systems, which typically operate on standardized platforms and protocols, IoT devices often lack consistent security standards. The lack of standardization in device design, communication protocols, and security practices across manufacturers creates vulnerabilities that hackers can exploit.

Challenges:

- **Proprietary Protocols**: Many IoT devices use proprietary or non-standard communication protocols that may not have been designed with security in mind. This can lead to vulnerabilities that are difficult to identify and patch.
- **Inconsistent Security Practices**: IoT manufacturers are often focused on functionality and cost efficiency, with security being an afterthought. As a result, many devices come with hardcoded credentials, weak or no encryption, and minimal security features, making them prime targets for cyberattacks.
- **Impact**: The absence of universally accepted security protocols in IoT devices increases the risk of exploitation, as vulnerabilities in one device can lead to cascading security failures across the network.

3. Device Authentication and Identity Management

Another critical challenge in IoT security is device authentication and identity management. In traditional IT networks, identity management is relatively straightforward—users and devices are authenticated using usernames, passwords, and certificates. However, in an IoT environment, there are often thousands or millions of devices that need to be securely authenticated to ensure that they are legitimate and not being spoofed by attackers.

Challenges:

- **Scale of Authentication**: The sheer number of IoT devices means that traditional methods of authentication, such as password-based systems or certificate management, become unwieldy. The ability to manage the identities of countless devices in real-time is a significant security hurdle.
- **Device Spoofing and Impersonation**: IoT devices are susceptible to impersonation attacks where an attacker mimics the identity of a trusted device to gain unauthorized access. This is especially concerning in environments like healthcare or industrial control systems where device authenticity is paramount.
- **Impact**: Weak or poorly implemented authentication mechanisms can open the door for attackers to impersonate legitimate devices, allowing them to execute malicious commands, exfiltrate data, or cause service disruptions.

4. Insecure Communication Channels

IoT devices often communicate with one another and with central servers over networks that may not be secure, making them vulnerable to eavesdropping, man-in-the-middle attacks, and data tampering. In many cases, IoT devices use open or unsecured communication protocols, which expose them to interception by malicious actors.

Challenges:

- **Unencrypted Communication**: Many IoT devices send data over unencrypted channels or use weak encryption, which can be intercepted by attackers to steal sensitive information or inject malicious code.
- **Man-in-the-Middle (MitM) Attacks**: Without proper encryption and authentication, IoT devices are vulnerable to MitM attacks, where an attacker intercepts and potentially alters the communication between devices or between a device and its cloud server.
- **Impact**: If communication channels are compromised, attackers can intercept sensitive data, alter device behaviors, or inject malicious commands that could

have catastrophic consequences, especially in critical systems like industrial automation or healthcare.

5. Limited Device Lifecycle Management and Updates

One of the most critical challenges in IoT security is ensuring that devices remain secure throughout their lifecycle. Many IoT devices are deployed with minimal or no capability for receiving firmware or software updates, which means that once a vulnerability is discovered, it often remains unpatched, making the device a target for attackers.

Challenges:

- **Limited Update Capabilities**: Many IoT devices are designed for simplicity and long-term use, but they often lack mechanisms for securely receiving and installing software or firmware updates.
- **Abandoned Devices**: Some IoT devices are no longer supported by their manufacturers after a few years, meaning that vulnerabilities in these devices remain unpatched indefinitely, providing an open door for attackers.
- **Vulnerable to Exploits**: If a device has known vulnerabilities and is not regularly updated, attackers can exploit these weaknesses, taking control of the device or using it as a point of entry to other systems.
- **Impact**: The inability to update IoT devices or the lack of ongoing support from manufacturers creates long-term security risks. As new vulnerabilities are discovered, unpatched devices become easy targets for exploitation.

6. Privacy Concerns and Data Protection

As IoT devices collect vast amounts of data—often including sensitive personal or business information—they raise significant privacy concerns. Many IoT devices, especially in consumer and healthcare sectors, gather information about users' habits, locations, and behaviors, which makes them prime targets for attackers seeking to steal this data.

Challenges:

- **Data Storage and Transmission**: IoT devices often store and transmit personal data, sometimes in an unencrypted form, which increases the risk of exposure during a data breach.
- **Lack of Data Anonymization**: Many IoT devices fail to anonymize the data they collect, making it more difficult to ensure that personal information is protected.

- **Impact**: Privacy breaches resulting from insecure IoT devices can have severe consequences, including identity theft, financial losses, and damage to an organization's reputation.

7. Difficulty in Implementing Centralized Security

IoT ecosystems are often highly decentralized, with devices distributed across different locations, environments, and networks. The lack of centralized security management makes it difficult to monitor, respond to, and mitigate security incidents in a unified manner.

Challenges:

- **Decentralized Nature**: IoT devices are frequently deployed in diverse locations, from smart homes to industrial sites, which makes centralized monitoring and control challenging.
- **Integration Issues**: IoT devices often operate in isolation from one another, using a variety of communication protocols and data formats, making it difficult to implement centralized security policies and controls.
- **Impact**: A decentralized IoT network increases the complexity of managing security at scale. Without centralized management and visibility, security teams may struggle to detect and respond to threats in real-time.

Securing IoT devices is an ongoing challenge due to their vast diversity, limited resources, and the growing complexity of their networks. As IoT continues to proliferate, it is essential that organizations adopt a multi-layered approach to IoT security, incorporating encryption, secure communication protocols, strong authentication, regular updates, and centralized management to mitigate risks. Addressing these unique security challenges requires collaboration between manufacturers, security professionals, and end users to develop and implement effective security solutions that can keep up with the rapid pace of innovation in the IoT space. Without these measures, the vulnerabilities inherent in IoT devices will continue to expose both consumers and organizations to significant security risks.

11.2 Using AI to Identify and Isolate Threats in IoT Networks

As the number of connected devices in the Internet of Things (IoT) ecosystem continues to grow, so do the security challenges. The interconnected nature of IoT networks, coupled with the sheer number of devices involved, makes them an attractive target for cybercriminals. These devices—ranging from simple sensors to complex machines—are often vulnerable to a variety of cyber threats, including unauthorized access, data breaches, and malware attacks. Due to the limitations in processing power and memory on many IoT devices, traditional security approaches often fall short in securing these devices. This is where Artificial Intelligence (AI) can play a transformative role in identifying, responding to, and mitigating threats within IoT networks.

In this section, we will explore how AI-powered systems are revolutionizing IoT security by enabling the identification and isolation of threats in real-time, effectively enhancing the protection of IoT environments.

1. Real-Time Threat Detection in IoT Networks Using AI

One of the most powerful ways AI is enhancing IoT security is through real-time threat detection. Traditional methods of threat detection, such as signature-based approaches, are less effective in dynamic and diverse IoT environments because they rely on pre-existing knowledge of attack patterns. IoT devices are constantly evolving, and new attack methods emerge regularly, making it challenging for signature-based systems to keep up.

AI-based solutions, particularly those using machine learning (ML) and deep learning (DL), offer a more adaptive and intelligent approach to threat detection. These systems can analyze large volumes of data from IoT devices and identify patterns that may indicate potential threats, such as unusual behavior, unauthorized access, or even zero-day attacks.

How AI Detects Threats:

- **Anomaly Detection**: AI systems continuously monitor the behavior of IoT devices, building a baseline of normal activity. Any deviation from this baseline, such as unusual data flows, unexpected communication patterns, or sudden changes in device activity, is flagged as potentially malicious.
- **Behavioral Profiling**: AI can create profiles for each device based on its typical behaviors. This enables it to detect irregularities such as a device trying to access resources it normally wouldn't, indicating a potential breach or compromise.
- **Pattern Recognition**: By leveraging machine learning algorithms, AI can identify patterns associated with known and unknown threats by analyzing historical attack data, making it capable of detecting novel attack types.
- **Example**: A smart thermostat in an IoT-enabled smart home typically sends data about temperature changes to a central hub. If the thermostat begins sending data at an unusually high rate, or starts transmitting information outside the home

network, an AI-powered security system would flag this activity as anomalous, prompting a closer inspection to determine whether the device has been compromised.

2. Automated Threat Isolation and Containment

Once a threat is detected, the next critical step is to isolate and contain it to prevent further damage or lateral movement across the network. In traditional IoT security systems, this process often requires manual intervention from security teams, which can be slow and error-prone, especially in large and complex networks.

AI can automate the process of threat isolation by using predefined rules and algorithms to quickly isolate compromised devices or sections of the network. This helps mitigate the risk of spreading the attack and minimizes damage by removing the affected devices from the network in real time.

How AI Isolates Threats:

- **Automated Response**: AI systems can be programmed to automatically take action when a threat is detected, such as cutting off network access to a device or segmenting it from the rest of the network. This minimizes response time and reduces the need for human intervention.
- **Segmentation**: By using AI, IoT networks can be dynamically segmented based on the threat level. Devices that exhibit suspicious activity can be isolated to a quarantined zone where they are unable to communicate with other critical systems until they have been properly assessed.
- **Self-Healing Networks**: Some AI-driven systems can not only detect and isolate threats but also take steps to self-heal the network. For instance, if a vulnerability is exploited, the system may automatically apply patches or reconfigure affected devices to restore them to a secure state.
- **Example**: In a large industrial IoT network, an AI-powered security system might detect that an industrial robot is behaving abnormally, trying to access unauthorized systems. The AI would immediately isolate the robot from the network, preventing any potential damage or data leakage, while security teams are alerted to investigate further.

3. Predictive Threat Modeling and Proactive Threat Prevention

One of the most exciting applications of AI in IoT security is its ability to go beyond reactive threat detection and offer predictive threat modeling. Using historical attack data and machine learning algorithms, AI can model and predict potential threats before they occur, allowing organizations to take a proactive approach to security.

How AI Predicts Threats:

- **Behavioral Predictions**: By analyzing vast amounts of data, AI can predict how certain IoT devices might behave under various conditions. If a device starts exhibiting behavior that aligns with patterns seen in past cyberattacks, the AI system can flag it as a potential threat, even if the attack hasn't happened yet.
- **Threat Intelligence Integration**: AI systems can integrate with external threat intelligence platforms to continuously learn about new attack techniques and evolving threat actors. This allows AI to predict and prepare for future threats based on emerging trends in cybercriminal tactics.
- **Example**: An AI-powered system may predict a potential attack on a fleet of connected medical devices based on emerging vulnerabilities in similar devices across the industry. The AI system might automatically update the device configurations or block specific ports to prevent exploitation, even before the attack materializes.

4. Enhanced Network Security Through AI-Driven Traffic Analysis

In many IoT environments, devices communicate over a network using various communication protocols. However, IoT devices often generate an overwhelming amount of traffic, making it difficult for security systems to differentiate between normal and malicious activity. AI can address this challenge by providing more advanced traffic analysis techniques that go beyond simple packet inspection.

How AI Enhances Traffic Analysis:

- **Deep Packet Inspection**: AI systems can use deep packet inspection (DPI) techniques to analyze the contents of data packets, looking for signs of malicious activity, such as exploit attempts, malicious code, or unusual patterns that could indicate a cyberattack.
- **Contextual Awareness**: AI algorithms can correlate data from multiple devices and communication channels to provide a more holistic view of the network. This context helps to identify threats that may be hidden in plain sight by linking events from different parts of the network that wouldn't be detected in isolation.
- **Example**: In an industrial IoT network, AI-powered systems can monitor traffic between machines, sensors, and control systems. If a machine starts sending unusually large data packets to a remote server, AI can flag this as suspicious

activity and isolate the device before it can exfiltrate sensitive data or spread malware.

5. Continuous Learning and Adaptation to Emerging Threats

One of the greatest strengths of AI in IoT security is its ability to continuously learn and adapt to new threats. Unlike traditional security systems, which often require manual updates and tuning, AI systems can improve their detection and response capabilities over time by incorporating new data and insights. This makes them highly effective at combating emerging and evolving threats in the fast-paced world of IoT.

How AI Continuously Learns:

- **Machine Learning**: AI systems can use machine learning models to continuously learn from new data, improving their detection accuracy and responsiveness to novel threats. The more data the system is exposed to, the better it becomes at identifying patterns and anomalies.
- **Model Refinement**: AI systems can be retrained with fresh datasets to adapt to new attack vectors or changes in device behavior. This allows the system to stay ahead of evolving threats in the dynamic world of IoT.
- **Example**: A smart city's IoT network that manages traffic lights, surveillance cameras, and environmental sensors can use AI to continuously monitor traffic patterns and sensor data. Over time, the AI system will refine its detection capabilities to identify not only technical threats like DDoS attacks but also anomalous behaviors, such as unauthorized access attempts to the traffic control systems.

The unique challenges of securing IoT networks require advanced, adaptive, and scalable solutions that can keep up with the dynamic nature of the Internet of Things. Artificial intelligence offers a powerful toolset for IoT security, providing real-time threat detection, automated isolation of threats, predictive threat modeling, advanced traffic analysis, and continuous adaptation to emerging threats. As the IoT landscape expands, AI's role in ensuring the integrity and security of these interconnected devices will only grow, providing essential protection for critical systems and sensitive data in an increasingly connected world. By harnessing the power of AI, organizations can enhance their IoT security posture and stay ahead of the ever-evolving cybersecurity challenges posed by IoT environments.

11.3 Real-Time Data Analysis from IoT Devices with ML

As the number of devices in the Internet of Things (IoT) continues to grow, the volume of data generated by these devices increases exponentially. In this highly connected world, ensuring the real-time security and efficiency of IoT networks has become a paramount concern. With thousands or even millions of devices transmitting data continuously, it's no longer feasible to rely on traditional methods of analyzing data in batches or on static datasets. Instead, Machine Learning (ML) has emerged as a powerful solution to help businesses and organizations analyze IoT device data in real-time, providing rapid insights and enabling timely responses to threats, anomalies, and inefficiencies.

In this section, we'll explore how ML algorithms are used for real-time data analysis in IoT environments, focusing on their applications for threat detection, predictive maintenance, performance monitoring, and anomaly identification.

1. Real-Time Anomaly Detection and Threat Identification

In any IoT network, one of the biggest challenges is to quickly identify and respond to potential security threats, such as unauthorized access, data breaches, or system intrusions. Traditional cybersecurity systems often struggle with the volume and complexity of the data IoT devices generate. However, ML algorithms can be applied to detect anomalous behaviors in real time, flagging any abnormal activity that could indicate a security breach.

How ML Improves Threat Detection in IoT:

- **Dynamic Baselines**: ML algorithms can learn normal behavior patterns of IoT devices by analyzing historical data. As new data flows in, the system continuously compares the current device behavior with the learned baseline, identifying deviations that could signal a potential threat.
- **Pattern Recognition**: Machine learning models, particularly those based on unsupervised learning methods, can identify complex patterns in large datasets, even when those patterns are indicative of subtle threats. For example, ML algorithms can identify when a device starts sending out unusual traffic or communicates with an unrecognized IP address, signaling a possible compromise.
- **Intrusion Detection Systems (IDS):** ML-based Intrusion Detection Systems (IDS) can analyze the data stream of connected IoT devices to flag potential security issues, such as unauthorized access attempts or the presence of malware. As these systems continuously learn from new data, they improve in detecting even the most sophisticated threats over time.

- **Example**: In an industrial IoT network, machines like PLC (Programmable Logic Controllers) and robotic arms continuously communicate with central control systems. If one of the devices begins transmitting unusual data—such as sending unexpected commands to other devices—an ML-based security system can immediately detect this anomaly and isolate the device before the situation escalates into a full-blown attack.

2. Predictive Maintenance and Fault Detection

IoT devices are increasingly being used in industries such as manufacturing, healthcare, and transportation, where continuous uptime and operational efficiency are critical. Predictive maintenance refers to the use of data analysis to predict and prevent equipment failures before they occur, reducing costly downtime and improving system reliability. Machine learning enables real-time monitoring of devices to detect early signs of malfunction or wear, allowing for more efficient maintenance operations.

How ML Powers Predictive Maintenance:

- **Sensor Data Analysis**: ML algorithms analyze data from various sensors embedded in IoT devices to track vital parameters like temperature, vibration, and pressure. If these parameters begin to deviate from their expected ranges, machine learning models can predict the likelihood of a malfunction occurring in the near future.
- **Failure Prediction**: By training on historical data, machine learning models can predict the remaining useful life (RUL) of a device or component. This enables operators to schedule maintenance activities just in time, preventing equipment failure and improving service reliability.
- **Anomaly Detection for Performance Monitoring**: Real-time analysis of data from IoT sensors can also be used to identify performance degradation. For example, a smart HVAC system might start consuming more power than usual, indicating a possible malfunction or inefficiency that requires immediate attention.
- **Example**: In a smart factory, multiple IoT sensors track the condition of equipment such as motors and pumps. Machine learning algorithms can monitor this data in real-time and detect early warning signs of wear and tear. For instance, if a motor shows signs of overheating or unusual vibrations, the system might predict a failure in the next few days, triggering maintenance crews to take preventive action before a costly breakdown occurs.

3. Real-Time Traffic and Data Flow Analysis

In an IoT ecosystem, devices often communicate with each other, sharing data across various networks. The large volume of traffic can make it difficult to detect security threats and ensure network efficiency. Machine learning helps IoT systems perform real-time traffic analysis, detecting patterns that might indicate inefficiencies or malicious activity, such as DDoS (Distributed Denial of Service) attacks or unauthorized data exfiltration.

How ML Improves Data Flow Analysis:

- **Traffic Pattern Recognition**: ML algorithms can detect abnormal network traffic by establishing baseline patterns for device communication. For example, a smart home system might regularly communicate with a cloud server to send temperature data. If, however, a device begins communicating with an unfamiliar external server, the system can identify this abnormality and raise an alert.
- **Anomaly-Based Intrusion Detection**: Instead of waiting for known attack signatures, ML systems can detect unusual data flows that might indicate the presence of an attack, even if it's novel or evolving. This helps in preventing attacks that traditional security systems would miss.
- **Traffic Optimization**: ML algorithms can also be used for load balancing and network optimization. By analyzing real-time data traffic, machine learning can help optimize the flow of data between IoT devices and control systems, ensuring efficient network performance even under heavy loads.
- **Example**: In a smart city environment, IoT devices such as streetlights, cameras, and sensors generate vast amounts of data. A machine learning-based system can monitor the traffic between these devices, flagging any traffic that deviates from typical patterns, such as large data packets being sent to unknown locations, signaling a possible breach or unauthorized data transfer.

4. Automated Response to Anomalies and Attacks

Real-time data analysis with ML not only helps in detecting and monitoring threats but also plays a critical role in automatically responding to incidents. Automated response systems enable faster reaction times, mitigating potential damage before human intervention is even needed.

How ML Automates Responses:

- **Self-Healing Systems**: In some IoT environments, machine learning models can be used to automatically isolate compromised devices or systems. For example, if a device begins exhibiting unusual behaviors that suggest it has been compromised (e.g., sending unauthorized requests), an AI system can automatically disconnect it from the network to prevent the spread of the attack.

- **Automated Threat Mitigation**: When an anomaly is detected, ML systems can trigger a set of predefined responses, such as blocking specific traffic, alerting administrators, or even reconfiguring affected devices. These automated responses help reduce the time between detection and mitigation, minimizing the impact of the attack.
- **Example**: In a smart home system, if one of the devices starts communicating with a suspicious external server, an ML system can automatically disconnect that device from the network to prevent data theft or further malicious activity, alerting the user to the threat.

5. Scaling and Adaptability for Large IoT Networks

The ability to scale is one of the most important features of real-time ML analysis in IoT networks. As the number of devices continues to grow, it becomes increasingly difficult to monitor them all manually or with traditional systems. ML allows for the automation of security tasks across large-scale IoT environments, enabling continuous, real-time data analysis across thousands or millions of devices.

How ML Scales for Large IoT Networks:

- **Distributed Machine Learning Models**: In large IoT networks, data from different devices can be processed in parallel using distributed ML models, allowing the system to scale and process massive volumes of data without compromising on performance.
- **Cloud Integration**: Cloud-based machine learning platforms can leverage the vast computing power available in the cloud to perform complex data analysis in real-time. This integration enables IoT networks to handle large data sets and complex models efficiently.
- **Example**: In a smart agriculture setup with thousands of sensors monitoring soil moisture, temperature, and crop conditions, a machine learning system can analyze data from all sensors in real-time, providing immediate feedback on the conditions of each farm. ML models can be scaled across multiple regions, allowing farmers to track the health of their entire crop network continuously.

Machine learning has become an indispensable tool for real-time data analysis in IoT environments, enabling organizations to detect anomalies, predict maintenance needs, optimize data traffic, and automate responses to security threats. The combination of AI-driven insights and real-time analysis ensures that IoT networks remain secure, efficient, and resilient, even as they grow in size and complexity. By leveraging the power of machine learning, businesses and industries can not only mitigate risks but also gain a competitive edge through more intelligent, adaptive systems that anticipate issues before they occur and respond immediately to emerging threats. As IoT ecosystems continue to expand, the role of ML in ensuring their security and performance will only become more critical.

11.4 Building Scalable AI-Driven IoT Security Frameworks

As the Internet of Things (IoT) continues to expand, with billions of devices interconnected in various environments—smart homes, industrial facilities, transportation networks, and healthcare—securing these devices becomes increasingly complex. The challenge lies in building security frameworks that not only ensure safety but can also scale to accommodate the massive growth of IoT devices. AI-driven IoT security frameworks have emerged as an essential solution for tackling this challenge, enabling organizations to manage security at scale while maintaining high performance and flexibility.

In this section, we will discuss how to design and implement scalable AI-driven IoT security frameworks that effectively address the unique security challenges of large-scale IoT environments, ensuring robust protection against threats without compromising on performance or efficiency.

1. The Need for Scalable IoT Security

IoT networks are inherently diverse, with a wide variety of devices, protocols, and use cases. From smart home systems with a few devices to industrial IoT (IIoT) networks with thousands of sensors and actuators, the sheer scale of interconnected devices creates enormous challenges for traditional security models. As the number of connected devices grows, so do the attack surfaces, making manual monitoring and static security measures less effective.

A scalable security solution needs to adapt to this dynamic landscape, providing real-time protection against evolving threats, while managing the large volumes of data generated by IoT devices. AI-driven frameworks are well-suited for this purpose because they can continuously learn, adapt, and scale without requiring massive human intervention.

2. Key Components of an AI-Driven IoT Security Framework

Building a scalable AI-driven IoT security framework involves several key components that work in tandem to ensure comprehensive protection:

a) Centralized Data Collection and Integration

One of the first steps in creating a scalable security framework is to establish a centralized platform that can collect data from various IoT devices, sensors, and systems across the network. This data serves as the foundation for AI and machine learning models to analyze in real-time.

- **Data Sources**: IoT devices generate vast amounts of heterogeneous data, including sensor readings, system logs, network traffic, and device states. Security frameworks must integrate these data sources into a centralized repository where they can be efficiently processed and analyzed.
- **Cloud or Edge Computing**: Depending on the IoT setup, data can either be processed locally (at the edge) or sent to a cloud-based platform for processing. Edge computing allows data to be analyzed close to the source, reducing latency and enhancing real-time threat detection capabilities.

b) AI and Machine Learning Models for Threat Detection

At the heart of an AI-driven security framework are the machine learning (ML) and artificial intelligence (AI) models that analyze the collected data for abnormal behavior, known attack signatures, and other indicators of compromise.

Anomaly Detection: AI models can continuously monitor the behavior of IoT devices and detect deviations from established baselines. By using unsupervised learning methods, the system can identify new and unknown threats without requiring explicit programming for every potential attack.

Predictive Analytics: AI can also be used to anticipate potential risks and vulnerabilities, helping organizations proactively secure their devices and networks. For example, predictive models can forecast equipment failures or identify vulnerable devices that are at high risk of being exploited.

Scalability in ML Models: To support the large and growing number of IoT devices, machine learning models need to be scalable and adaptable. Distributed learning frameworks allow the AI models to be trained on data across multiple devices or geographic locations, ensuring that the security solution can scale with the network.

c) Real-Time Response and Automation

A scalable AI-driven security framework is not only about detecting threats but also taking real-time action to mitigate them. Automation plays a crucial role in this process.

- **Automated Threat Mitigation**: Once an anomaly or threat is detected, the system must automatically take predefined actions, such as isolating compromised devices, blocking malicious traffic, or applying security patches. This reduces the response time to threats and ensures that the system can react even without human intervention.
- **Self-Healing Mechanisms**: Some AI-driven security frameworks are designed with self-healing capabilities, enabling the system to restore affected IoT devices to their secure state automatically after a detected attack, thus minimizing disruption to normal operations.

d) Device Authentication and Identity Management

In large IoT networks, managing the identities and authenticity of devices is critical for security. AI-driven frameworks can automate and enhance device authentication, ensuring that only legitimate devices are allowed to access the network.

Dynamic Authentication Models: With AI, security frameworks can continuously assess the trustworthiness of devices based on their behavior and interactions with the network. This ensures that a compromised device, even if initially authenticated, is quickly detected and isolated.

e) Scalable Threat Intelligence Sharing

AI-driven IoT security frameworks can also integrate threat intelligence feeds from external sources, enabling them to stay updated on the latest attack techniques and vulnerabilities affecting IoT devices.

Distributed Threat Intelligence: By leveraging machine learning models, frameworks can quickly adapt to new threats as they emerge, sharing relevant threat data with other devices or organizations in a real-time manner. This creates a dynamic, adaptive ecosystem where IoT networks can collectively respond to security threats.

3. Challenges in Building Scalable AI-Driven IoT Security Frameworks

While the potential of AI-driven IoT security frameworks is clear, there are several challenges that organizations must consider when building scalable solutions:

a) Data Privacy and Security Concerns

The widespread deployment of AI across IoT networks raises significant concerns about the privacy and security of the data being collected and analyzed. The more data that is shared between devices, cloud platforms, and third-party services, the greater the risk of sensitive information being compromised. Ensuring that AI systems are designed with strong encryption, secure data transmission, and privacy-preserving techniques is essential.

b) Device Diversity and Interoperability

IoT devices come from a wide range of manufacturers, each with its own protocols, standards, and communication methods. This heterogeneity can make it difficult to integrate devices into a unified AI-driven security framework. To address this, security frameworks must be designed to handle multiple device types, protocols, and operating systems.

c) High Volume of Data

The sheer volume of data generated by IoT devices can overwhelm traditional data-processing systems. Building scalable frameworks requires advanced data processing techniques, such as distributed computing and cloud-based architectures, to manage the influx of data and ensure real-time analysis.

d) Latency and Real-Time Processing

In IoT networks, particularly those in time-sensitive environments (such as healthcare or industrial applications), low-latency processing is crucial. AI models must be optimized for fast response times to detect and mitigate threats as quickly as possible. Implementing low-latency, distributed AI solutions across edge devices and centralized cloud systems can help minimize delays in real-time decision-making.

4. Future Directions for Scalable AI-Driven IoT Security

The future of scalable AI-driven IoT security frameworks lies in continued advancements in machine learning, cloud computing, and edge AI. As IoT networks continue to expand and evolve, AI will play an increasingly critical role in securing them, providing the necessary automation, real-time threat detection, and adaptive responses to ensure safety.

- **Edge AI Expansion**: As more IoT devices move to the edge, processing data locally will become more common. AI will be implemented directly on edge devices, ensuring real-time responses without overburdening the network or introducing latency.
- **AI in Autonomous Security**: AI systems will continue to evolve toward autonomous cybersecurity solutions, where decision-making and responses are carried out without the need for human intervention.
- **Federated Learning**: The rise of federated learning will enable AI models to be trained across multiple devices without the need for data centralization, ensuring better privacy and reducing the burden on centralized data processing systems.

Building scalable AI-driven IoT security frameworks is essential to managing the growing risks and complexities of securing vast, interconnected IoT networks. By leveraging AI and machine learning, organizations can implement real-time threat detection, automated responses, and dynamic defense mechanisms that scale to meet the needs of diverse IoT environments. While challenges remain—such as privacy concerns, device diversity, and real-time processing requirements—continued innovations in AI will help pave the way for more effective and resilient IoT security architectures. As IoT devices proliferate, the importance of these AI-driven frameworks will only continue to grow, safeguarding critical infrastructure and sensitive data across industries.

11.5 Case Studies of Successful IoT Security Solutions

As the Internet of Things (IoT) continues to evolve, securing these interconnected devices and systems has become increasingly vital to protect sensitive data, prevent cyberattacks, and ensure smooth operation across industries. Across the globe, organizations are successfully implementing AI-driven security solutions to address the unique challenges of IoT security. In this section, we will explore case studies that highlight the effective use of AI and machine learning in IoT security, showcasing real-world applications, challenges faced, and how these solutions helped protect against increasingly sophisticated threats.

1. Case Study: Smart Home Devices and AI-Powered Threat Detection

Organization: A global smart home technology company

Challenge: Securing a range of interconnected smart home devices, such as smart thermostats, cameras, lights, and voice assistants, from cyberattacks targeting vulnerabilities in the devices and home networks.

Solution:

The company integrated AI-based threat detection models into its IoT security platform, which was designed to monitor and secure smart home devices in real-time. Using machine learning (ML), the system could continuously analyze the data streams from smart devices, identifying abnormal behavior, such as unusual access patterns or attempts to compromise a device through brute-force login attacks.

Behavioral Analytics: The system utilized behavioral analytics to establish baseline patterns of device usage, allowing it to quickly detect deviations indicative of a potential attack. For example, a sudden surge in network traffic to a smart camera or unauthorized remote access attempts were flagged for immediate action.

Automated Responses: Once a threat was identified, the system automatically initiated security protocols, such as isolating the compromised device, restricting its access to the home network, or sending alerts to the homeowner and the central security team for further investigation.

Results:

The AI-powered solution successfully identified and mitigated several threats, including credential stuffing attacks on voice assistants and remote exploitation of vulnerable devices. By continuously monitoring device activity and leveraging machine learning to detect new patterns, the system significantly reduced the risk of IoT device breaches and improved overall security for users.

2. Case Study: Industrial IoT (IIoT) Security in Manufacturing

Organization: A large industrial manufacturing company

Challenge: Protecting industrial IoT devices used in manufacturing facilities, including sensors, controllers, and automated machines, from cyberattacks that could disrupt production or cause equipment failures.

Solution:

To safeguard its Industrial IoT (IIoT) network, the company implemented an AI-powered security solution designed to monitor and analyze data from sensors and operational systems. The system used deep learning models trained on vast datasets from industrial equipment to recognize normal operational patterns and detect anomalies that might indicate an attack or malfunction.

AI-Driven Intrusion Detection: Using AI-based intrusion detection systems (IDS), the security solution detected unauthorized attempts to access industrial control systems. The system also identified signs of advanced persistent threats (APTs) that targeted critical infrastructure.

Predictive Maintenance and Threat Prevention: The AI models predicted potential mechanical failures and identified cyber-physical attacks by analyzing real-time data from industrial machines. These predictive insights helped the company proactively address vulnerabilities before they could be exploited.

Network Segmentation: The security solution also used AI to segment the IIoT network into isolated zones, reducing the attack surface and preventing lateral movement of threats between devices.

Results:

The AI-powered security solution significantly reduced downtime in the manufacturing facility by preventing attacks on critical systems. In one instance, the AI system detected an attempt to tamper with machine control software, which could have led to a production halt. By isolating the affected system and alerting security personnel, the system prevented a potential cyberattack, ensuring smooth operations and protecting valuable assets.

3. Case Study: Healthcare IoT Security for Patient Monitoring Systems

Organization: A healthcare provider with an IoT-enabled patient monitoring network

Challenge: Ensuring the privacy and security of sensitive patient data being transmitted across IoT devices, such as heart rate monitors, glucose meters, and wearable health devices, while safeguarding against attacks that could jeopardize patient safety.

Solution:

The healthcare provider adopted an AI-powered security solution to protect its IoT-enabled medical devices. The solution focused on securing the communication channels between medical devices, patient data storage systems, and healthcare providers' networks.

Real-Time Data Monitoring: The AI system continuously analyzed the data transmitted between IoT devices and healthcare systems, identifying potential signs of malware infections or attempts to intercept data during transmission.

Anomaly Detection: The AI-driven system leveraged machine learning algorithms to detect abnormal health readings or unexpected device behavior that could indicate a compromised device. For example, if a wearable device sent out inconsistent or incorrect health data, the system flagged it as a potential malware infection or data tampering attempt.

Access Control and Authentication: The AI solution also applied continuous authentication checks for users accessing medical devices, ensuring that only authorized personnel could view or modify patient data.

Results:

The implementation of AI-powered security helped prevent a series of ransomware attacks targeting connected healthcare devices, where hackers attempted to lock down critical patient information. By identifying irregular communication patterns and unauthorized access attempts, the AI system allowed the healthcare provider to act quickly, avoiding significant data breaches and ensuring patient safety.

Additionally, the solution improved patient trust by ensuring data privacy and integrity, while also streamlining regulatory compliance with standards such as HIPAA (Health Insurance Portability and Accountability Act).

4. Case Study: Securing Smart Grids with AI-Powered Threat Detection

Organization: A utility company managing a smart grid network

Challenge: Securing a complex smart grid infrastructure composed of thousands of IoT-enabled sensors and devices that monitor and control energy distribution and consumption, while safeguarding critical systems against cyberattacks.

Solution:

The utility company deployed an AI-driven security framework to monitor its smart grid infrastructure, which was vulnerable to cyberattacks such as denial-of-service (DoS), spoofing, and malicious data injection attacks. By implementing AI algorithms, the system was able to continuously analyze data from IoT devices, identify vulnerabilities, and detect attacks in real-time.

Predictive Analytics for Attack Prevention: The AI solution used predictive analytics to forecast potential attack vectors and identify devices or components that were at higher risk. This enabled the company to proactively address vulnerabilities before attackers could exploit them.

Anomaly Detection in Energy Consumption Patterns: The system also monitored energy consumption patterns across the grid, using machine learning to detect abnormal spikes or drops in power usage, which could indicate an attack or tampering with the smart meters.

AI for Incident Response: When a cyberattack was detected, the AI solution initiated automatic responses, such as shutting down vulnerable devices, isolating compromised sensors, or triggering manual interventions by security teams.

Results:

The AI-driven security framework enabled the utility company to detect and mitigate several advanced attacks, including an attempted DoS attack aimed at disabling the grid. By using real-time analytics and automated responses, the company was able to maintain service continuity, prevent costly disruptions, and safeguard critical infrastructure from both internal and external threats.

5. Case Study: Smart City IoT Security for Urban Infrastructure

Organization: A municipality implementing IoT-enabled smart city infrastructure

Challenge: Protecting the interconnected IoT devices deployed across various urban services, including traffic management systems, smart streetlights, waste management systems, and public surveillance cameras, from cyberattacks and ensuring privacy for citizens.

Solution:

The city's smart city initiative involved the deployment of IoT sensors and devices in key infrastructure areas. To protect these assets, the city government implemented a scalable AI-powered IoT security solution that used machine learning and real-time monitoring to secure smart city networks.

Traffic Management and Smart Streetlights: The AI system monitored traffic sensors and smart streetlights for malicious behavior, such as attempts to manipulate traffic signals or disrupt service. The system flagged unusual patterns, such as sudden traffic signal changes or unauthorized access to traffic data.

Public Surveillance and Privacy Protection: With privacy concerns at the forefront, the AI solution ensured that public surveillance cameras did not violate privacy regulations by continuously monitoring camera activity for unauthorized access attempts or data manipulation.

Threat Intelligence Sharing: The security system also integrated threat intelligence feeds from other smart cities and IoT security networks, helping the city to stay ahead of emerging threats that targeted urban infrastructure.

Results:

The AI-powered security framework successfully thwarted multiple attempts to compromise traffic management systems and access sensitive surveillance data. By using machine learning to predict attack vectors and taking automated actions to secure devices, the city was able to provide uninterrupted public services while protecting the privacy and safety of its citizens.

These case studies demonstrate how AI-driven IoT security solutions are being successfully implemented across various industries to protect vulnerable devices and critical systems. Whether in smart homes, healthcare, industrial environments, or smart cities, AI is proving to be an invaluable tool in detecting threats, preventing attacks, and ensuring the continued safe operation of IoT networks. As IoT devices proliferate, the need for scalable, intelligent, and automated security systems will only grow, with AI playing a central role in shaping the future of IoT security.

12. Adversarial Machine Learning: The Next Battlefield

As machine learning becomes increasingly integrated into cybersecurity defenses, it also becomes a target for sophisticated attacks designed to manipulate AI models. This chapter dives into the emerging field of adversarial machine learning, where attackers intentionally craft inputs to deceive or mislead AI systems, causing them to make incorrect predictions or misclassify data. From poisoning training datasets to exploiting vulnerabilities in AI algorithms, adversarial attacks are a growing threat to the integrity of machine learning models. Readers will explore common adversarial techniques, real-world examples, and strategies for defending against them, such as adversarial training and robust model design. This chapter provides essential knowledge for securing AI systems, highlighting the need for a proactive approach to protect the AI models that power modern cybersecurity.

12.1 What Is Adversarial ML and Why It Matters

Adversarial Machine Learning (AML) refers to the field of study and practice that explores how machine learning (ML) models, particularly those used in AI applications, can be deliberately manipulated or misled through adversarial attacks. These attacks typically involve crafting carefully designed inputs or data points that deceive the machine learning system, causing it to make incorrect predictions or decisions. These attacks exploit the vulnerabilities in the design, training, or deployment of ML models, often undermining their reliability and security.

In the context of cybersecurity, adversarial ML presents a significant threat, as it can enable attackers to bypass defense mechanisms, evade detection, or manipulate automated systems in ways that could compromise security. As AI and machine learning become integral to various sectors — including cybersecurity, finance, healthcare, and autonomous systems — the potential for adversarial attacks grows. The ability of attackers to influence AI behavior poses a substantial risk, making adversarial ML a critical area of concern for developers, security experts, and organizations at large.

Understanding Adversarial ML: How It Works

At its core, adversarial ML relies on the manipulation of inputs to fool machine learning algorithms. This is achieved by introducing small, often imperceptible changes to the input data — these changes might be so subtle that they are almost invisible to the human eye, but they can be enough to confuse AI systems.

For example, in image recognition tasks, an adversarial attack might involve slightly altering the pixels in an image of a cat so that the machine learning model misclassifies it as a dog. Similarly, adversarial attacks on natural language processing (NLP) models could involve modifying text data in ways that mislead AI systems into providing incorrect responses or classifications.

There are several types of adversarial attacks, including:

Evasion Attacks: These attacks involve manipulating inputs to an already-deployed ML model to cause incorrect outputs without the model realizing it. Attackers may attempt to bypass detection systems (such as intrusion detection systems or spam filters) by altering malicious input to avoid detection.

Poisoning Attacks: In this scenario, attackers inject harmful data into the training dataset, effectively "poisoning" the model during its development process. This can lead to incorrect predictions or weaken the model's overall performance.

Model Inversion Attacks: These attacks attempt to extract sensitive information about the underlying model, such as its structure or the training data it was exposed to. Attackers can use this information to craft further attacks or gain unauthorized access.

Why Adversarial ML Matters in Cybersecurity

The rise of AI-driven cybersecurity solutions, such as intrusion detection systems, malware detection, and phishing defenses, has made adversarial ML a pressing concern. Attackers who understand the vulnerabilities of machine learning models can target these systems to bypass security measures or manipulate outcomes in their favor. For instance, adversarial ML attacks could cause a security system to misidentify a malicious file as safe or allow an attacker to sneak past an intrusion detection system undetected.

Here are a few reasons why adversarial ML is particularly critical in the context of cybersecurity:

AI in Threat Detection Systems: Many cybersecurity defenses, such as intrusion detection systems (IDS), firewalls, and anti-malware systems, rely on machine learning to detect and respond to cyber threats. If attackers can exploit adversarial ML vulnerabilities within these systems, they can bypass detection and evade security measures.

Automated Decision Making: AI-powered systems are increasingly used for automated decision-making processes, such as fraud detection, risk assessment, or incident response. Adversarial attacks on these systems can undermine their accuracy and effectiveness, leading to incorrect decisions that may cause harm or fail to detect a cyberattack in time.

Manipulating AI-Driven Autonomous Systems: Autonomous vehicles, drones, and robots are increasingly powered by machine learning models. Adversarial ML attacks on these systems could compromise their ability to function safely, potentially leading to accidents or dangerous behavior.

Complexity of Defending Against Attacks: Adversarial ML poses unique challenges for security professionals because these attacks are often subtle and difficult to detect. Traditional security measures, such as signature-based detection systems, are not equipped to handle adversarial manipulation of input data.

Ethical and Legal Implications: Adversarial attacks can lead to privacy violations (e.g., revealing sensitive information through model inversion) and can have significant ethical and legal consequences. For example, adversarial attacks that manipulate AI-powered medical diagnosis systems could result in misdiagnoses, leading to harm to patients or legal liabilities for healthcare providers.

The Growing Importance of Adversarial ML Research

As the role of AI in cybersecurity continues to grow, understanding and defending against adversarial ML attacks becomes increasingly vital. Research into adversarial machine learning is focused on identifying the ways in which AI models can be attacked, developing defenses against such attacks, and ensuring that AI systems are robust and secure.

Several approaches are being explored to defend against adversarial ML:

Adversarial Training: This technique involves training models with adversarial examples so that the model learns to recognize and resist adversarial inputs. This can improve the model's robustness against attacks, though it is an ongoing area of research and may not fully eliminate vulnerabilities.

Detection and Mitigation: There are techniques aimed at detecting when an adversarial attack has occurred by analyzing the model's outputs or the input data. These methods can flag suspicious behavior and trigger defensive measures to prevent the attack from succeeding.

Certified Defenses: Researchers are working on developing certified defenses that provide mathematical guarantees that a model will perform correctly even in the presence of adversarial inputs. This is an emerging area aimed at providing more robust protection against attacks.

Model Explainability: By improving the explainability of AI models, researchers can better understand how adversarial attacks affect model behavior. Transparency in model decisions can also make it easier to spot signs of tampering or unusual input patterns.

Robustness in Training: Developing more robust ML algorithms that are resistant to small perturbations in the input data is crucial. This involves designing models that can still perform correctly despite adversarial noise.

Adversarial Machine Learning is a critical area of research and development, especially as AI and machine learning become more ingrained in cybersecurity. The ability for attackers to exploit vulnerabilities in AI models presents a new frontier in the ongoing battle between cybercriminals and defenders. Understanding adversarial ML — its methods, implications, and potential defenses — is essential for building secure, reliable, and trustworthy AI-powered systems. As cybersecurity solutions increasingly rely on machine learning, addressing the challenges posed by adversarial attacks is paramount to ensuring that these systems remain effective in the face of evolving threats.

12.2 Common Techniques to Exploit AI Models

As artificial intelligence (AI) and machine learning (ML) models become more integrated into security systems, decision-making processes, and everyday applications, their vulnerability to exploitation increases. Adversarial attacks, which seek to exploit weaknesses in AI models, can have significant consequences, from bypassing security measures to manipulating outcomes for malicious purposes. Understanding the common techniques used to exploit AI models is crucial for developing defensive strategies and ensuring the security and robustness of AI-driven systems.

In this section, we will explore the most prevalent techniques used to exploit AI models, focusing on how attackers can manipulate the model's inputs, parameters, or behavior to achieve their objectives.

1. Evasion Attacks

Evasion attacks involve modifying the input data in a way that causes the AI model to make incorrect predictions or classifications, without the attacker needing access to the model itself. These attacks are often subtle, making it difficult for the system to detect manipulation.

How Evasion Attacks Work:

- **Image Classification**: In the case of image recognition, attackers might apply small, imperceptible changes to the pixels of an image (e.g., adding noise or altering certain patterns) that are virtually invisible to humans but cause the AI model to misclassify the object in the image.
- **Text Manipulation**: In natural language processing (NLP), attackers may tweak words or characters in a sentence, altering the meaning in such a way that the model misinterprets the text while remaining relatively coherent to human readers.

Example:

An attacker could design a manipulated file that appears to be benign to a machine learning-based malware detection system, but is actually a malicious program that executes once inside a network.

2. Poisoning Attacks

Poisoning attacks involve introducing misleading or harmful data into the training dataset of a machine learning model. By manipulating the data used to train the AI, attackers can alter the model's behavior or introduce bias into its predictions. This type of attack is particularly dangerous because it can influence the model's output even before it is deployed, allowing the attacker to control or disrupt its operation.

How Poisoning Attacks Work:

- **Training Data Corruption**: Attackers may insert erroneous or malicious samples into the training set, causing the model to learn incorrect patterns or associations.

This can degrade the model's overall performance or lead it to make poor decisions when exposed to real-world data.

- **Targeted Poisoning**: In some cases, attackers may target specific parts of the model's functionality by poisoning the data related to particular features or classes. For instance, poisoning a facial recognition system's training data could make it less accurate at recognizing certain faces or groups of people.

Example:

In a recommendation system, poisoning the training data could cause the system to make biased suggestions, potentially leading to financial fraud or the promotion of malicious content.

3. Model Inversion Attacks

Model inversion attacks aim to reverse-engineer the AI model to extract sensitive information about its training data, architecture, or parameters. This technique exploits the outputs of an AI model, such as its predictions or decision boundaries, to infer private or confidential information that was used to train the model. These attacks pose a significant threat to privacy and security, particularly when AI models are used for sensitive applications like healthcare, finance, or legal matters.

How Model Inversion Attacks Work:

- **Querying the Model**: Attackers typically interact with the AI model by submitting queries or inputs and observing the responses. By analyzing the output for different inputs, the attacker can infer patterns about the model's decision-making process and potentially deduce sensitive information from the training data.
- **Reconstructing Training Data**: In some cases, adversaries may attempt to reconstruct the original training data by using the model's predictions to approximate the data points it was trained on.

Example:

An attacker could use model inversion to extract private patient data from a healthcare AI system, such as details of medical conditions or treatments, based on the model's predictions about an individual's health status.

4. Data Poaching (Data Extraction Attacks)

Data poaching refers to the theft of proprietary data or sensitive information directly from an AI model. Unlike model inversion, which seeks to extract training data indirectly through outputs, data poaching involves directly accessing a model's parameters or learned weights.

How Data Poaching Works:

- **Stealing Weights or Parameters**: Attackers may target machine learning models that are deployed in the cloud or on vulnerable systems. By gaining unauthorized access to the model's storage, they can steal the model's internal parameters (such as weights in a neural network), which may contain valuable insights or confidential data.
- **Shadow Models**: Attackers can also create shadow models that mimic the behavior of the target model. These models can be trained using publicly available data or stolen data to infer sensitive information about the target model's functioning.

Example:

An attacker could steal the trained weights of an AI-powered fraud detection system and use the extracted knowledge to design more sophisticated fraudulent transactions that bypass the system.

5. Membership Inference Attacks

In a membership inference attack, the goal is for the attacker to determine whether a particular data point was used to train a specific AI model. This type of attack exploits the overfitting that can occur in some machine learning models, where the model becomes too tailored to the training data and exhibits "memorization" behavior.

How Membership Inference Attacks Work:

- **Model Queries**: Attackers use a set of known inputs and query the target AI model. By observing how the model responds to these inputs (such as the confidence level or likelihood of certain outputs), they can infer whether a particular data point was part of the training dataset.
- **Confidence Estimation**: Models that are overfit or highly confident in their predictions may reveal clues that can help an attacker determine if a data point was included in the training set.

Example:

An attacker might query a machine learning-based credit scoring model to determine if a specific individual's financial data was part of the model's training set, potentially revealing sensitive information about the person's financial history.

6. Backdoor Attacks

A backdoor attack involves embedding a hidden "trigger" or "backdoor" in the AI model, which causes the model to behave differently when specific, often innocuous, input patterns are encountered. The attacker's goal is to manipulate the model's output at a specific moment, often when certain conditions are met.

How Backdoor Attacks Work:

- **Inserting Triggers**: The attacker adds a hidden feature to the training data, known as a "trigger," which is not visible in normal usage. When this trigger appears in the input data, the model is manipulated to produce a specific, pre-determined output.
- **Targeted Misclassification**: Backdoors can be particularly dangerous because they allow attackers to control the model's behavior under certain conditions, while the model appears to work normally under other circumstances.

Example:

An attacker could insert a backdoor into a facial recognition system that causes the system to incorrectly classify the face of the attacker as an authorized user when a particular trigger (e.g., a specific pair of glasses or hat) is present.

7. Exploiting Transfer Learning

Transfer learning allows models trained on one task or dataset to be applied to similar tasks, saving time and computational resources. However, this feature also opens up the possibility for attackers to exploit transferred models by manipulating the original model and then transferring the attack to a new model.

How Transfer Learning Attacks Work:

- **Model Reuse**: If a malicious actor can manipulate an AI model trained for one purpose, they can transfer the attack to other models that use the same architecture or share similar features.
- **Exploiting Shared Weights**: Attackers may target commonly used pre-trained models, inserting adversarial inputs or backdoors that can propagate across different applications that reuse the model.

Example:

An attacker could tamper with a pre-trained image classification model used by multiple organizations, inserting a backdoor that only activates in certain settings, enabling them to evade detection in all instances where the model is reused.

As AI and machine learning continue to shape modern cybersecurity systems, understanding the common techniques used to exploit these technologies is essential for defending against adversarial threats. Whether through evasion, poisoning, or backdoor attacks, the potential for malicious actors to manipulate AI models and disrupt security measures is ever-growing. Organizations must be vigilant and employ advanced detection, mitigation, and model-hardening techniques to ensure their AI systems remain resilient against these emerging threats.

12.3 Defending AI Systems Against Adversarial Attacks

Adversarial attacks represent one of the most pressing challenges for the security of AI systems. These attacks can manipulate AI models by subtly altering inputs to mislead the system into making incorrect predictions or classifications. Defending AI systems against these attacks is essential to maintain the integrity and reliability of AI applications in critical areas such as cybersecurity, healthcare, finance, and autonomous systems. In this section, we will explore various strategies and techniques for defending AI systems against adversarial threats, focusing on both preventative and reactive measures.

1. Adversarial Training

Adversarial training is one of the most widely recognized and effective techniques for defending AI models against adversarial attacks. The core idea is to train AI models with adversarial examples — deliberately crafted inputs designed to trick the model. By exposing the model to these perturbations during the training phase, the model becomes more robust and capable of handling similar manipulations in real-world scenarios.

How Adversarial Training Works:

- **Generating Adversarial Examples**: During training, adversarial examples are generated using techniques like the Fast Gradient Sign Method (FGSM) or Projected Gradient Descent (PGD), which perturb the model's input data to maximize the prediction error.
- **Model Retraining**: These adversarial examples are incorporated into the training dataset, allowing the model to learn how to correctly classify these adversarial inputs alongside normal data.
- **Continuous Improvement**: Adversarial training can be an iterative process, where the model is periodically retrained with newly generated adversarial examples to enhance its robustness over time.

Example:

In image classification, adversarial training can help a model learn to recognize objects even when small, imperceptible noise is added to the images, preventing the model from misclassifying adversarially altered images.

2. Defensive Distillation

Defensive distillation is another technique used to defend AI models, particularly deep neural networks, against adversarial attacks. The primary goal of this method is to make the model more resistant to perturbations by modifying its internal structure and how it learns.

How Defensive Distillation Works:

- **Knowledge Transfer**: The process involves training a secondary model (a "student" model) on the softened outputs of a pre-trained model (the "teacher"). Instead of directly using the hard predictions (e.g., class labels) from the teacher model, the student model is trained using the probability distribution of the teacher's predictions.
- **Softer Decision Boundaries**: The distillation process smoothens the decision boundaries of the model, making it less sensitive to small input changes or perturbations.
- **Improved Robustness**: As a result, the student model tends to be more resilient against adversarial examples because it learns from the less confident, more generalized outputs of the teacher model.

Example:

A deep neural network used for facial recognition might undergo defensive distillation, where the system learns to be less certain about its predictions, thereby making it more difficult for adversarially altered facial images to cause misclassification.

3. Input Transformation and Preprocessing

Input transformation involves modifying or preprocessing inputs before they are passed into the AI model in order to reduce the impact of adversarial perturbations. These transformations aim to neutralize or filter out the changes made by adversarial attacks while preserving the integrity of the input data.

Common Input Transformation Techniques:

- **Image Preprocessing**: In computer vision, techniques such as JPEG compression, random resizing, or grayscale conversion can be used to reduce the effectiveness of adversarial perturbations in images.
- **Smoothing**: Applying filters such as Gaussian blur or median filtering to inputs can help smooth out small adversarial changes, making them less likely to mislead the model.
- **Feature Squeezing**: This technique involves reducing the precision of the input features, such as lowering the bit-depth of images or quantizing the features, making adversarial perturbations more difficult to achieve.

Example:

In NLP, techniques like text denoising or spell checking can be applied to remove small adversarial manipulations, ensuring the model receives a clean input that is less likely to be misclassified.

4. Regularization Techniques

Regularization methods are used to prevent overfitting in machine learning models by adding constraints or penalties during training. Some regularization techniques can help improve the robustness of AI models against adversarial attacks by ensuring the model generalizes better and does not become overly sensitive to small changes in the input data.

Key Regularization Techniques for Defending AI:

- **Weight Regularization**: This technique penalizes large weights in the model, encouraging the model to develop simpler decision boundaries that are less likely to be influenced by small adversarial perturbations.
- **Dropout**: Dropout is a regularization technique that randomly disables certain neurons during training, forcing the model to become more robust by learning more generalizable patterns and reducing its reliance on specific features.
- **Data Augmentation**: By artificially expanding the training dataset with various transformations, such as rotation or flipping, the model becomes less sensitive to specific input configurations and is less likely to be tricked by adversarial modifications.

Example:

In an autonomous vehicle system, regularization techniques could prevent the model from becoming too specialized on specific road conditions, making it less susceptible to adversarial examples designed to confuse the system during a real-world driving scenario.

5. Robust Optimization and Certifiable Defenses

Robust optimization focuses on making AI models not only resistant to adversarial attacks but also capable of certifying their robustness under certain conditions. This involves modifying the training process so that the model can guarantee correct classification within a given perturbation budget.

How Robust Optimization Works:

- **Robust Training**: During training, adversarial examples are generated within a specific perturbation budget (e.g., small changes within a defined range), and the model is trained to correctly classify data even within these constraints.
- **Certifiable Robustness**: After training, some models can be certified to be robust to adversarial attacks within a certain range of perturbations. This can be achieved through formal verification methods that mathematically prove the model's resilience to certain types of attacks.
- **Verification Tools**: Tools like Verifiable Robustness and Certified Defenses allow AI developers to assess how vulnerable their models are and optimize them to withstand adversarial manipulation.

Example:

In healthcare, a certified model could ensure that a medical diagnosis system remains reliable even when adversarially crafted medical images are presented to it, minimizing the chances of misdiagnosis.

6. Adversarial Detection

Adversarial detection focuses on identifying adversarial inputs before they are processed by the model. This approach acts as a first line of defense by preventing adversarial examples from reaching the model in the first place.

How Adversarial Detection Works:

- **Anomaly Detection**: One common technique is to train a secondary model to detect unusual or abnormal patterns in the input data that deviate significantly from normal, unperturbed examples.
- **Feature Analysis**: Anomalous inputs can be flagged by analyzing discrepancies in key features, such as pixel values in images or semantic structure in text.
- **Confidence Scores**: AI models can be equipped with confidence scores for each prediction, where a low-confidence score could trigger a warning that an adversarial input might be present.

Example:

In financial fraud detection, a secondary system could monitor incoming transaction data for unusual patterns that indicate possible adversarial manipulation, such as an altered account number or a suspiciously modified payment amount.

7. Model Ensembling

Model ensembling involves combining the predictions of multiple models to make more robust and accurate decisions. By using an ensemble of models, each potentially trained on different data or using different algorithms, the likelihood that all models are simultaneously vulnerable to the same adversarial input is reduced.

How Model Ensembling Works:

- **Diverse Models**: An ensemble can consist of different types of models, such as decision trees, neural networks, and support vector machines, that offer varying perspectives on the data.

- **Majority Voting or Averaging**: The final decision is often based on a majority vote (in classification tasks) or an averaging method (in regression tasks), ensuring that adversarial inputs are less likely to fool the entire ensemble.

Example:

In fraud detection systems, using an ensemble of models trained on different features (e.g., transaction history, user behavior, geographic location) can help mitigate the risk of adversarial manipulation targeting only one particular feature set.

Defending AI systems against adversarial attacks is an ongoing challenge that requires a multi-faceted approach. Strategies like adversarial training, defensive distillation, and input transformation can enhance the robustness of AI models by preventing or mitigating the impact of adversarial perturbations. As AI continues to play an increasingly critical role in cybersecurity, healthcare, finance, and other sectors, ensuring the security of AI models through these defenses will be crucial to maintaining trust and reliability in AI-driven systems. Additionally, continuous research and development in adversarial defense mechanisms will be necessary to stay ahead of evolving attack techniques and ensure the resilience of AI systems in the face of new threats.

12.4 Detecting Poisoned Data in Training Sets

Data poisoning is a significant and emerging threat to machine learning (ML) models, where malicious actors intentionally introduce misleading, erroneous, or biased data into a training dataset to corrupt the model's learning process. In the context of cybersecurity, poisoned data can undermine the model's performance, leading to vulnerabilities that can be exploited by attackers. Detecting poisoned data is therefore essential for maintaining the integrity and security of AI-driven systems.

In this section, we will explore the concept of poisoned data, its impact on machine learning systems, and the various strategies and techniques used to detect and mitigate the effects of poisoned data in training sets.

1. What Is Data Poisoning?

Data poisoning occurs when adversaries manipulate a machine learning model's training data in such a way that the model learns from incorrect, misleading, or intentionally crafted examples. These poisoned examples are often designed to cause the model to make wrong predictions or to degrade its overall performance in a subtle manner. There are two main types of data poisoning:

Targeted Poisoning: In this scenario, attackers inject poisoned data that causes the model to make a specific erroneous prediction or classification for a particular input. The objective is usually to compromise the model's ability to make correct decisions under specific conditions.

Untargeted Poisoning: This approach aims to degrade the general performance of the model without necessarily targeting a specific input or decision. It focuses on causing a broad reduction in accuracy or increasing the likelihood of error across a range of inputs.

For instance, in a facial recognition system, poisoned data could be inserted into the training set that causes the model to misidentify certain individuals, potentially allowing unauthorized access to secure systems.

2. Identifying Signs of Poisoned Data

Detecting poisoned data involves identifying anomalies in the training dataset that deviate from the normal distribution or expected patterns. The goal is to isolate and flag suspicious data points that may be subtly altering the model's behavior without being immediately apparent. Several common indicators suggest poisoned data:

Outlier Detection: Poisoned data points are often outliers that do not match the general distribution of the dataset. Outliers, especially those that do not fit any logical pattern, can be an indication that the data has been tampered with.

Label Inconsistencies: In supervised learning, poisoned data can often be identified by checking for inconsistencies between the features and the labels. For instance, if certain data points have feature-label pairs that are unreasonably mismatched, they may have been intentionally poisoned.

Model Behavior Anomalies: Sudden changes in model performance, particularly drops in accuracy, can indicate that poisoned data has influenced the learning process. Inconsistent or unexpected changes in decision boundaries can also signal that the model has been influenced by adversarial data.

Small Gradients in Training: When poisoned data is introduced to a model, the gradients during training may behave unusually. For example, adversarial data points may cause the loss function to stagnate or behave in ways that are different from the norm.

3. Techniques for Detecting Poisoned Data

There are several methods and techniques that can be employed to detect poisoned data during the model training phase. Some of these methods include:

1. Data Validation and Preprocessing

Anomaly Detection Algorithms: Before training, statistical or machine learning-based anomaly detection methods can be applied to the dataset. These algorithms look for data points that deviate significantly from the expected distribution and flag them for further investigation.

Outlier Detection: Methods such as Isolation Forest, k-nearest neighbors (KNN), and local outlier factor (LOF) can be used to detect outliers in the data that may suggest poisoning. These algorithms work by assessing the relative distance between data points and flagging those that are far removed from others as potential poisons.

Cross-Validation: Cross-validation is a process where the dataset is split into multiple subsets, and the model is trained on different combinations of these subsets. By validating performance across different folds, any discrepancies in model behavior can point to the influence of poisoned data. For example, if performance significantly differs between subsets, it could indicate that specific subsets contain poisoned examples.

2. Robust Learning Methods

Robust Statistical Techniques: When poisoned data is present in a dataset, it may introduce biases or inconsistencies that can be detected using robust learning methods. For example, Huber loss functions, which are less sensitive to outliers, can help reduce the impact of poisoned data by assigning less weight to anomalous points during training.

Robust Optimizers: Algorithms like gradient clipping or gradient regularization are designed to minimize the influence of large gradient updates, which can be caused by poisoned data. By controlling the gradient step size, these techniques can limit the impact of poisoned data during the learning process.

3. Ensemble Methods

Model Averaging: Using ensemble techniques like bagging and boosting can help identify poisoned data by comparing the predictions of multiple models. If a certain set of data points consistently causes model predictions to deviate in the same way across the ensemble, those points may be flagged as poisoned.

Multiple Training Runs: Training multiple versions of the model with slightly different datasets can help identify discrepancies caused by poisoned data. Models that consistently perform poorly on certain data points or exhibit unexpected behavior can help pinpoint corrupted data.

4. Sensitivity Analysis

Gradient-Based Analysis: Sensitivity analysis involves studying how small changes in the input data (such as adding noise or small perturbations) affect the model's output. If a particular data point leads to large changes in the model's behavior, it may be an indication that the data point is poisoned.

Influence Functions: Influence functions help quantify the impact of individual data points on the final model. By using influence functions, it is possible to track how much a specific data point contributes to changes in the model's predictions. If a data point has an unusually high influence on the model's output, it may be a sign that the data point has been poisoned.

5. Outlier Detection During Deployment

After a model has been deployed, detecting poisoned data may become more difficult, as the dataset is constantly changing. To address this, post-deployment anomaly detection techniques can be used to identify poisoned data in real-time.

Online Anomaly Detection: Real-time anomaly detection tools can help identify unexpected input data patterns that deviate from the model's learned distribution. These tools can continuously monitor incoming data and flag suspicious inputs for further inspection.

Drift Detection: Over time, the data distribution may change, and this phenomenon is known as concept drift. Monitoring for drift in the input data or the model's performance can help identify poisoned data that might affect the system's stability.

4. Countermeasures and Mitigation Techniques

Once poisoned data has been detected, it is essential to remove or correct the compromised data points to restore the integrity of the model. Some mitigation strategies include:

Data Cleansing: This involves manually or algorithmically removing suspicious data points from the training set and retraining the model.

Model Recalibration: After detecting poisoned data, recalibrating the model or retraining it on a clean dataset can help restore accuracy and prevent further corruption.

Defensive Data Collection: Ensuring that data is collected from reliable, verified sources and implementing validation checks during data collection can prevent poisoned data from entering the system in the first place.

Detecting and mitigating poisoned data is a critical challenge in securing AI models. By employing strategies like anomaly detection, robust learning methods, sensitivity analysis, and post-deployment monitoring, organizations can safeguard their models from malicious manipulation. These techniques not only enhance the resilience of AI systems but also ensure that machine learning models operate as intended, delivering accurate, reliable, and secure results even in the face of adversarial attempts to corrupt their training data. As AI continues to grow in importance across industries, the ability to detect and counter poisoned data will remain a key component of maintaining robust and trustworthy systems.

12.5 Building Robust and Resilient AI Models

In the evolving world of artificial intelligence (AI) and machine learning (ML), building robust and resilient models is critical for safeguarding them against adversarial attacks, data poisoning, and other forms of manipulation that can compromise their integrity and effectiveness. Robustness in AI models refers to their ability to maintain high performance and reliability, even when exposed to imperfect, noisy, or adversarial inputs. Resilience, on the other hand, involves the ability to recover from disturbances or attacks, ensuring that the model continues to function in a secure and dependable manner.

As AI models become increasingly integral to critical applications, such as cybersecurity, healthcare, finance, and autonomous systems, ensuring their robustness and resilience is paramount. This section explores the strategies and techniques used to build AI models that can withstand adversarial threats and perform reliably in real-world, dynamic environments.

1. Understanding Model Robustness and Resilience

Before diving into the methods of building robust and resilient AI models, it's important to understand the fundamental differences between these two characteristics:

Robustness refers to a model's ability to maintain its performance when faced with noisy or adversarial data. For example, in a cybersecurity system, a robust AI model should be able to identify malicious activity even when faced with misleading or altered attack data.

Resilience is the model's capacity to recover from disruptions such as adversarial attacks, data corruption, or environmental changes. A resilient model should continue to function effectively even after it has been subjected to deliberate attempts to degrade its performance.

Together, robustness and resilience ensure that AI models can operate effectively in unpredictable environments, making them more secure and reliable.

2. Key Principles for Building Robust AI Models

1. Adversarial Training

Adversarial training is one of the most effective strategies for improving model robustness. It involves intentionally exposing the AI model to adversarial examples—inputs designed to fool the model—and training it to correctly classify or respond to these inputs. By doing this, the model becomes more adept at identifying adversarial inputs during its actual deployment.

Method: During the training process, adversarial perturbations are generated and added to the training data. This allows the model to learn not only the correct labels for normal inputs but also to recognize and resist attempts to manipulate the data.

Effectiveness: Adversarial training improves the model's generalization ability and ensures that it performs well even when presented with unseen adversarial inputs. While adversarial training can be computationally expensive, it significantly enhances the model's resilience to attacks.

2. Regularization Techniques

Regularization is a technique used to prevent overfitting, which occurs when a model becomes too closely fitted to the training data and fails to generalize to new, unseen data. Regularization techniques help AI models remain robust by ensuring that they do not become overly sensitive to small variations in input data.

Common Regularization Methods:

- **L2 regularization (Ridge):** Adds a penalty term to the loss function that discourages large weights in the model, promoting simpler, more generalized models.
- **Dropout**: A method where random subsets of neurons or parameters are dropped during training, preventing the model from relying too heavily on any single input feature.
- **Data Augmentation**: By artificially increasing the diversity of the training data through transformations such as rotation, cropping, or flipping, models become less sensitive to small changes in input data, which helps build robustness.

3. Robust Optimization Techniques

Robust optimization techniques aim to improve the performance of AI models under uncertainty. These techniques adjust the optimization process during model training to ensure that the model performs well under a range of different conditions, including the presence of noisy or adversarial data.

Robust Loss Functions: Loss functions such as Huber loss and quantile loss are less sensitive to outliers and noisy data. These loss functions help the model maintain stable performance even when some data points are anomalous or corrupted.

Min-Max Optimization: This approach is designed to optimize a model to perform well across the worst-case scenarios. The model is trained to minimize the maximum possible loss, making it more resilient to unexpected data variations.

4. Explainable AI (XAI)

While building robust models is essential, it is equally important that these models are transparent and interpretable. Explainable AI (XAI) techniques make AI models more understandable by humans, which is critical for identifying why the model makes specific predictions and whether it is being influenced by adversarial or corrupted data.

Model Interpretability: Using methods like SHAP (SHapley Additive exPlanations) and LIME (Local Interpretable Model-agnostic Explanations), practitioners can inspect how various features influence the model's predictions. This can help in identifying potential vulnerabilities or biases in the model that might be exploited by attackers.

Advantages of XAI: With explainability, security experts can better understand model behavior, detect adversarial manipulations, and make informed decisions about further strengthening the system.

5. Data Provenance and Integrity Checks

Ensuring that the training data is accurate and not compromised by adversarial manipulation is a critical component of building resilient models. One way to safeguard against data poisoning and ensure data integrity is to implement robust data provenance and integrity checks.

Data Provenance: This refers to the tracking of the data's origin and history throughout the AI model's lifecycle. By maintaining accurate records of where the data comes from and how it has been processed, AI developers can identify and exclude any corrupted or malicious data.

Integrity Verification: Techniques such as cryptographic hashing or digital signatures can be applied to verify the integrity of the training data. These checks help ensure that the data has not been tampered with or altered in a way that could introduce vulnerabilities.

3. Building Resilient AI Systems

In addition to enhancing robustness, resilience is essential for ensuring that AI systems continue to function effectively in the face of adversarial attacks or real-world challenges. The following practices are key to building AI models that can recover from disturbances:

1. Continuous Monitoring and Feedback Loops

Once an AI model is deployed, continuous monitoring is necessary to detect any degradation in performance, unusual patterns, or indications that the system has been compromised. Monitoring systems should track both the performance metrics and the inputs being fed into the system.

Real-Time Monitoring: Continuous monitoring enables the early detection of attacks or anomalies, such as data poisoning or adversarial inputs. With real-time alerts, security teams can take immediate action to mitigate potential risks.

Feedback Loops: Feedback loops involve updating the model based on newly observed data and performance results. This iterative process ensures that the model adapts to changes in the environment and recovers from any vulnerabilities or issues that arise during operation.

2. Redundancy and Failover Systems

In critical applications, AI models should be designed with redundancy and failover mechanisms to ensure that the system continues to function even if one model or component fails. This can include using multiple models in parallel (ensemble methods) or building backup systems that can take over in the event of an attack or failure.

Ensemble Methods: By using multiple models and combining their outputs, the overall system becomes more resilient to individual model failures or attacks. If one model is compromised, others can still provide accurate predictions, reducing the risk of a complete system failure.

Failover Mechanisms: Having redundant systems in place, such as backup servers or alternative model architectures, ensures that the system can recover quickly and continue operating normally.

3. Regular Model Updates and Patch Management

The landscape of AI threats is constantly evolving, and attackers continuously develop new techniques to circumvent defenses. To ensure that AI models remain resilient over time, regular updates and patching are essential. This includes updating the models with new data, applying security patches, and improving defense mechanisms to address new threats.

Model Retraining: As adversaries learn to bypass existing defenses, retraining the model with new data and adversarial examples helps to maintain its robustness. This approach ensures that the model stays up to date with the latest attack vectors and data patterns.

Building robust and resilient AI models is an ongoing process that requires a combination of strong foundational practices, such as adversarial training, regularization, robust optimization, and explainability, along with continuous monitoring, redundancy, and adaptability to new threats. By employing these strategies, organizations can ensure that their AI systems remain secure, reliable, and capable of handling unexpected challenges, while also protecting against adversarial attacks, data poisoning, and other vulnerabilities. Robust and resilient AI models are crucial to maintaining trust in these systems as they continue to play an increasingly important role in cybersecurity, healthcare, autonomous vehicles, and a wide range of other critical applications.

13. Ethics and Privacy in AI-Powered Cybersecurity

As AI and machine learning increasingly shape cybersecurity practices, they bring with them a host of ethical and privacy challenges. This chapter explores the delicate balance between utilizing AI to enhance security and ensuring the protection of individuals' privacy rights. Topics covered include the ethical implications of AI surveillance, the potential for bias in AI models, and the risks of overreach in automated decision-making. Additionally, it examines how AI-powered systems must comply with global data protection regulations, such as GDPR, and the importance of transparency in AI-driven security measures. Readers will gain insight into the ethical dilemmas that arise when AI is used to defend against cyber threats, while also considering the broader societal impacts of these technologies in ensuring a fair and accountable cybersecurity landscape.

13.1 Ethical Challenges in AI-Driven Cyber Defense

As artificial intelligence (AI) and machine learning (ML) continue to revolutionize cybersecurity, they also present a host of ethical challenges that must be carefully considered. While AI-driven cyber defense systems can significantly improve the ability to detect, prevent, and respond to threats, they also introduce new complexities related to privacy, fairness, accountability, and transparency. The rapid adoption of AI in cybersecurity raises important ethical questions, as the consequences of deploying these technologies extend beyond technical performance to encompass broader social and moral implications. This chapter explores the primary ethical challenges in AI-powered cyber defense, with an emphasis on their potential impact on individuals, organizations, and society at large.

1. Privacy Concerns in AI-Powered Cybersecurity

One of the most significant ethical challenges in AI-driven cyber defense is the potential for violations of privacy. Cybersecurity systems often require extensive access to personal data, such as network activity, communications, and user behavior, in order to identify threats and anomalous patterns. AI algorithms may analyze this data in real-time to detect potential breaches or attacks, but this level of surveillance can raise concerns about the excessive collection of sensitive information and its potential misuse.

Data Collection and Surveillance: In many AI-powered cybersecurity systems, the sheer volume of data being collected for analysis could inadvertently lead to violations of individual privacy. Continuous monitoring of users' digital activities may not only invade their personal privacy but also lead to the erosion of trust between users and organizations.

Data Use and Retention: The way that collected data is used and stored also poses significant ethical dilemmas. For example, if AI systems access sensitive personal information to detect potential threats, it is important to ensure that this data is not retained for longer than necessary and that individuals are informed about the scope of data collection.

To address these concerns, organizations must implement strict data protection policies, such as data minimization, where only the essential data needed for threat detection is collected. In addition, AI systems should be designed to respect user privacy by ensuring that personal data is anonymized and encrypted, reducing the risk of misuse.

2. Bias and Fairness in AI Algorithms

AI algorithms, including those used in cybersecurity, are not immune to the biases that may be present in the data used to train them. These biases can manifest in a variety of ways, potentially leading to unfair or discriminatory outcomes. For example, if an AI system is trained on biased datasets, it could inadvertently give disproportionate attention to certain types of threats, or, conversely, fail to detect others.

Data Bias: If the data used to train AI models reflects societal biases or imbalances (such as overrepresentation of certain demographic groups or types of attacks), the AI system may learn these biases and perpetuate them in its decision-making processes. In cybersecurity, this could mean that the system is less effective at detecting threats originating from certain regions, groups, or attack vectors.

Algorithmic Bias: Even if the data is relatively unbiased, AI models can still exhibit bias due to the way they process and analyze the data. For example, an AI system trained to identify malicious network traffic might misclassify legitimate activity as a threat because the algorithm has learned to prioritize certain patterns of behavior.

To mitigate bias, AI systems should be trained on diverse, representative datasets that capture a wide range of attack scenarios, user behaviors, and demographic groups. Additionally, ongoing audits and testing of AI models for fairness and equity should be conducted to ensure that they do not disproportionately impact certain groups or lead to false positives/negatives in threat detection.

3. Accountability and Responsibility

As AI systems become more autonomous, determining who is responsible when these systems fail or make incorrect decisions becomes a key ethical issue. In cybersecurity, this is particularly pertinent, as errors in AI-driven threat detection systems could result in undetected breaches, data leaks, or compromised security.

Automated Decision-Making: AI systems are increasingly tasked with making real-time decisions based on data inputs. However, these systems may not always make the correct call, particularly in complex or novel situations. When an AI system fails to detect an attack or inaccurately flags a legitimate action as malicious, it raises questions about who is accountable for the mistake.

Accountability of Developers and Organizations: In cases where AI systems malfunction or cause harm, it can be difficult to assign responsibility. Should accountability lie with the developers who built the system, the organizations deploying the technology, or the AI system itself? This ambiguity poses significant ethical concerns, as individuals and organizations may try to shift blame rather than take responsibility for AI failures.

To address accountability issues, organizations must establish clear lines of responsibility for the development, deployment, and monitoring of AI-driven cybersecurity systems. This includes maintaining transparency about the functioning of the AI system, implementing human-in-the-loop mechanisms to oversee decisions, and ensuring that appropriate remedial actions are taken in the event of an error or failure.

4. Transparency and Explainability of AI Systems

AI-driven systems often operate as "black boxes," meaning their decision-making processes are not always easily understood or explainable by humans. This lack of transparency can create ethical concerns in cybersecurity applications, particularly when individuals or organizations are affected by the outcomes of AI decisions without knowing how those decisions were made.

Explainability of Decisions: In cybersecurity, it is crucial to understand why an AI system flagged an activity as malicious or benign. If an AI system cannot explain its reasoning, it becomes difficult to assess its accuracy, identify potential biases, or challenge incorrect conclusions. For example, if an AI system blocks a user's access to certain data or systems, the lack of transparency could lead to frustration and distrust.

Trust in AI: Users and stakeholders need to trust that the AI system is making decisions based on sound reasoning and accurate data. Lack of explainability undermines that trust and makes it harder to identify and fix flaws in the model.

To address these challenges, developers should implement explainable AI (XAI) principles, which prioritize transparency and interpretability. By providing clear, human-understandable explanations of how decisions are made, organizations can foster trust in the system, ensure fairness, and improve accountability.

5. Security and Integrity of AI Models

Another ethical concern in AI-powered cyber defense is the security and integrity of the AI models themselves. As cybersecurity is a primary application for AI, these models can become prime targets for adversaries. Attackers may attempt to manipulate AI systems using adversarial tactics to deceive or trick them into making incorrect decisions.

Adversarial Attacks: Attackers may craft malicious inputs designed to exploit vulnerabilities in AI models. These adversarial inputs can cause the system to misidentify threats or fail to detect attacks, thereby undermining the security of the entire system.

Model Integrity: If an AI model is compromised, it could be subverted to perform malicious actions, such as allowing a hacker to bypass security protocols or enabling persistent vulnerabilities in a network. The challenge is ensuring that the models themselves are secure and resistant to manipulation.

Organizations must implement strong defenses to protect AI models from adversarial attacks, such as adversarial training, robustness testing, and model verification processes. This will help preserve the integrity and effectiveness of AI-powered cybersecurity systems, ensuring that they can continue to detect and prevent cyber threats effectively.

While AI has the potential to dramatically enhance cybersecurity defenses, it also brings with it a range of ethical challenges that must be carefully addressed. Privacy concerns, algorithmic bias, accountability, transparency, and model security are just a few of the critical ethical issues organizations must consider when deploying AI in cyber defense. Striking the right balance between leveraging AI for improved security and safeguarding individual rights and freedoms is essential. By prioritizing ethical considerations in the design, development, and deployment of AI-driven cybersecurity systems, organizations can build more robust, trustworthy, and responsible defenses against an increasingly sophisticated cyber threat landscape.

13.2 Balancing Security and Privacy: The Trade-offs

In the rapidly evolving world of cybersecurity, the growing reliance on artificial intelligence (AI) and machine learning (ML) has introduced new challenges in striking a delicate balance between security and privacy. As organizations implement more advanced AI-driven security measures, such as real-time threat detection, anomaly detection, and automated response systems, they must navigate the trade-offs between ensuring robust digital protection and respecting individuals' right to privacy. This chapter delves into the tension between security and privacy, exploring how these two critical components of digital protection can sometimes conflict and how organizations can strive to achieve an ethical, fair, and effective balance.

1. The Growing Demand for Cybersecurity and Privacy Concerns

In today's hyper-connected digital world, the demand for enhanced cybersecurity measures has never been greater. With cyberattacks becoming more frequent and sophisticated, organizations are investing heavily in AI-driven solutions to detect, prevent, and respond to these threats. From intrusion detection systems to behavioral analytics, AI technologies are being used to scrutinize vast amounts of user data and network activity in real time, ensuring that potential threats are identified and mitigated as quickly as possible.

However, these efforts to enhance security can sometimes infringe on privacy rights. The very mechanisms used to safeguard against cybercrime, such as monitoring user activity, collecting and analyzing personal data, and identifying abnormal behaviors, raise concerns about how much personal information is being exposed in the name of security. For example, AI systems may require access to sensitive data, such as communications, browsing habits, or device usage patterns, to accurately assess whether a security breach is occurring.

While security is crucial to protecting sensitive information, the data used to detect and respond to threats may itself contain sensitive personal or business information. Privacy advocates argue that constant surveillance and data collection for cybersecurity purposes can lead to overreach and a loss of autonomy for individuals and organizations. Finding the right balance between robust security measures and protecting privacy is essential for building trust and maintaining compliance with regulations.

2. Data Collection and Surveillance: The Privacy Dilemma

One of the most significant challenges in balancing security and privacy is the data collection required for effective AI-driven cybersecurity systems. Machine learning algorithms rely on vast datasets to identify patterns and anomalies that may indicate a cyberattack. These datasets may include information about network traffic, user behaviors, and even personal data such as emails, passwords, or location data. To detect emerging threats, organizations often have to gather and analyze enormous amounts of information in real-time, making it easier for sensitive personal data to be exposed.

Security Surveillance: AI systems typically need to monitor user behavior and interactions with digital platforms to detect malicious actions. However, this can quickly cross the line from security monitoring to intrusive surveillance, raising concerns about who has access to this data and how it is being used. The issue is particularly relevant in the context of employee monitoring in organizations, where constant tracking of digital activities can lead to a perception of a "big brother" environment, diminishing trust between employees and employers.

Over-Collection of Data: Many AI-powered systems collect far more data than is necessary for cybersecurity purposes. The data can often include sensitive personal information that may not be required for threat detection but is nevertheless processed and stored. This "over-collection" of data can leave individuals vulnerable to potential breaches, as it increases the attack surface that adversaries can exploit.

Organizations need to be mindful of the principle of data minimization, which emphasizes the collection of only the necessary information for a specific purpose. Implementing anonymization and encryption techniques can also help ensure that sensitive data is not exposed during security checks, thus enhancing privacy protection.

3. The Need for Transparency in AI Systems

As AI becomes increasingly integrated into cybersecurity frameworks, the complexity and opacity of these systems present another challenge to maintaining privacy. Many AI-driven security technologies operate as "black boxes," meaning their decision-making processes are not easily understood by humans. This lack of transparency is especially concerning when personal or sensitive data is involved, as users may not be aware of how their data is being used or what specific actions are being taken on their behalf.

Opacity of AI Decision-Making: The very nature of AI systems, particularly those that rely on deep learning models, can make it difficult for users or administrators to explain how a given decision was made. For example, AI models may flag certain user behaviors as suspicious, but without transparency in how those behaviors were evaluated, it is hard to ensure that the AI is acting fairly or accurately. Users whose actions are flagged as suspicious may feel that their privacy has been violated without sufficient understanding of why their data was accessed.

Accountability and Control: In cases where an AI system makes a mistake or raises false alarms, users and organizations must be able to trace the cause of the error. If the decision-making process is opaque, it becomes much harder to correct or mitigate these issues, undermining both the privacy and security of the system.

To mitigate these concerns, organizations should prioritize the development of explainable AI (XAI) systems. By offering clear, interpretable explanations of how AI systems arrive at their decisions, organizations can increase trust and transparency while still benefiting from enhanced security.

4. Privacy Laws and Regulations: Navigating Compliance

As organizations adopt AI-powered cybersecurity solutions, they must also navigate the complex landscape of privacy laws and regulations, which can vary significantly across regions and industries. In many jurisdictions, privacy regulations like the General Data Protection Regulation (GDPR) in the European Union or the California Consumer Privacy Act (CCPA) in the United States impose strict guidelines on how personal data can be collected, stored, and processed.

Data Processing and Consent: Privacy laws often require organizations to obtain explicit consent from users before collecting their personal data, including for cybersecurity purposes. This can be challenging in AI systems, where data may be analyzed in real time without users being fully aware of what data is being processed. Striking the right balance between real-time threat detection and respecting user consent is a critical aspect of this trade-off.

Data Minimization and Purpose Limitation: Privacy laws also require organizations to limit data collection to only what is necessary for a specific purpose. In the context of cybersecurity, this means that organizations must ensure that AI systems are only collecting the data required to detect and mitigate security threats, rather than engaging in unnecessary surveillance or data over-collection.

To remain compliant with privacy laws while benefiting from AI-driven cybersecurity solutions, organizations must invest in privacy-preserving technologies like differential privacy, encryption, and decentralized data storage. These tools can help ensure that personal data is not misused or exposed while still allowing AI systems to function effectively in detecting and responding to threats.

5. The Ethical Dilemma: Sacrificing Privacy for Security?

At its core, the issue of balancing security and privacy presents a broader ethical dilemma. Should organizations prioritize the security of systems, networks, and data over individual privacy rights? Or should privacy always take precedence, even if it means sacrificing some aspects of security? This question is central to the design and deployment of AI-powered cybersecurity systems.

On one hand, enhanced security is essential to protect against the growing threat of cyberattacks. A breach in an organization's security could have severe consequences, including financial loss, reputational damage, and even risks to national security. AI-driven cybersecurity systems, if implemented properly, can help prevent such breaches by identifying vulnerabilities and stopping attacks before they can cause harm.

On the other hand, individuals have the right to privacy, and overreach in surveillance or the collection of personal data can undermine this fundamental right. Excessive data collection and AI surveillance can lead to a "surveillance society," where individuals feel constantly watched, which can erode trust in organizations and harm relationships between consumers and companies.

Organizations must be guided by ethical principles and adopt a privacy-by-design approach, where privacy is embedded into the design of AI systems from the outset. Striking a balance between protecting both privacy and security requires careful consideration of these competing interests, with the ultimate goal being to protect individuals without infringing on their rights.

Balancing security and privacy is one of the most challenging ethical dilemmas facing organizations as they adopt AI-driven cybersecurity systems. While the need for robust cybersecurity measures is undeniable, protecting personal privacy and adhering to ethical guidelines are equally important. By prioritizing transparency, accountability, and privacy-preserving technologies, organizations can create cybersecurity solutions that provide strong protection against cyber threats while respecting individuals' privacy rights. It is only through this balance that organizations can build trust, foster user confidence, and ensure the ethical deployment of AI in cybersecurity.

13.3 Mitigating Risks of AI Misuse in Surveillance

As artificial intelligence (AI) technologies continue to advance, they have increasingly been integrated into surveillance systems for enhanced security and threat detection. While AI can greatly improve the efficiency and effectiveness of surveillance in areas like crime prevention, border security, and cybersecurity, its misuse can lead to significant ethical, privacy, and societal concerns. These concerns are particularly relevant when it comes to AI-powered surveillance systems, as they can easily be exploited for invasive monitoring, mass data collection, and even manipulation. This chapter explores the risks associated with AI misuse in surveillance and outlines strategies for mitigating these risks to ensure ethical, transparent, and responsible use.

1. Understanding the Potential for Misuse in AI-Driven Surveillance

AI-powered surveillance systems leverage technologies like facial recognition, object detection, and behavior analysis to monitor individuals and activities in real-time. These systems have been adopted by governments, law enforcement agencies, and private organizations, offering capabilities such as identifying criminal activities, tracking movements, and detecting anomalies in digital or physical spaces.

However, AI's ability to continuously analyze vast amounts of data raises serious concerns about privacy, consent, and human rights. The key risks related to AI misuse in surveillance include:

Invasive Monitoring: AI systems can be used to monitor individuals without their knowledge or consent, leading to a sense of constant surveillance. This can result in violations of privacy and the erosion of personal freedoms, particularly in public spaces.

Bias and Discrimination: AI systems, particularly facial recognition technology, have been shown to have biases in their algorithms, leading to incorrect identification, especially among marginalized groups such as racial minorities. Misuse of AI in surveillance could exacerbate these biases, leading to discrimination and unfair targeting.

Lack of Accountability: AI-driven surveillance systems can operate without human oversight, leading to decisions made by algorithms that cannot be easily questioned or challenged. This lack of transparency can undermine trust and accountability in law enforcement and government agencies.

Potential for Authoritarianism: The ability to use AI for mass surveillance could be exploited by authoritarian regimes or even democratic governments, leading to the suppression of dissent and the curtailing of individual rights. In such contexts, AI may be weaponized to track and monitor political activists, journalists, or dissenters.

Given these risks, it is essential to proactively address the potential for AI misuse in surveillance, ensuring that the technology is used in a way that aligns with ethical standards and respects individual rights.

2. Ethical Frameworks and Regulations to Guide AI Surveillance

The first step in mitigating the risks of AI misuse in surveillance is the development of robust ethical frameworks and legal regulations that guide the deployment of AI technologies. By establishing clear guidelines, organizations and governments can help prevent abuses while ensuring AI is used responsibly and transparently.

Data Protection and Privacy Laws: Regulations such as the General Data Protection Regulation (GDPR) in the European Union provide clear guidelines on data collection, processing, and storage. These regulations prioritize privacy by limiting the type and amount of data that can be collected and requiring explicit consent from individuals. For AI surveillance, the implementation of data protection laws ensures that personal information is not misused or over-collected.

Transparency and Accountability: One of the most critical aspects of mitigating AI misuse in surveillance is ensuring transparency in how AI systems operate. Organizations must disclose the purpose of surveillance, the data being collected, and how it will be used. Additionally, accountability measures should be implemented so that decisions made by AI systems can be traced back and reviewed by human oversight bodies. These measures help prevent the unchecked use of AI for mass surveillance.

Independent Oversight: Establishing independent bodies or regulatory agencies to monitor AI surveillance practices can help ensure that AI systems are not being misused. These bodies should be empowered to audit AI systems, review the data collected, and investigate potential abuses. Independent oversight acts as a safeguard to ensure compliance with ethical standards and laws.

Human Rights Protections: AI surveillance technologies must be deployed in a manner that does not infringe upon fundamental human rights, such as the right to privacy, freedom of expression, and freedom of assembly. International human rights organizations, such as the United Nations, have called for the regulation of AI surveillance technologies to protect individuals from misuse by both state and non-state actors.

By embedding ethical frameworks and regulations into the design and implementation of AI surveillance systems, the risks associated with misuse can be significantly reduced.

3. Designing Privacy-Preserving AI Surveillance Systems

Another key strategy for mitigating AI misuse in surveillance is the development of privacy-preserving technologies. These technologies focus on minimizing data collection, ensuring that sensitive personal information is not exposed, and preserving individuals' privacy while still enabling effective surveillance. Some of these technologies include:

Data Anonymization: Anonymization techniques remove or obfuscate personally identifiable information (PII) from data sets, ensuring that surveillance systems cannot track individuals back to their identity. For example, facial recognition systems can be designed to blur or anonymize faces when performing general surveillance, only retaining identifiable features when needed for specific investigations or security alerts.

Edge Computing: Instead of transmitting all surveillance data to central servers for processing, edge computing allows AI to process data locally on the devices or cameras where it is collected. This reduces the amount of personal data being sent to centralized databases, making it more difficult for sensitive data to be misused or exposed. It also helps minimize the risk of large-scale data breaches.

Differential Privacy: Differential privacy techniques add noise to the data before it is processed, ensuring that the information cannot be traced back to an individual. In AI surveillance, this could involve adding random variations to data about individuals' movements or behaviors, making it impossible to identify them while still enabling valuable analysis.

Minimal Data Retention: Surveillance systems should be designed with data retention policies that limit the amount of time personal data is stored. Instead of keeping surveillance data indefinitely, AI systems should delete or anonymize data after a specified period, reducing the risk of abuse or unauthorized access.

By incorporating privacy-preserving technologies into the design of AI surveillance systems, organizations can significantly reduce the impact on individuals' privacy rights and limit the potential for misuse.

4. Mitigating Bias and Discrimination in AI Surveillance

One of the most concerning risks associated with AI-powered surveillance is the potential for biased decision-making, particularly in facial recognition and behavioral analysis. If AI systems are trained on biased data sets or if their algorithms are not designed to account for diversity, they can disproportionately target certain groups, leading to discriminatory practices.

Bias Mitigation in Training Data: To reduce bias, organizations must ensure that the data sets used to train AI systems are diverse and representative of all demographic groups. This can involve collecting data from a wide range of sources and ensuring that marginalized communities are not underrepresented in the training sets. Regular audits should also be conducted to check for emerging biases in AI models.

Bias Detection and Auditing Tools: Developers should integrate bias detection tools into AI systems, allowing for real-time monitoring of algorithmic decisions. These tools can identify whether certain groups are being unfairly targeted or misidentified. If any issues are detected, the models should be retrained or adjusted to correct for biases.

Continuous Model Evaluation: AI surveillance systems should undergo continuous evaluation and re-calibration to ensure that their accuracy remains unbiased and that their decisions are consistently fair across all demographics. This helps prevent discriminatory behavior from being entrenched over time.

5. Engaging the Public in AI Surveillance Decisions

Another critical aspect of mitigating AI misuse in surveillance is public engagement. As AI surveillance becomes more widespread, it is important for organizations and governments to be transparent with the public about how AI systems are being used and to engage citizens in discussions about the ethical implications.

Public Consultation and Debate: Governments and organizations should conduct public consultations before deploying AI surveillance systems, allowing citizens to voice their concerns and opinions. This can help build public trust and ensure that AI surveillance policies align with societal values.

Education and Awareness: Public awareness campaigns can help individuals understand how AI surveillance works, what data is being collected, and how their rights are being protected. Educating the public empowers them to make informed decisions about their privacy and participate in debates about AI surveillance.

Transparency Reports: Organizations should issue transparency reports detailing the use of AI surveillance technologies, the data being collected, and how that data is being used. These reports should also disclose any privacy violations, bias-related issues, or incidents of misuse.

AI-driven surveillance technologies offer immense potential for improving security and detecting threats, but their misuse can lead to significant privacy violations, biases, and the erosion of civil liberties. To mitigate the risks of AI misuse, organizations must implement ethical guidelines, legal regulations, and privacy-preserving technologies, ensuring that AI surveillance systems are deployed transparently, responsibly, and in accordance with human rights standards. Through these efforts, AI can be harnessed for positive purposes while safeguarding individual privacy and preventing abuses of power.

13.4 Ensuring Transparency in AI Cybersecurity Systems

As artificial intelligence (AI) continues to play an integral role in cybersecurity, it is crucial to maintain transparency in its design, deployment, and operation. Transparency in AI systems ensures that stakeholders, including security professionals, users, and regulatory bodies, can understand how decisions are made, how data is handled, and how risks are mitigated. In cybersecurity, where decisions can have profound impacts on privacy, security, and trust, transparency is essential for fostering confidence in AI technologies and ensuring they are used ethically and effectively. This chapter explores the importance of transparency in AI-powered cybersecurity systems and offers strategies for achieving it.

1. The Importance of Transparency in AI Cybersecurity Systems

AI-driven cybersecurity solutions, such as intrusion detection systems, malware analysis tools, and threat intelligence platforms, are becoming increasingly sophisticated and critical to protecting digital infrastructures. However, these systems operate as "black boxes," where the inner workings of AI algorithms are not always visible or understandable to end users. This lack of transparency can create several risks:

Loss of Trust: When users or organizations cannot understand how AI systems make decisions, they may question their reliability or fear that the system might behave unpredictably. Without trust, cybersecurity professionals might resist integrating AI tools, reducing their effectiveness in protecting systems.

Difficulty in Accountability: In the event of a security breach, it is essential to understand how an AI system made its decisions. If AI systems are not transparent, it becomes difficult to assess whether the system made errors or if its behavior was aligned with the intended cybersecurity protocols. Lack of accountability can prevent proper investigation, leading to undetected weaknesses in security measures.

Ethical and Legal Concerns: AI systems can inadvertently exhibit biases, leading to unfair or discriminatory outcomes. Without transparency, such biases can go unnoticed and result in unequal protection across different groups. Additionally, transparency is necessary to ensure that AI systems comply with data protection and privacy laws, such as the General Data Protection Regulation (GDPR) in Europe.

Ensuring transparency in AI cybersecurity systems addresses these concerns by enabling scrutiny, accountability, and alignment with ethical standards.

2. How Transparency Benefits AI-Driven Cybersecurity

Transparency in AI systems brings several benefits to cybersecurity, which ultimately enhance the security posture of organizations and individuals. These benefits include:

Enhanced Trust and Adoption: When AI systems are transparent about how they function, users can better understand how decisions are made and what factors influence those decisions. This clarity encourages adoption and reliance on AI systems for cybersecurity tasks, which is essential given the growing complexity of cyber threats.

Improved Decision-Making: Transparency allows security professionals to review and challenge AI decisions, helping to fine-tune algorithms and improve overall system performance. This iterative feedback process enhances decision-making, ensuring AI systems adapt to evolving threats and remain accurate in detecting malicious activity.

Accountability and Auditability: Transparent AI systems offer clear insight into the rationale behind their actions, enabling detailed audits of decisions and actions taken. If an AI system detects a security threat, being able to trace the reasoning behind its detection allows cybersecurity teams to assess whether the alert is valid and to identify potential weaknesses in the system.

Compliance with Regulations: Transparency ensures that AI systems in cybersecurity comply with various regulations that mandate clear, understandable processes for collecting and processing data. Compliance with standards such as GDPR, the California Consumer Privacy Act (CCPA), and other privacy laws is crucial for organizations operating in regulated environments. Transparency allows organizations to demonstrate that they are handling data responsibly.

3. Approaches to Achieving Transparency in AI Cybersecurity Systems

To ensure transparency, AI cybersecurity systems must be designed, deployed, and managed with clear communication and accessibility of processes. There are several strategies to achieve transparency:

Explainable AI (XAI): One of the primary methods for achieving transparency is Explainable AI (XAI), which refers to techniques that make AI models more interpretable to humans. Instead of presenting results as opaque black-box outputs, XAI provides explanations for decisions made by AI systems, showing which factors or features influenced the model's predictions. For example, an intrusion detection system that flags a suspicious activity could explain that the detection was based on an unusual login time and IP address location, along with certain behavioral patterns that resemble past attack attempts.

Model Interpretability: While deep learning models are often considered to be difficult to interpret due to their complexity, there are tools and techniques that can be used to enhance the interpretability of AI models. Techniques such as LIME (Local Interpretable Model-agnostic Explanations) and SHAP (Shapley Additive Explanations) allow for the breakdown of model decisions into human-readable explanations, making it easier to understand why certain cybersecurity actions are recommended or taken by the AI system.

Transparent Data Practices: Transparency must extend to how data is handled, processed, and used in AI cybersecurity systems. Data privacy is a critical component of transparency, and users should be informed about what data is being collected, how it is being processed, and how long it will be retained. For example, an AI-driven firewall should clearly outline what information is collected (e.g., network traffic logs) and how that data contributes to identifying potential threats.

Audit Trails and Documentation: A comprehensive audit trail for AI cybersecurity systems ensures that every decision, action, and change is logged and can be reviewed later. This documentation should include information such as the input data used, the specific AI model or algorithm applied, and the rationale behind the AI's conclusions. This makes it possible to trace any anomalies or errors back to the decision-making process and ensures accountability.

Human-in-the-Loop Systems: Incorporating human oversight into AI systems is another way to increase transparency. Human-in-the-loop (HITL) systems allow cybersecurity experts to monitor and verify AI's actions before any significant decisions are made. For instance, while AI may identify a potential malware attack, a cybersecurity expert can review the findings, assess the severity, and decide on the appropriate response. This collaborative approach ensures that the human factor remains central to important security decisions.

4. Challenges in Implementing Transparency in AI Cybersecurity

While transparency is crucial, implementing it in AI cybersecurity systems presents several challenges:

Complexity of AI Models: AI systems, particularly deep learning models, can be incredibly complex. The more intricate the model, the harder it can be to explain how specific decisions are made. Balancing the power of advanced AI models with the need for transparency can be a difficult trade-off, especially when high levels of accuracy are required for threat detection.

Data Sensitivity and Privacy: Making AI systems transparent requires sharing data and decision-making processes, which can create conflicts with privacy and security concerns. Ensuring that sensitive data is not exposed during the explanation process is a critical challenge. For instance, revealing certain patterns in threat detection might inadvertently expose weaknesses in the system or in the organization's security practices.

Lack of Standardization: There is currently a lack of widely accepted standards for transparency in AI-driven cybersecurity systems. Without established frameworks and benchmarks, it can be challenging for organizations to know how best to achieve transparency while balancing technical complexity, user understanding, and security requirements.

Resistance to Transparency: Some organizations may be hesitant to make their AI systems fully transparent due to concerns about proprietary algorithms, intellectual property, or competitive advantages. While transparency is important for ethical and legal reasons, there may be resistance due to commercial interests or fear of exposing vulnerabilities.

5. The Future of Transparency in AI Cybersecurity

The future of AI in cybersecurity is likely to see increasing demands for transparency, as both users and regulators become more focused on accountability and trust in automated systems. As AI technology advances, transparency will need to evolve alongside innovations in AI models and data privacy concerns. We can expect the following trends:

Integration of AI Transparency Standards: Regulatory bodies will likely introduce more formalized standards for transparency in AI cybersecurity systems, helping to ensure that companies comply with best practices for explainability, auditability, and data protection.

Collaboration Between AI Developers and Cybersecurity Experts: Future AI systems will see closer collaboration between AI developers and cybersecurity professionals to create explainable models that meet the needs of both domains. This partnership will help ensure that AI systems are not only effective at detecting threats but also understandable and trustworthy.

AI Transparency Tools and Frameworks: We may see the development of more advanced tools and frameworks to facilitate transparency, including improved explainability algorithms, real-time monitoring tools, and automated auditing processes.

Transparency in AI cybersecurity systems is essential for fostering trust, accountability, and ethical behavior in the use of AI to protect digital infrastructures. Through the adoption of explainable AI techniques, transparent data practices, and continuous human oversight, organizations can ensure that AI-driven cybersecurity systems are both effective and aligned with societal values. Although there are challenges in implementing transparency, the long-term benefits in terms of trust, compliance, and improved security outcomes make it a critical goal for the future of cybersecurity.

13.5 Compliance with Global Data Protection Regulations

As the digital landscape continues to evolve and AI technologies become integral to cybersecurity, compliance with global data protection regulations has become a significant concern for organizations. Data protection laws ensure that individuals' privacy is respected, and sensitive data is handled appropriately, particularly when it comes to the vast amounts of data processed by AI systems. This chapter examines the importance of ensuring compliance with international data protection regulations, how AI cybersecurity systems can be designed to align with these laws, and the strategies organizations can employ to meet regulatory requirements.

1. The Importance of Data Protection Regulations in Cybersecurity

With AI and machine learning becoming increasingly central to cybersecurity, organizations must handle large amounts of data, some of which may be sensitive or personal in nature. For instance, personal information, login credentials, financial data, and health records are often part of the datasets processed by AI models used in security systems like intrusion detection, threat intelligence platforms, and behavioral analytics tools.

Data protection regulations aim to safeguard individuals' rights over their personal data, prevent unauthorized access, and ensure that data is processed fairly and securely. For cybersecurity, these regulations are crucial as AI systems often require access to vast amounts of data to detect patterns, identify threats, and respond in real time. Non-compliance can lead to severe penalties, reputational damage, and loss of customer trust. Consequently, aligning AI-powered cybersecurity tools with data protection regulations is not just a legal obligation but also a vital part of responsible data management.

2. Key Global Data Protection Regulations Impacting AI Cybersecurity

Several international and regional data protection laws shape how AI systems must handle personal and sensitive data. Understanding these regulations is essential for ensuring that AI cybersecurity systems comply with legal requirements.

General Data Protection Regulation (GDPR): The GDPR is one of the most well-known and comprehensive data protection regulations globally, applicable to all organizations processing personal data of European Union (EU) citizens. GDPR imposes strict rules on data collection, storage, processing, and sharing, and it grants individuals rights over their personal data, such as the right to access, rectification, and erasure. GDPR also places emphasis on data minimization, transparency, and security measures, all of which affect AI systems used for cybersecurity.

Implications for AI Cybersecurity: AI systems must be designed to respect data privacy rights under GDPR, including ensuring data minimization, obtaining explicit consent for data processing, and providing mechanisms for data subjects to access or delete their data. For example, when an AI-based intrusion detection system processes network traffic logs, it must do so in a way that does not unnecessarily store or expose personal data. Additionally, AI models used in threat detection must be explainable to meet the transparency requirements under GDPR.

California Consumer Privacy Act (CCPA): The CCPA is a state-level regulation in California, USA, that provides consumers with the right to control their personal data. It includes provisions for the right to know what data is being collected, the right to delete data, and the right to opt-out of data sales.

Implications for AI Cybersecurity: Under the CCPA, organizations using AI-driven cybersecurity tools must disclose the types of data being collected and processed and provide users with clear options to manage or delete their data. For example, organizations must ensure that threat intelligence platforms powered by AI do not violate users' rights by selling personal data without proper consent.

Asia-Pacific Privacy Laws (e.g., Australia's Privacy Act, Japan's APPI): In the Asia-Pacific region, countries have their own data protection regulations, such as Australia's Privacy Act and Japan's Act on the Protection of Personal Information (APPI). These laws generally focus on personal data processing, user consent, and data breach notification.

Implications for AI Cybersecurity: AI-powered cybersecurity systems must align with the local laws in each region where the data is being processed. For instance, AI systems designed to protect data in Australian organizations must comply with the Privacy Act's provisions on data security, the rights of individuals to access their data, and ensuring data is not used for purposes beyond those consented to by the data subject.

Brazil's Lei Geral de Proteção de Dados (LGPD): The LGPD is Brazil's data protection regulation, modeled after the GDPR. It applies to any organization that processes personal data of Brazilian citizens, regardless of the organization's location. It includes provisions related to consent, data minimization, data security, and individual rights to access, correct, and delete personal data.

Implications for AI Cybersecurity: AI systems used by organizations operating in Brazil must be designed to comply with LGPD's strict consent requirements and data security provisions. For example, AI-driven cybersecurity tools that collect and analyze personal data must implement adequate security controls and ensure transparency in their data processing operations.

China's Personal Information Protection Law (PIPL): China's PIPL, effective from 2021, is another example of a stringent data protection law that focuses on personal data privacy, security, and cross-border data transfer restrictions. This law applies to organizations processing data of Chinese citizens and mandates that businesses obtain clear consent from individuals before processing personal data.

Implications for AI Cybersecurity: Organizations using AI cybersecurity tools to protect systems in China must ensure that their data handling practices comply with the PIPL. This includes getting explicit consent for the use of personal data, securing data during processing, and adhering to specific rules regarding data transfers across borders.

3. Strategies for Achieving Compliance in AI Cybersecurity Systems

Organizations can adopt various strategies to ensure that their AI-powered cybersecurity solutions comply with global data protection regulations.

Data Minimization and Purpose Limitation: AI systems should only collect and process the minimum amount of data necessary to perform their functions. For instance, in threat detection, AI systems should focus on processing metadata or anonymized data, rather than sensitive personal information, unless absolutely necessary for accurate threat identification.

By adhering to the principles of data minimization and purpose limitation, organizations can reduce the risk of non-compliance and protect individuals' privacy rights.

Privacy by Design and Default: AI systems should be built with privacy as a core feature from the outset. This concept, known as Privacy by Design, requires that data privacy be integrated into the design of AI models, algorithms, and security processes. Additionally, Privacy by Default ensures that, by default, AI systems do not process more data than necessary and provide robust data protection controls without requiring users to take action.

Incorporating these principles into the development of AI cybersecurity tools ensures that privacy is safeguarded throughout the lifecycle of the system.

Transparent Data Processing Practices: Transparency is key to compliance with many data protection laws. Organizations must be clear about how AI systems collect and process personal data, the purposes for which the data is used, and how it will be protected. Privacy policies and terms of service should provide clear information about AI tools and their data processing practices.

Additionally, organizations should consider providing users with control over their data, allowing them to opt-out or request deletion, in line with regulations like GDPR and CCPA.

Data Anonymization and Pseudonymization: Where possible, organizations should employ techniques like anonymization and pseudonymization to reduce the risks associated with processing personal data. By anonymizing data, AI systems can continue to detect and respond to threats without exposing sensitive personal information, helping organizations remain compliant with regulations.

Conducting Privacy Impact Assessments (PIAs): To comply with data protection laws, particularly under GDPR, organizations are required to conduct regular Privacy Impact Assessments (PIAs) or Data Protection Impact Assessments (DPIAs). These assessments evaluate the risks associated with AI systems, particularly when handling sensitive or personal data, and help identify potential compliance issues before they become problems.

Cross-Border Data Transfer Considerations: AI cybersecurity systems often require transferring data across borders, which can be complicated due to various regulatory requirements. Organizations should ensure that any cross-border data transfers comply with regulations such as GDPR's restrictions on transferring personal data outside the EU. Techniques like using Standard Contractual Clauses (SCCs) or Binding Corporate Rules (BCRs) can help ensure that data transfers comply with legal requirements.

As AI continues to revolutionize cybersecurity, ensuring compliance with global data protection regulations is paramount for both ethical and legal reasons. Organizations must carefully design and implement AI-driven cybersecurity systems that adhere to regulations such as GDPR, CCPA, PIPL, and others, to protect personal data, maintain trust, and avoid costly penalties. By adopting strategies like data minimization, transparency, privacy by design, and conducting privacy impact assessments, organizations can create AI cybersecurity systems that not only defend against evolving threats but also respect and safeguard users' privacy rights.

14. Building a Resilient Cybersecurity Ecosystem with AI

In an increasingly interconnected world, building a resilient cybersecurity ecosystem is more critical than ever. This chapter explores how AI can be integrated into broader cybersecurity strategies to create a proactive, adaptive, and robust defense network. By combining AI-driven tools such as intrusion detection systems, threat intelligence, and automated incident response with human expertise, organizations can develop a multi-layered security approach that continuously evolves to combat emerging threats. Readers will learn how to foster collaboration between AI technologies and cybersecurity professionals, ensuring that AI enhances decision-making and strengthens defenses without compromising human oversight. The chapter also discusses the importance of scalability and adaptability in creating systems that can withstand future challenges, preparing organizations to thrive in an ever-changing digital landscape.

14.1 Integrating AI with Human Expertise

The integration of Artificial Intelligence (AI) with human expertise represents one of the most powerful approaches to strengthening cybersecurity. While AI brings advanced capabilities, such as rapid data processing, pattern recognition, and predictive analytics, human expertise remains essential in providing context, ethical decision-making, and nuanced judgment. This chapter explores how the combination of AI and human professionals can create a more resilient, adaptive, and effective cybersecurity framework.

1. The Complementary Strengths of AI and Human Experts

AI excels at automating complex tasks, processing vast amounts of data, and identifying patterns that would be challenging for humans to detect. Machine learning models, for example, can analyze network traffic in real-time to identify anomalies, while AI-driven systems can predict potential threats based on historical data and emerging trends. These systems can scale and operate continuously, offering efficiency and speed far beyond human capabilities.

However, human experts bring critical skills to the table that AI cannot replicate. These include:

Contextual Understanding: Humans can understand the broader implications of a cybersecurity threat or a data breach. While AI might flag an anomaly, it may not be able to grasp the political, legal, or social context behind an attack. Cybersecurity professionals can interpret these threats within a larger context and make informed decisions on how to respond.

Ethical and Legal Judgment: AI operates based on the data it's trained on and the algorithms that drive it. It does not have the capability to make ethical decisions or understand the legal ramifications of its actions. Human professionals play an essential role in ensuring that security measures align with legal frameworks and ethical guidelines, especially in complex situations where privacy and rights are at stake.

Creative Problem Solving: While AI can identify threats and suggest responses based on past patterns, it lacks the creativity and intuition that cybersecurity experts bring to the table. Human experts are critical in developing new defense strategies, responding to novel attacks, and fine-tuning AI models to handle increasingly sophisticated threats.

By combining the strengths of AI and human expertise, organizations can better address the challenges posed by modern cybersecurity threats and create a defense mechanism that is both dynamic and effective.

2. Enhancing Decision-Making with AI-Driven Insights

AI's ability to provide actionable insights is a significant advantage in cybersecurity. AI systems are capable of processing large datasets in real time, identifying threats much faster than human teams could on their own. By analyzing historical data and ongoing security events, AI can predict and detect a variety of attack types, such as zero-day exploits, ransomware attacks, and advanced persistent threats (APTs).

However, AI is most effective when used as a decision-support tool rather than a replacement for human decision-making. For example, an AI-powered intrusion detection system may flag suspicious activity, but it is up to a human expert to assess the severity, determine the potential risks, and decide the appropriate course of action. This decision could include manual intervention, a response strategy, or a combination of automated and human-driven actions. AI helps by filtering out the noise and presenting only the most relevant data, thereby streamlining the decision-making process for cybersecurity professionals.

Moreover, as cyber threats evolve, human cybersecurity experts can continuously improve the AI models by feeding them new data and adjusting algorithms to address emerging threats. This continuous feedback loop between AI and human expertise enhances the system's accuracy and efficacy over time.

3. Collaboration Between Security Operations and AI Systems

In modern cybersecurity operations, Security Operations Centers (SOCs) are integral to managing and responding to security incidents. AI can be integrated into the SOC ecosystem to improve threat detection, automate routine tasks, and support incident response.

For example, AI can be used to monitor networks 24/7, automatically detecting potential security breaches such as phishing attempts, malware infections, or unauthorized access. AI-powered systems can escalate the most critical incidents to human security professionals, who then assess the situation and decide on the appropriate response. This collaboration ensures that human experts can focus on high-priority threats, while AI handles repetitive tasks such as scanning logs, monitoring traffic, or identifying known attack patterns.

Additionally, AI can be employed in security orchestration, automation, and response (SOAR) platforms. These platforms integrate AI into the incident response process by automating repetitive tasks and coordinating responses across different security tools. In this collaborative model, AI handles routine tasks and the automation of initial responses, while human experts can intervene when deeper investigation or sophisticated decision-making is needed.

4. Continuous Learning and Adaptation

One of the critical ways to integrate AI and human expertise is through a continuous learning process. While AI models are incredibly powerful, they require ongoing training and refinement to stay effective. Humans play a pivotal role in this process by providing feedback and oversight to ensure that the AI systems remain up-to-date with the latest security threats and industry trends.

Cybersecurity professionals can provide the AI models with new training data, based on emerging threat patterns, attack vectors, and security vulnerabilities. They can also adjust models to reflect changing business objectives, technological environments, and legal requirements. AI, in turn, offers human experts a more accurate and comprehensive understanding of the evolving threat landscape.

Moreover, cybersecurity professionals can use AI-driven systems to monitor and assess vulnerabilities across an organization's entire IT infrastructure, providing valuable insights that help to proactively address potential weaknesses before they are exploited. AI-based threat intelligence platforms, for example, can gather and analyze global threat data, providing human experts with relevant, timely insights to guide their defensive strategies.

5. The Role of Human Expertise in AI Model Development and Maintenance

AI and machine learning models are only as good as the data they are trained on. While AI systems can process and analyze data autonomously, it's human experts who are responsible for curating and preparing the data. They must ensure that data is clean, diverse, and representative of the threat landscape to prevent AI systems from being biased or ineffective.

Human experts also play a crucial role in evaluating the performance of AI models and fine-tuning them as necessary. AI-based systems may encounter challenges, such as misclassifying a benign activity as a threat or failing to recognize new, unknown attack vectors. Security professionals can adjust the models, retrain them on new data, and introduce corrective measures. They may also provide insights into how AI systems could be further improved to handle more complex or targeted attacks.

6. Addressing Ethical Concerns with AI

The integration of AI into cybersecurity raises several ethical considerations, such as privacy concerns, fairness, transparency, and accountability. Human experts play a vital role in ensuring that AI-driven systems adhere to ethical standards, comply with regulations, and respect user privacy.

For instance, AI systems may require access to sensitive personal data for threat detection and mitigation. Human professionals must ensure that the system operates within the boundaries of ethical guidelines, protecting individuals' rights and preventing abuse. Additionally, cybersecurity teams should provide transparency regarding how AI models make decisions and ensure that there is human oversight to prevent algorithmic bias or other harmful outcomes.

Moreover, in situations where AI-driven cybersecurity systems have to make decisions about data access or privacy (e.g., during a data breach investigation), human professionals must evaluate the situation and decide the best course of action in accordance with ethical principles and legal requirements.

7. The Future of AI and Human Collaboration in Cybersecurity

Looking ahead, the role of AI in cybersecurity is expected to grow, but so will the need for human expertise. As AI becomes more sophisticated, human cybersecurity professionals will be required to take on roles as overseers, trainers, and decision-makers. The most effective cybersecurity teams will consist of human experts working alongside AI-driven systems to build more resilient defenses, create proactive strategies, and respond to threats in real-time.

The future will likely see an even more integrated approach, where AI systems are embedded into every layer of cybersecurity, from threat detection to incident response. Human experts will continuously refine these systems, ensuring that they remain effective against evolving threats while adhering to ethical, legal, and privacy standards.

The integration of AI with human expertise is essential to the future of cybersecurity. While AI offers remarkable capabilities in automating tasks, analyzing vast amounts of data, and detecting threats, human professionals bring the critical elements of context, judgment, and creativity that AI alone cannot provide. Together, AI and human expertise form a symbiotic relationship, creating a more powerful, adaptive, and resilient cybersecurity ecosystem capable of addressing the challenges posed by an increasingly sophisticated digital threat landscape.

14.2 Building AI-Driven Collaborative Defense Networks

The complexity and scale of modern cyber threats demand a shift towards collaborative, dynamic defense strategies that leverage the strengths of AI to protect digital assets in real-time. Traditional cybersecurity efforts often rely on siloed, individual defense measures that are reactive and often unable to scale in response to the increasingly sophisticated and evolving threat landscape. In contrast, AI-driven collaborative defense networks allow organizations to work together to share knowledge, resources, and intelligence to create a more cohesive and adaptive defense mechanism.

This chapter delves into the key components and strategies for building AI-powered collaborative defense networks, examining how AI can be integrated into cross-organization and multi-layered defense systems to enhance proactive threat detection, faster response times, and overall resilience.

1. The Need for Collaborative Defense Networks

In the face of evolving cyber threats, collaboration between organizations, sectors, and even nations has become increasingly important. Cyber threats do not respect borders, industries, or organizational boundaries—what threatens one entity can often be a precursor to threats that affect many others. With cybercriminals using increasingly sophisticated methods, such as advanced persistent threats (APTs), coordinated ransomware attacks, and AI-driven exploits, cybersecurity must evolve beyond traditional, isolated defense mechanisms.

Collaborative defense networks enable organizations to work together by sharing critical threat intelligence, early warning signals, and defensive strategies. These networks allow for a unified approach where the actions of one organization can directly benefit others. AI plays a central role in this approach by enabling rapid communication, real-time data sharing, and automated decision-making processes that enhance collective defense efforts. AI technologies can analyze vast amounts of threat intelligence data, identify emerging attack patterns, and facilitate the exchange of information across the network, ensuring that all participants are better equipped to prevent or mitigate threats.

2. Leveraging AI for Threat Intelligence Sharing

Threat intelligence sharing is at the heart of any collaborative defense network. Traditional threat intelligence sharing has often been slow, inefficient, and reactive. However, with the integration of AI, organizations can automate the exchange of threat data and generate real-time alerts based on shared intelligence, thereby creating a more agile defense posture.

AI can process threat intelligence data from multiple sources—such as malware hashes, indicators of compromise (IOCs), network traffic patterns, and attack signatures—at an unprecedented speed and scale. It can identify correlations and trends across different attack vectors and translate this information into actionable intelligence. Furthermore, AI-powered systems can aggregate data from global sources, including private and public sector entities, creating a more comprehensive and up-to-date view of the threat landscape.

In a collaborative network, AI enables the automated dissemination of relevant information to all stakeholders. For example, when a new malware strain is discovered, the AI system can instantly analyze it, share IOCs with other organizations, and provide guidance on mitigating or blocking the threat. This shared intelligence benefits all participants in the network by allowing them to take proactive steps to defend against emerging attacks.

3. Automating Incident Response and Decision Making

Effective incident response requires swift action, coordination, and accurate decision-making. AI can enhance the speed and precision of these processes by automating routine tasks, assessing security incidents, and making recommendations for responses based on learned patterns from historical data.

In a collaborative defense network, AI-driven incident response systems can work in tandem across multiple organizations. When a cybersecurity incident occurs, the AI system can immediately analyze the situation, identify the nature of the threat, and recommend or even initiate predefined response actions. These automated responses could include isolating affected systems, blocking malicious traffic, or patching vulnerabilities.

In a collaborative setting, these AI systems can leverage data from other organizations' networks to improve incident response. For example, if one organization detects a new attack vector, its AI system can instantly share the information with others in the network, allowing them to implement countermeasures before the attack spreads further. This real-time collaboration enables faster mitigation and containment, reducing the overall impact of cyber incidents.

4. Building Trust and Transparency in Collaborative Networks

One of the primary challenges in building collaborative defense networks is ensuring trust among participating organizations. For AI-driven networks to be effective, organizations must trust that the information being shared is accurate, reliable, and protected. Establishing trust is essential to encourage information sharing and ensure that sensitive data is not misused.

Blockchain technology can be integrated into collaborative networks to provide a secure, transparent, and immutable record of shared threat intelligence. By using blockchain, organizations can ensure that information is exchanged in a tamper-proof manner, and participants can verify the authenticity and origin of shared data. This technology helps build trust by ensuring that data is not altered and can be traced back to its source, fostering a higher level of confidence in the collaborative defense system.

Moreover, organizations need to adhere to legal and ethical standards regarding data sharing. Data privacy regulations, such as the General Data Protection Regulation (GDPR) in Europe or the California Consumer Privacy Act (CCPA), must be taken into account when building collaborative defense networks. AI systems can help enforce compliance by ensuring that shared data is anonymized where necessary and that privacy concerns are addressed before sensitive information is exchanged.

5. Enhancing Cross-Sector Collaboration

The threat landscape is increasingly diverse, and cybercriminals often target critical sectors such as finance, healthcare, energy, and government. A collaborative defense network should extend beyond individual organizations to include entire industries or sectors. By working together, organizations can better defend against cross-sector threats and ensure that critical infrastructure remains protected.

For instance, in the financial sector, banks and financial institutions can share real-time threat intelligence related to financial fraud, phishing schemes, or ransomware attacks. AI-powered systems can identify trends, vulnerabilities, and emerging threats across the sector, allowing institutions to act quickly and prevent widespread damage. Similarly, in healthcare, hospitals, pharmaceutical companies, and healthcare providers can exchange data on malware and ransomware targeting medical devices, patient data, and critical infrastructure.

Cross-sector collaboration benefits all participants by providing a more comprehensive defense system that is capable of addressing the diverse nature of cyber threats. AI can be used to aggregate sector-specific threat data and provide actionable insights that enhance the resilience of entire industries.

6. The Role of Machine Learning in Adaptive Defense

Machine learning (ML) plays a pivotal role in adaptive cybersecurity by allowing AI systems to continuously learn from data, adapt to new threats, and improve their effectiveness over time. In collaborative defense networks, ML algorithms can be employed to analyze data from multiple organizations and adapt the network's defense strategies accordingly.

For example, if an AI system detects a new attack technique that is successful in one organization, it can automatically update its models to recognize similar attacks in other organizations within the network. As the network grows and more organizations contribute data, the machine learning models become more refined, allowing the defense network to stay ahead of evolving cyber threats.

Moreover, ML algorithms can help detect previously unknown attack vectors by analyzing patterns in incoming data that would be invisible to traditional, signature-based detection systems. This capability is especially important in collaborative defense networks, where new and evolving threats can be shared and addressed quickly through AI's adaptive learning capabilities.

7. Future Directions and Challenges in Building Collaborative Defense Networks

While the potential for AI-driven collaborative defense networks is vast, several challenges remain in fully realizing this vision. Some of the key hurdles include:

Data Privacy and Security: Ensuring the privacy and security of shared data is critical. Collaboration between organizations must not compromise individual privacy, proprietary information, or sensitive data. Advanced encryption techniques and data anonymization methods are essential to mitigate these risks.

Scalability and Interoperability: Collaborative defense networks need to scale effectively and work across diverse organizations with different security protocols, systems, and infrastructures. Achieving interoperability between these different environments is a technical challenge that must be addressed to ensure seamless collaboration.

Legal and Regulatory Considerations: Organizations must navigate legal and regulatory complexities when sharing threat intelligence across borders, especially in a global collaborative defense network. Adherence to data protection regulations and international cybersecurity laws is essential to avoid legal pitfalls.

Building AI-driven collaborative defense networks represents the future of cybersecurity. By leveraging AI to automate threat intelligence sharing, enhance decision-making, and enable adaptive, real-time responses, organizations can create a more resilient and proactive defense system. Through cross-organization collaboration, shared intelligence, and collective action, these networks can mitigate the impact of cyberattacks and prevent emerging threats from spreading. As AI and machine learning technologies continue to evolve, they will play an increasingly central role in building dynamic and adaptive cybersecurity ecosystems capable of addressing the challenges posed by today's rapidly changing digital landscape.

14.3 Addressing Scalability Challenges in AI Systems

As organizations scale their operations and digital environments become more complex, the demands on cybersecurity systems grow exponentially. This is particularly true when implementing Artificial Intelligence (AI) and Machine Learning (ML) solutions for cybersecurity, which require not only robust infrastructure but also the capacity to process vast amounts of data in real-time across increasingly distributed networks. Scalability is one of the key challenges that must be addressed to ensure that AI-driven cybersecurity solutions can effectively protect against evolving and sophisticated cyber threats. In this chapter, we will explore the various scalability challenges that arise when deploying AI systems in cybersecurity, and propose strategies for overcoming these hurdles.

1. The Need for Scalability in AI-Powered Cybersecurity Systems

AI and ML technologies have demonstrated great potential in enhancing cybersecurity by automating threat detection, reducing response times, and improving predictive capabilities. However, as businesses expand and data volumes increase, the demand for more powerful AI systems capable of handling larger datasets, more diverse sources of information, and more complex network environments becomes critical.

Scalability in AI systems refers to the ability of these systems to maintain or improve performance as the size of the data, the complexity of the networks, or the number of users grows. In the context of cybersecurity, this includes processing large amounts of network traffic, analyzing vast quantities of threat intelligence data, and managing the increased load from distributed IoT devices, cloud environments, and multi-cloud systems.

With the increasing adoption of cloud computing, Internet of Things (IoT), and connected devices, organizations are faced with larger attack surfaces and higher volumes of cybersecurity data to monitor. AI systems need to be designed to adapt to this scale, ensuring that they can continue to provide accurate and timely threat analysis without compromising efficiency or performance.

2. Data Volume and Velocity: Handling Large Datasets in Real-Time

One of the most significant scalability challenges in AI-powered cybersecurity is the sheer volume and velocity of data that must be processed. Modern networks generate terabytes of data every day, including logs, network traffic, and user behavior data. As organizations grow, so does the data they need to protect and analyze. The challenge lies in not only gathering this data but also processing it in real-time to identify potential threats quickly.

AI systems in cybersecurity rely on machine learning models to identify anomalies and detect threats. These models require large, high-quality datasets to learn and generate accurate predictions. However, as data volumes increase, training AI models becomes more resource-intensive. If the systems cannot scale to handle these large datasets, they may struggle to deliver timely insights, leading to delays in threat detection and response.

To address this challenge, organizations can deploy distributed AI architectures and cloud-based infrastructure that allows for horizontal scaling—enabling systems to spread processing workloads across multiple servers or data centers. This approach can increase computational power without needing to upgrade individual hardware components, ensuring the AI system can scale with the growing data load.

Furthermore, organizations can implement techniques like streaming data analytics and edge computing to process data closer to its source, reducing latency and enabling faster decision-making. By processing data at the edge, AI systems can identify and mitigate threats before they propagate throughout the network.

3. Computational Power and Model Complexity

As AI models become more sophisticated, their computational requirements increase. Deep learning models, for instance, require powerful processing units (GPUs or TPUs) to train and run efficiently. These models, which excel at identifying complex patterns in data, can be particularly demanding in terms of computational power, especially as they are trained on massive datasets that grow larger over time.

The complexity of these models can also make scaling more difficult. While a small dataset might require only a few hours or days of processing on a single machine, as the dataset grows in size and complexity, the resources needed to train the model multiply accordingly. This computational burden can slow down training times and even limit the AI system's ability to learn in real-time from continuously streaming data.

To address these scalability issues, organizations can consider distributed machine learning and parallel computing. These techniques allow large models to be broken down into smaller tasks and processed concurrently across multiple machines or processing units, speeding up both training and inference times. Additionally, model pruning—which reduces the size and complexity of a deep learning model without sacrificing accuracy—can help decrease computational demands, allowing AI systems to scale more effectively.

Using cloud-based AI platforms that offer elastic computing resources is another key strategy. With cloud infrastructure, organizations can easily scale up or down their computational resources based on demand, enabling them to quickly adapt to changing workloads without significant upfront capital investment.

4. Real-Time Decision-Making and Latency Issues

In cybersecurity, the ability to make real-time decisions is critical to protecting against threats. However, as AI models become more complex and data flows increase, the time it takes to process and analyze this information can introduce significant latency. High latency can result in slower response times, allowing cyberattacks to progress before mitigation strategies are deployed.

Reducing latency while maintaining model accuracy is a key challenge when scaling AI systems for cybersecurity. AI solutions need to process large datasets in real-time and make decisions based on this data—whether it's identifying an intrusion attempt, analyzing a suspicious network pattern, or stopping a phishing attack before it succeeds. Delays in processing can render the entire security system ineffective, leaving networks vulnerable to attack.

One solution to this problem is implementing edge computing and distributed AI models, which allows data processing to occur closer to the source (such as at the device level or on local servers) rather than relying solely on centralized cloud infrastructure. This can significantly reduce latency by minimizing the time it takes for data to travel across networks. Additionally, real-time model optimization techniques can be used to update AI models quickly, ensuring that the system stays responsive without sacrificing performance.

5. Ensuring Interoperability Across Diverse Systems and Platforms

Modern organizations use a wide range of technologies, platforms, and security tools—each with their own architectures, APIs, and data formats. Scaling AI systems to work seamlessly across these diverse environments while maintaining consistent performance can be a major challenge.

For example, an AI system designed for a corporate data center may struggle to integrate with cloud-based infrastructure, or an AI solution built for a specific endpoint might not work across an entire network of IoT devices. Ensuring that AI systems can communicate and share data effectively across different platforms is essential for scalability, especially as organizations grow and diversify their tech stacks.

To address this challenge, organizations can adopt open-source frameworks and standardized data formats for AI integration. These tools help ensure that AI systems can interact with a wide range of platforms and services, promoting interoperability. Additionally, using containerized applications (such as Docker) and microservices architecture can enable organizations to scale their AI systems flexibly across different environments, without compromising on functionality or performance.

6. Addressing Data Quality and Availability

As organizations scale, maintaining the quality and availability of data becomes increasingly complex. AI systems rely heavily on high-quality, clean data to make accurate predictions and detect threats effectively. However, as data volumes grow, it becomes more difficult to ensure that all data is accurate, relevant, and accessible.

Poor data quality, inconsistent formats, or missing data can hinder the AI system's ability to perform at scale, leading to incorrect predictions, false positives, or missed threats. Additionally, ensuring that the AI model has access to data in real-time across a distributed network of systems and devices becomes more challenging as the attack surface grows.

To overcome these challenges, organizations can implement data normalization processes, which help standardize and clean data before it is fed into the AI system. Data lakes can be used to store large volumes of raw data in a centralized repository, while data pipelines ensure that the data is consistently collected, processed, and made available for analysis.

Scalability challenges in AI-powered cybersecurity systems are complex and multifaceted, but they can be overcome with a combination of advanced techniques and technologies. By leveraging distributed architectures, parallel processing, cloud resources, and edge computing, organizations can ensure that their AI systems can scale effectively to meet the growing demands of modern cybersecurity. As businesses continue to evolve and digital environments expand, addressing these scalability challenges will be crucial for maintaining robust, adaptive, and responsive security measures capable of defending against the ever-increasing volume and complexity of cyber threats.

14.4 Future-Proofing Against Emerging Threats

As the digital landscape continues to evolve, so too does the nature of cyber threats. With the rapid advancement of technologies like artificial intelligence (AI), machine learning (ML), the Internet of Things (IoT), and quantum computing, cybersecurity professionals must adopt strategies to future-proof their defense systems against increasingly sophisticated and unpredictable threats. The traditional methods of cybersecurity are no longer sufficient to keep pace with these advancements, and proactive measures must be taken to ensure systems remain secure against emerging challenges.

In this chapter, we will explore how organizations can prepare for future cybersecurity challenges by adopting a proactive, agile approach to AI and cybersecurity systems. We'll examine the key trends that are shaping the future of cyber threats and offer strategies for fortifying defenses to safeguard against these evolving dangers.

1. The Rise of Quantum Computing: A Game-Changer for Cybersecurity

Quantum computing represents a paradigm shift in computing power, with the potential to break traditional encryption methods that have long been the cornerstone of cybersecurity. While quantum computers are still in their infancy, their future capabilities raise serious concerns about the security of sensitive data. Quantum algorithms, such as Shor's algorithm, can efficiently factor large numbers and break widely used public-key encryption schemes, such as RSA and ECC, rendering current encryption protocols obsolete.

To future-proof against quantum threats, organizations must begin exploring quantum-resistant cryptography (also known as post-quantum cryptography). This emerging field focuses on developing encryption algorithms that can withstand attacks from quantum computers. Governments and industries are already investing in quantum-safe encryption standards, and businesses must stay ahead of the curve by evaluating and adopting quantum-resistant solutions.

2. AI-Driven Cyberattacks: The Need for Evolving Defenses

AI and ML are not only tools for defending against cyber threats but are also being used by cybercriminals to develop more advanced and evasive attacks. AI-powered malware can adapt in real-time to bypass traditional security measures, while automated tools can be used to exploit vulnerabilities faster than human defenders can react. Similarly, AI-driven social engineering attacks, such as highly convincing phishing campaigns, are becoming more prevalent.

To future-proof against these AI-driven attacks, organizations must integrate adaptive cybersecurity systems that can respond to novel and evolving threats. AI and ML models must be trained to recognize patterns and behaviors indicative of AI-powered attacks. These models should also be continuously updated to detect new attack methods, and anomaly detection systems must be flexible enough to account for previously unknown threat vectors.

In addition, the integration of collaborative defense mechanisms can help organizations share threat intelligence and insights across industries and sectors, creating a more robust collective defense against AI-driven cybercriminal activities.

3. Securing the Expanding Attack Surface: IoT, 5G, and Cloud

The proliferation of IoT devices, the rollout of 5G networks, and the increasing adoption of cloud technologies are all expanding the attack surface, creating new vulnerabilities for cybercriminals to exploit. While these technologies offer tremendous benefits in terms of connectivity, efficiency, and data sharing, they also create new entry points for malicious actors.

To future-proof against threats arising from these technologies, organizations must implement zero-trust architectures that assume no device, user, or system is inherently trusted. This approach ensures that every request for access is verified before being granted, regardless of whether it originates from inside or outside the network. Additionally, AI-powered network monitoring systems can continuously analyze traffic patterns and detect suspicious activity, even if the attack comes from a previously trusted source.

For IoT, businesses should adopt device authentication protocols and ensure that each connected device is secure, using techniques such as machine learning for anomaly detection on IoT networks. Similarly, with the increased use of cloud services, organizations must adopt cloud-native security strategies, such as AI-driven cloud monitoring and the enforcement of strong encryption standards for data in transit and at rest.

4. Ensuring Privacy in a Data-Driven Future

As data becomes more central to business operations, safeguarding privacy becomes even more challenging. The increasing volume and complexity of personal data collected by organizations, combined with growing concerns about data breaches and misuse, mean that organizations must future-proof their privacy practices. Advances in AI and ML can help identify and mitigate privacy risks by analyzing vast amounts of data to detect patterns indicative of privacy violations.

In addition to the ongoing application of data protection regulations such as GDPR and CCPA, businesses must implement AI-driven privacy frameworks that can autonomously detect potential privacy violations, including unauthorized data access or misuse.

Organizations can leverage differential privacy techniques, which ensure that data remains anonymous while still providing valuable insights, to prevent inadvertent exposure of sensitive information.

Moreover, AI can be used to enhance data minimization practices, ensuring that only the necessary amount of data is collected and processed, reducing the risk of breaches and misuse.

5. The Importance of Agility in Cybersecurity

One of the most critical components of future-proofing cybersecurity systems is ensuring that they are agile and adaptable. The nature of cyber threats is constantly changing, and static defenses are ill-suited to address these dynamic challenges. Organizations must be prepared to quickly adjust to new threats, regulatory changes, and technological innovations.

To enhance agility, businesses should embrace DevSecOps practices that integrate security directly into the development lifecycle. By adopting a security-first mindset and continuously testing and updating AI-powered defense systems, organizations can ensure that their defenses remain relevant in an ever-changing threat landscape.

Agility also requires investing in cybersecurity automation tools, which can enable rapid identification and mitigation of threats without relying on manual intervention. AI-driven automation can help organizations scale their response to large volumes of security events, allowing security teams to focus on more complex tasks while automated systems handle routine detection and response.

6. Fostering a Culture of Cybersecurity Awareness and Education

As cyber threats become more sophisticated, it is crucial to invest in building a cybersecurity-conscious culture within organizations. Employees are often the first line of defense against phishing, social engineering, and other types of human-targeted attacks. Therefore, preparing employees for emerging threats, especially those involving AI-driven tactics, is essential for future-proofing an organization's defenses.

Regular training programs should be implemented, focusing on AI-enhanced cybersecurity awareness, including educating employees about the latest AI-powered phishing attacks and how to recognize them. Additionally, cybersecurity training should be an ongoing process, as threats evolve rapidly.

Moreover, organizations should consider red teaming exercises, where employees simulate cyberattacks to identify vulnerabilities and reinforce learning about emerging threats. This hands-on approach allows employees to understand the latest attack techniques and prepare accordingly.

7. Continuous Innovation in Threat Detection and Response

To stay ahead of cybercriminals, cybersecurity systems must constantly evolve to meet the challenges of the future. This means investing in ongoing research and development of AI and ML technologies, exploring new methods for detecting and responding to threats faster and more effectively. Collaboration with academic institutions, industry experts, and cybersecurity firms can help organizations stay at the forefront of cybersecurity innovation.

Developing a cybersecurity innovation lab within the organization can foster creativity and experimentation, allowing for the testing of new AI models and techniques in a controlled environment before they are deployed in real-world systems. This forward-thinking approach enables organizations to rapidly adapt to emerging threats and create effective countermeasures in real-time.

As cyber threats continue to grow in sophistication and scale, organizations must embrace a proactive approach to future-proofing their cybersecurity defenses. By staying ahead of technological trends such as quantum computing, AI-powered attacks, and the expanding attack surface of IoT and cloud technologies, businesses can ensure that their security systems remain effective in the face of emerging challenges. Adopting scalable, flexible, and innovative solutions, while fostering a culture of continuous improvement and cybersecurity awareness, is key to building resilient defense systems capable of adapting to the future cyber threat landscape.

14.5 Preparing for Quantum Computing's Impact on Cybersecurity

Quantum computing represents a revolutionary advancement in technology that has the potential to transform many industries, including cybersecurity. While the promise of quantum computing in fields such as data analysis, drug discovery, and artificial intelligence is immense, it also brings significant challenges, particularly in the realm of cybersecurity. Quantum computers, when fully realized, could pose a serious threat to existing cryptographic systems, which underpin the security of much of the world's digital infrastructure. In this chapter, we will explore the potential impact of quantum computing on cybersecurity and the proactive steps organizations can take to prepare for this inevitable shift.

1. The Threat Quantum Computing Poses to Traditional Encryption

At the heart of current cybersecurity practices lies encryption, specifically public-key cryptography. This method of encryption, which includes algorithms like RSA (Rivest-Shamir-Adleman) and ECC (Elliptic Curve Cryptography), is the foundation of secure communications, online banking, and the protection of sensitive data. The security of these algorithms relies on the difficulty of certain mathematical problems, such as factoring large prime numbers (RSA) or solving discrete logarithms (ECC).

However, quantum computers, with their ability to perform complex calculations at exponentially faster speeds compared to classical computers, have the potential to break these encryption methods. Quantum algorithms like Shor's Algorithm could efficiently solve these mathematical problems, rendering public-key cryptography obsolete. This would expose encrypted data to interception and decryption by malicious actors, undermining the integrity of secure communications, financial transactions, and personal privacy.

Preparing for quantum computing's impact on encryption requires a shift toward post-quantum cryptography (PQC), which involves developing encryption algorithms that can withstand attacks from quantum computers. Governments and industry bodies worldwide are already researching and standardizing these new cryptographic protocols, but organizations must begin evaluating and integrating PQC into their cybersecurity strategies well before quantum computers become widely available.

2. The Transition to Post-Quantum Cryptography (PQC)

While the full-scale deployment of quantum computers capable of breaking traditional encryption is still years away, cybersecurity experts agree that the transition to post-quantum cryptography must begin now. As quantum computing progresses, data that is encrypted today may become vulnerable in the future. For example, sensitive data transmitted or stored today may be intercepted and stored by adversaries with the expectation that it can be decrypted once quantum computing becomes powerful enough.

To future-proof against this threat, organizations should adopt a quantum-resistant cryptography strategy, which includes the following steps:

Cryptographic Assessment: Evaluate existing cryptographic systems and assess their vulnerability to quantum computing attacks. This involves identifying which encryption methods are critical to the organization and may be at risk from quantum algorithms.

Adoption of Post-Quantum Algorithms: Start testing and implementing PQC standards that are resistant to quantum-based attacks. The National Institute of Standards and Technology (NIST) is leading efforts to standardize PQC algorithms, and organizations should begin integrating these new protocols into their systems. These algorithms, such as lattice-based, hash-based, and code-based cryptography, provide secure alternatives to current methods.

Hybrid Cryptography Solutions: In the interim, organizations may use hybrid cryptographic schemes, which combine traditional encryption with quantum-resistant algorithms. This dual approach ensures that sensitive data remains secure even in a quantum-enabled future.

Encryption Key Management: Ensuring the secure storage and management of cryptographic keys is essential. With the potential for quantum computing to break encryption algorithms, it's vital that organizations adopt secure key management protocols that are resistant to quantum-enabled attacks. Key rotation and forward secrecy should be prioritized as part of the transition to PQC.

3. Impact of Quantum Computing on Digital Signatures and Authentication

Digital signatures, used to verify the authenticity and integrity of electronic documents, software updates, and digital communications, are also based on public-key cryptography. As quantum computers gain the ability to break RSA and ECC, digital signatures relying on these systems will be at risk of forgery, undermining trust in the integrity of transactions and communications.

In response, organizations should prepare for quantum-resistant alternatives for digital signatures, such as hash-based digital signatures or lattice-based schemes, which are considered more resistant to quantum attacks. These new systems will need to be adopted gradually to ensure that digital signatures remain secure and trusted.

Similarly, authentication mechanisms like multi-factor authentication (MFA) and identity management systems may also require a rethinking in the face of quantum computing. Quantum-resistant algorithms must be integrated into these systems to maintain the confidentiality and integrity of user identities and access privileges.

4. Quantum Key Distribution (QKD): A Quantum-Safe Communication Solution

In addition to advancing cryptography, quantum computing also opens up new possibilities for secure communication. One promising solution is Quantum Key Distribution (QKD), a method that uses the principles of quantum mechanics to create a secure communication channel. QKD enables two parties to securely share a cryptographic key, with the inherent properties of quantum mechanics ensuring that any attempt to intercept or eavesdrop on the communication will be immediately detectable.

While QKD is not yet widely deployed due to technical and infrastructure challenges, it offers a potential quantum-safe alternative to traditional key exchange methods. Organizations with high-security needs—such as government agencies or financial institutions—should begin exploring QKD as part of their long-term quantum-resilience strategy.

5. Training and Education for Quantum-Ready Cybersecurity Teams

As quantum computing continues to advance, there will be an increasing demand for cybersecurity professionals who understand the implications of quantum technology and how to protect against quantum-enabled threats. Organizations must invest in training and upskilling their cybersecurity teams to ensure they are equipped with the knowledge and tools to respond to the challenges posed by quantum computing.

Cybersecurity teams should become familiar with the basics of quantum computing, as well as the specific risks it poses to encryption, authentication, and secure communications. Moreover, they should stay up-to-date with the latest research in post-quantum cryptography and be prepared to test and deploy new cryptographic algorithms.

Collaboration with quantum computing researchers, cryptographers, and industry groups will be crucial for ensuring a smooth transition to quantum-resistant systems. Participation in industry standards bodies and conferences on quantum computing will allow organizations to stay ahead of the curve and be part of the ongoing conversation about future-proofing cybersecurity.

6. Long-Term Strategies for Quantum-Resilient Cybersecurity

The transition to a quantum-resilient cybersecurity landscape will not happen overnight. It will require long-term planning, investment, and collaboration across sectors. In addition to implementing post-quantum cryptography, organizations must develop strategies to monitor and defend against the unique challenges posed by quantum computing, including the ability to detect potential quantum attacks and the integration of quantum computing with existing cybersecurity defenses.

Organizations must also consider the lifecycle of their data in a quantum-enabled world. Data that remains sensitive for years, even decades, may need to be encrypted with quantum-resistant protocols today to ensure its security in the future. Businesses with long-term data retention policies—such as those in healthcare, finance, or government—must prioritize quantum-safe practices now to mitigate future risks.

Quantum computing presents both tremendous opportunities and significant threats to cybersecurity. While the full impact of quantum computing on cryptographic systems is still several years away, organizations cannot afford to wait until the technology matures before preparing. By adopting post-quantum cryptography, embracing hybrid encryption solutions, and investing in training and education, organizations can build a future-proof cybersecurity framework that safeguards against the risks posed by quantum-enabled cyberattacks. The proactive steps taken today will ensure that tomorrow's digital infrastructure remains secure, resilient, and ready to face the challenges of the quantum computing era.

Writing **Next-Gen Cybersecurity: AI and ML Innovations** for Digital Protection has been an incredible journey, and I owe my gratitude to the many individuals who made it possible.

First and foremost, I want to thank my family and friends for their unwavering support and encouragement throughout this project. Your belief in me gave me the motivation to see this book through to completion.

To my colleagues, mentors, and peers in the cybersecurity and AI communities—your insights, challenges, and collaborations have been invaluable. This book is a reflection of the collective knowledge and innovation that we strive to push forward in our field.

A special thanks to the readers who inspire authors like me to share ideas and knowledge. Your curiosity and passion for learning are the driving forces behind works like this.

Finally, to everyone working tirelessly to make the digital world a safer place: this book is dedicated to you. Together, we are shaping a future where technology empowers rather than endangers.

With gratitude,

Davide Mancuso